Campaigning for Napoleon

Campaigning for Napoleon

The Diary of a Napoleonic
Cavalry Officer 1806–13

Maurice de Tascher

Translated and Edited by Rosemary Brindle

Project Editor: Christopher Summerville

Pen & Sword
MILITARY

First published in Great Britain in 2006 by
Pen & Sword Military
an imprint of
Pen & Sword Books Ltd
47 Church Street
Barnsley
South Yorkshire
S70 2AS

ISBN 1-84415-457-2

A CIP catalogue record for this book is available from the British Library.

Typeset in 11/13 Ehrhardt by Concept, Huddersfield, West Yorkshire
Printed and bound in England by CPI UK

Pen & Sword Books Ltd incorporates the imprints of Pen & Sword Aviation,
Pen & Sword Maritime, Pen & Sword Military, Wharncliffe Local History,
Pen & Sword Select, Pen & Sword Military Classics and Leo Cooper.

For a complete list of Pen & Sword titles please contact
Pen & Sword Books Limited
47 Church Street, Barnsley, South Yorkshire, S70 2AS, England
E-mail: enquiries@pen-and-sword.co.uk
Website: www.pen-and-sword.co.uk

Contents

Chronology of Major Events

1804

18 May:	Napoleon Bonaparte becomes Napoleon I, Emperor of the French. His imperial status is later confirmed by plebiscite. Napoleon's star waxes . . .
2 December:	Napoleon is crowned at Notre Dame.

1805

9 August:	Third Coalition formed by Britain, Austria and Russia with the aim of defeating Napoleon and restoring the Bourbon monarchy.
10 September:	Austrian forces invade Bavaria, initiating the War of the Third Coalition.
7 October:	Napoleon's Grand Army crosses the Danube to meet the Austrians.
20 October:	Capitulation of Ulm (in present-day Württemberg, southern Germany). Napoleon encircles Mack's Austrian Army, which is obliged to capitulate, some 30,000 Austrians marching into captivity.
21 October:	Battle of Trafalgar. Admiral Nelson destroys the combined fleets of France and Spain, securing British naval supremacy at the cost of his own life.
2 December:	Battle of Austerlitz (present-day Czech Republic). Napoleon crushes the armies of Austria and Russia.
26 December:	The Peace of Pressburg ends the War of the Third Coalition, leaving Napoleon master of mainland Europe.

1806

15 February:	Napoleon demands and receives concessions from Prussia.
16 May:	British Royal Navy begins its blockade of French ports.
20 June:	Louis Bonaparte, Napoleon's brother, made King of Holland.
12 July:	Napoleon takes control of Germany's patchwork of independent states by forming the pro-French Confederation of the Rhine.
6 August:	The Austrian Kaiser, Francis II, abdicates as Holy Roman Emperor, becoming Francis I of Austria. The Holy Roman Empire of German States is dissolved.
9 August:	Alarmed by French ascendancy in Germany and Central Europe, Prussia secretly mobilizes for war against Napoleon.
1 October:	Prussia delivers an ultimatum to France, provoking a swift military response from Napoleon.

6 October:	The Fourth Coalition is formed by Britain, Russia and Prussia to combat Napoleon's new-found Empire.
10 October:	The Prussians are defeated by Marshal Lannes at Saalfeld (present-day eastern Germany).
14 October:	Battles of Jena–Auerstädt (present-day eastern Germany). Napoleon and Marshal Davout crush the Prussian Army, which suffers some 50,000 casualties in the two separate battles. The occupation of Berlin follows, as King Frederick William III flees, seeking sanctuary with the Russians.
21 November:	Berlin Decrees. Napoleon initiates economic war with Britain by closing European ports to British goods: the start of his ruinous 'Continental System'.
16 December:	The French enter Warsaw in an attempt to head off a Russian force marching to the aid of Prussia.
26 December:	Having advanced from Warsaw, French troops clash inconclusively with the Russians at the Polish settlements of Golymin and Pultusk.

1807

8 February:	Battle of Eylau (present-day Bagrationovsk in the Russian Baltic enclave of Kaliningrad). A costly clash with the Russian Army, which is augmented by a Prussian corps. Napoleon claims a victory but the outcome is a draw at best.
18 March:	French besiege the port of Danzig (present-day Gdansk), which falls on 27 May.
10 June:	Battle of Heilsberg (present-day Polish town of Lidzbark Warminski). Napoleon evicts the Russian Army but at the cost of some 10,000 casualties.
14 June:	Battle of Friedland (present-day Pravdinsk in Kaliningrad). Napoleon annihilates the Russian Army, causing Tsar Alexander to sue for peace.
7 July:	Peace of Tilsit. Napoleon dismantles Prussia, creating new French satellites, including the Grand Duchy of Warsaw and the Kingdom of Westphalia. Russia enters into an alliance with France and the Fourth Coalition is consequently dissolved. Napoleon's star is at its zenith . . .
27 October:	Treaty of Fontainebleau. Napoleon secures the assistance of his Spanish allies in a secret plan to invade Portugal. But the project is merely an excuse to flood the Iberian Peninsula with French troops, prior to a full takeover.

1808

20 February:	Marshal Murat becomes Napoleon's 'Lieutenant' in Spain.

29 February:	French forces seize Barcelona, leaving their Spanish 'allies' confused, bewildered and outraged.
16 April:	Conference of Bayonne. With Portugal and much of Spain occupied by French troops, the Spanish royal family are obliged to surrender their throne to Napoleon, who gives it to his brother Joseph on 6 June.
2 May:	Spanish outrage at Napoleon's cynical coup boils over into a violent anti-French uprising in Madrid. The 'Dos de Mayo' marks the start of a long, savage campaign – Napoleon's 'Spanish Ulcer'.
15 June:	First Siege of Zaragoza begins. The French launch several unsuccessful attempts to take the Spanish city, which will eventually fall in February 1809.
14 July:	Battle of Medina del Rio Seco. French forces under Marshal Bessières defeat the Spaniards of General Blake's Army of Galicia.
22 July:	Capitulation of Bailén. A French army under General Dupont – fresh from the plunder of Cordova – is entrapped by Spaniards under General Castaños. Dupont capitulates, enraging Napoleon, who quits Paris to march on Madrid at the head of his Imperial Guard.
21 August:	Battle of Vimiero. In Portugal, General Junot's French Army is defeated by a small British expeditionary force under Sir Arthur Wellesley, later first Duke of Wellington.
30 August:	Convention of Cintra. British generals achieve the bloodless evacuation of Junot's French from Portugal. A British force under Sir John Moore will soon cross into Spain to cooperate with the Central Junta.
5 November:	Napoleon takes personal command of French forces in Spain.
23 November:	Battle of Tudela. Marshal Lannes inflicts a heavy defeat on the Spaniards.
30 November:	Battle of Somo Sierra. Napoleon pushes General San Juan's Spaniards aside on the march to Madrid – thanks to the celebrated charge of his Polish Lancers.
4 December:	Napoleon enters Madrid at the head of a veteran army, determined to crush all Spanish resistance and drive the British into the sea.
20 December:	Second Siege of Zaragoza begins.
21 December:	Battle of Sahagun. Sir John Moore, having marched into Spain, inflicts a surprise defeat on elements of Marshal Soult's corps.

1809

1 January:	The British under Moore, threatened by superior French forces, begin their epic retreat to La Coruña.

16 January:	Battle of La Coruña. Moore's troops hold off Marshal Soult and successfully evacuate – thanks to the Royal Navy. Moore is killed at the height of the battle.
24 January:	Napoleon quits Spain for Paris amid rumours of Austrian rearmament.
20 February:	Zaragoza finally falls to the French.
29 March:	Battle of Medellin. Marshal Victor defeats the Spaniards of General Cuesta's Army of Estremadura, which sustains losses of some 10,000 men.
9 April:	Having joined a new anti-French coalition, Austria invades Napoleon's ally Bavaria, unleashing a new war.
20 April:	Battle of Abensberg (south-eastern Bavaria). French forces defeat the Austrians under Archduke Charles, pushing them onto the defensive.
21 April:	Storming of Landshut (south-eastern Bavaria). Marshals Lannes and Masséna smash the rearguard of General Hiller's Austrian force, capturing the city as well as Hiller's baggage train and guns.
22 April:	Battle of Eckmühl (present-day south-eastern Germany). Napoleon defeats the Austrians, who retire behind the Danube.
23 April:	Storming of Ratisbon (present-day Regensburg in south-eastern Germany). Napoleon takes this Austrian stronghold on the Danube but the Austrian Army makes good its escape.
26 April:	British troops return to Portugal under Wellesley, who lands at Lisbon.
12 May:	Battle of Opporto (Portugal). Marching north from Lisbon, Wellesley surprises Marshal Soult and takes the city. French losses are high in the ensuing evacuation and retreat.
13 May:	Napoleon enters Vienna.
21–22 May:	Battle of Aspern–Essling (Austria, east of Vienna). Having elected to pursue the Austrian Army eastwards, Napoleon is checked by Archduke Charles in one of history's bloodiest battles.
5–6 July:	Battle of Wagram (Austria, 6 miles/9.6 km east of Vienna). Napoleon recovers his strength and inflicts a decisive defeat on Archduke Charles. An armistice follows.
10 July:	Action of Znaim (in present-day Slovak Republic). Marshal Masséna charges a vastly superior Austrian force, shunting them back through Znaim with heavy loss.
28 July:	Battle of Talavera. A victory over the French in Spain for the recently returned British under Wellesley.
14 October:	Treaty of Schönbrunn. An ultimatum from Napoleon obliges Austria to sue for peace, ending the War of the Fifth Coalition.

19 October:	Treaty of Vienna and Peace of Schönbrunn. Austria loses 3 million subjects as Napoleon redraws the map of Europe in France's favour. Austria agrees to join the Continental System.
15 December:	Napoleon divorces Josephine.

1810

2 April:	Having divorced the Empress Josephine – who cannot produce an heir – Napoleon marries the Archduchess Marie-Louise of Austria.
17 April:	Marshal Masséna takes command of French troops in Portugal.
16 June:	Siege of Ciudad Rodrigo begins (fortress in western Spain). A French victory over the Spaniards.
16 August:	Siege of Almeida begins (fortress in eastern Portugal). A French victory over the Portuguese.
21 August:	Marshal Bernadotte becomes Crown Prince of Sweden.
27 September:	Battle of Busaco (fortified village in central Portugal). French forces under Marshal Masséna are checked by Wellesley, who though victorious, expects to be outflanked and retreats on Lisbon.
10 October:	Massena's pursuit of Wellesley (now Wellington) is halted at the Lines of Torres Vedras.

1811

1 March:	Unable to feed his army due to Wellington's 'scorched earth' policy, Masséna retreats from Portugal.
5 March:	Fortress of Badajoz (western Spain) falls to the French.
3–5 May:	Battle of Fuentes d'Oñoro (village in western Spain). Masséna is narrowly defeated by Wellington.
16 May:	Battle of Albuera (south-western Spain). Beresford's British 'diehards' drive Soult's Frenchmen off the battlefield.
24 May:	French forces besiege Tarragona, a fortified harbour in eastern Spain. The place will fall four weeks later.
25 September:	Battle of El Bodon (western Spain). Inconclusive battle between French and British forces.
28 October:	Battle of Arroyo dos Molinos (south-western Spain). General Hill's British catch and defeat a French division under General Girard, inflicting heavy casualties.
23 December:	Napoleon and Alexander prepare for war as diplomatic relations between the two Emperors plummet. Among the bones of contention are: the Continental System, which has ruined the Russian economy; and the Grand Duchy of Warsaw, which has developed into a militarized zone right on Russia's doorstep.

1812

26 February:	Napoleon obtains an alliance with Prussia, which is obliged to supply troops for Napoleon's Grand Army.
10 March:	Napoleon obtains an alliance with Austria, which also provides troops for the Grand Army preparing to invade Russia.
16 March:	In Spain, Wellington besieges French troops at Badajoz – the fortress will fall on 6 April.
17–28 May:	Conference of Dresden. Napoleon gathers the crowned heads of Europe in a thirteen-day show of strength, designed to overawe Tsar Alexander.
18 June:	War breaks out between Great Britain and the United States.
20 June:	A Sixth Coalition is formed by Russia and Britain.
24 June:	Napoleon invades Russia without bothering to declare war.
28 June:	Battle of Vilna (present-day Vilnius). Vastly outnumbered, the Russians retreat, avoiding a major battle.
22 July:	Battle of Salamanca (Spain, north-west of Madrid). Wellington achieves a decisive victory over Marshal Marmont in Spain.
23 July:	Battle of Mogilev (present-day Belarus). Marshal Davout defeats Bagration, as the Russians slip across the River Dniepr. The Russians continue to retreat, pulling the Grand Army after them.
28 July:	Battle of Vitebsk (present-day Belarus). A minor clash between Franco-Polish forces and the retreating Russians.
17–19 August:	Battle of Smolensk (western Russia). Napoleon takes the city but the Russian Army evacuates, the Grand Army following. Meanwhile, on Napoleon's northern flank, French forces under Saint-Cyr defeat Wittgenstein's Russians at the First Battle of Polotsk (present-day Belarus).
7 September:	Battle of Borodino (western Russia), known to the French as 'the Moskova'. A monstrous – though inconclusive – clash on the road to Moscow. Napoleon, having inflicted over 40,000 losses on Kutusov's Russians, claims a victory, but his army is too exhausted to pursue the Russians. Kutusov decides to abandon Moscow and regroup south of the city.
14 September:	Napoleon enters Moscow. The city is torched by Russian arsonists, the flames spread by equinoctial gales. Meanwhile, Alexander refuses to treat with Napoleon.
15 September:	In Moscow the great fire burns for four days, destroying three-quarters of the old city.
18 October:	Battle of Vinkovo (western Russia). Murat's outposts – in a vulnerable position some 40 miles/64 km south-west of Moscow – are caught napping by a surprise Russian counter-attack.

19 October:	Napoleon orders the evacuation of Moscow.
24–25 October:	Battle of Maloyaroslavets (western Russia). A strategic victory for the Russians, who block Napoleon's southern line of march. The Grand Army is now forced to retreat through territory devastated by the invasion of the previous summer.
26 October:	Napoleon formally orders the Grand Army to retreat via the main Smolensk road.
4 November:	Winter begins in earnest with the first snowfall. Harassed by the Russians, the Grand Army begins to disintegrate.
14 November:	Second Battle of Polotsk. St Cyr's Franco-Bavarian force is defeated by Wittgenstein in a 'return match' and obliged to evacuate.
16–18 November:	Battle of Krasnöe (western Russia). The French fend off Kutusov's pursuing Russians on the road to Smolensk, but sustain heavy casualties.
25 November:	The remnants of the Grand Army reach the River Berezina, the last major obstacle before quitting Russian territory.
26–29 November:	Battle of the River Berezina (present-day Belarus). The battlefield encompasses a cluster of towns and villages between Minsk and Mogilev. Napoleon effects a miracle, crossing the river on extemporized bridges in the grip of three separate Russian armies. The French fighters escape but thousands of stragglers are stranded on the hostile bank. Some sources give Napoleon's total losses at the Berezina at over 40,000.
5 December:	Napoleon takes his leave of the Grand Army and returns to Paris, leaving Murat in command.
14 December:	French rearguard reaches the River Niemen on the Polish border. Kutusov abandons his pursuit.
18 December:	Napoleon reaches Paris.
30 December:	Convention of Tauroggen. The Prussian contingent of the Grand Army defects. A reluctant ally, Prussia will soon become an open enemy, seeking revenge for humiliating defeats of 1806–7.

1813

26 February:	Treaty of Kalisch sees Prussia join the Sixth Coalition against France. Finally adopting a common front against Napoleon and carefully coordinating their efforts, this coalition of major European powers will prove fatal to Napoleon's empire.
16 March:	Prussia declares war on France. The War of German Liberation begins. Napoleon's star is on the wane . . .

Translator's Preface

The de Tascher family can be traced back to the marriage of a Guillaume de Tascher to Jeanne de Chaumont in 1462. The elder son of this union, one Imbert, took the title of the lordship of La Pagerie in the parish of Sainte Mandé (Loire et Cher), and it was from this line that Napoleon's Empress Josephine descended. The younger brother of Imbert, Pierre, gave rise to the du Perche or de Pourvrai branch of the family, from which Maurice de Tascher descended.

Thus Maurice de Tascher's relationship to the Empress Josephine was distant, but nonetheless, was always recognized by her, for she had a strong feeling for family ties. Maurice's father, Pierre-Jean Alexandre, Count de Tascher, born in 1745, served in the army of the King of France; however, he did not emigrate during the Revolution, and commanded the National Guard in Orléans, so avoiding Robespierre's Terror. His marriage to Flore Bigot de Chérelles produced five sons and two daughters. It was due to the patronage of Josephine that Pierre de Tascher became a senator and officer of the Légion d'Honneur in 1804. He became a count of the Empire in 1808 and a peer of France in 1814.

The writer of this journal, Maurice-Charles-Marie de Tascher, was born at Orléans on 4 December 1786, and was educated at home, under the direction of the Abbé Fousset, until he was old enough to enter the Fontainebleau School. There he began the necessary training at the depôt before being appointed a 'sous-lieutenant' – a second lieutenant in British Army terms – in the 8th Hussars. It is from the date of his departure from the depôt that the diary entries begin.

Wherever he went, de Tascher carried with him a small notebook in which, even on a battlefield, he wrote brief entries, which he afterwards, at leisure, transcribed in more detail into larger exercise books. These he took home with him on his infrequent leaves, with the exception of the final one, which was stolen from him during the dreadful retreat from Moscow. We are left, as a result, with only the small notebook containing the brief but moving notes he managed to write in the midst of appalling suffering, both mental and physical, during this final terrible period.

His elder brother, Ferdinand de Tascher (born in 1779), faithfully transcribed the original text of the diary into a large volume of 537 pages, bound in black calf, each page containing twenty-one lines of elegant, legible writing. This book was handed to Madame Clémentine de Chaboud de la Tour (née de

Tascher), the daughter of Benjamin de Tascher, the youngest of Maurice's brothers. Ferdinand de Tascher wrote: 'When he left our family home to start his military career, my brother, Maurice, adopted the custom, continued until his last days, of writing a daily account of his campaigns, these became less detailed during the interludes of peace. Anxious to render into a single, compact form the various notebooks of which the journal of my brother is composed, I have been careful to transcribe them with the utmost exactness and by doing so, I have felt the sad pleasure of being drawn close to him who is no longer with us.'

Throughout the journal, Maurice de Tascher refers to his family home, his siblings and parents with great affection, and they are clearly in his mind as he writes, especially in times of danger and privation: but he never expresses regret for his choice of career, nor does he lose his determination to be in action. The words of his elder brother, following the above quoted remarks, help to explain the stern sense of duty that never failed the younger man, and which must have been an integral part of his education and family life:

> 'If there was a worthy custom that obliged each well-born individual to write down the various circumstances of his life, and if such writings were preserved like a sacred trust in each family; if, before embarking on and following in the footsteps of their fathers, young men could draw from these observations respect for religion, honour and love of duty, then there would no longer be, as is the case now, so many individuals dishonouring their names and their birth by conduct unworthy of their forebears. They would show themselves ready to take up arms against the enemies of our ancient nobility, the support of the monarchy, so that their honourable sentiments would be in accord with those of their birth. If such a custom was established, the fine maxim, expressed by our forebears when facing death, "Remember whose son you are, and commit no disgrace," would not have fallen into disuse.'

These sentiments perfectly express the outlook of Maurice de Tascher, his concepts of honour and duty, which govern his actions and support his morale in all circumstances.

This is the journal of a young man from the age of twenty till his death at just twenty-seven: it was never revised, as were so many contemporary diaries, with the advantage of mature reflection and hindsight. As the diary was written during the events recorded, it cannot suffer from the problems that may beset a memoir: failure of, or false, recollection. Spanning the period from July 1806 to January 1813, a time of upheaval and uncertainty, Maurice de Tascher's diary confronts us with the dreadful reality of the campaigns in which he fought.

The early entries depict a young man filled with enthusiasm, longing for glory and unquestioning of the rightness of his country's cause. Apart from the fiasco in Egypt, Napoleon's progress had been virtually unchecked on land and France was still inspired and elated by the triumphs he continually proclaimed. The popular view was that, threatened by invading foreigners, French frontiers and the Revolution needed aggressive protection. Over the years, the tone of the journal entries subtly changes, as de Tascher learns that death, destruction and cruelty are the price that is inevitably paid in the quest for glorious victory. Towards the end, in 1813, only duty and patriotism remain to inspire his dogged endurance.

It is noteworthy that no admiring or affectionate reference is, at any time, made to the Emperor, and while in Spain, Maurice becomes very conscious that he is now fighting a war of aggression, rather than one in defence of his homeland; it is this that provokes some less than flattering references to Napoleon's policies. Was there a lingering Royalist regret in the de Tascher family for the passing of the old order? If this was so, he avoids any direct criticism of the Emperor, even during the terrible months of the retreat from Russia.

There are times when there is an almost dream-like quality in the journal entries. Vivid depictions of scenes of the utmost horror are sometimes abruptly juxtaposed with a lively description of a magnificent church or a beautiful landscape. Disgust and admiration struggle in Maurice's mind; he tries to reconcile the cruelty and waste of war with duty to his country and the bravery and endurance of the soldiers. The sight of the dead and wounded, left on the battlefield, abandoned to the depredations of the ravens, appal him; and he laments the homelessness and hardship to which miserable peasants are condemned by the burning of their villages and the destruction of their crops.

De Tascher marched across Europe and back again – and from Bayonne to the south of Spain – in the course of the campaigns which he fought, embarking on what would now be called 'a steep learning curve'. Promotion brought responsibility; he stoically endured great hardship and frustration, as well as enjoying the pleasures of new sights and experiences. Wounded in his first brush with the enemy at Jena, he was out of action for a month, and after being subjected to the unpleasant realities of a field hospital, enjoyed the comforts of convalescence at Leipzig. As he himself remarks, his experiences are like the flickering pictures in a magic lantern.

It was at his own request that Maurice de Tascher was sent to Spain, having been transferred to the 2nd (Provisional) Regiment of Chasseurs. He asked for this transfer in order to be with his friend, Sainvilliers. There is no explanation in his diary to account for the deep friendship he clearly feels for this individual, and few references are made to him thereafter, but this wish to be near his friend was instrumental in his involvement in one of the most catastrophic battles of the Peninsular War, the encounter with the Spaniards at Bailén.

In his first two campaigns, Maurice had been in the company of seasoned, battle-hardened officers and men, when his chief anxiety had been fear of failing to live up to their expectations: but his experience of the war in Spain illustrates how the drain on manpower of the preceding years had changed the French Army. An unanticipated blow to Napoleonic ambitions fell early in the incursion into Spain, and de Tascher had the misfortune to witness it first-hand. The endless demand for men had meant that half-trained, raw troops were sent into the campaign, frequently, as in de Tascher's case, with more experienced officers to lead them. Napoleon had misread the temperament of his one-time Spanish allies: neither he nor his generals were prepared for the fury that the population directed against the French troops sent to enforce the rule of Joseph Napoleon, who had been thrust upon them in place of the deposed Spanish King. Everything that went wrong with the Spanish campaign later was implicit in this first foray to the south, which was a disaster from the first.

This new French Army, composed to a great extent of 'provisional' regiments, filled with young conscripts lacking the stamina of the experienced veterans of previous campaigns, marched, under the command of General Dupont, into Andalusia to capture Cadiz to complete the occupation of the Peninsula. The celebrated French memoirist, Marbot,[1] who saw these troops, noted that they looked 'young and puny'. Also, there were many among the French in Spain who shared Marbot's feeling that he 'knew in his heart that the cause was wrong and that the Spaniards were right to try to repel foreigners who, having represented themselves as friends, had dethroned their King and tried to take his kingdom by force'. Morale suffered as a result.

Not only were these troops inexperienced in battle but, even more fatally, they lacked discipline, and paid dearly for their behaviour when they fell into the power of the Spanish people following the astonishing surrender by General Dupont after his defeat at Bailén. Then, the native population, enraged by the sacking of Cordova and the terrible brutality of the invading force, rose as one man in bitter anger. The officers and men of the French Army had plundered everything they could lay their hands on, not even sparing sacred objects seized from looted churches; nunneries and monasteries were plundered and despoiled. Burdened with their loot, French Army columns, toiling slowly through unfamiliar territory, failed to strike the rapid blow for which Napoleonic armies were renowned. Dupont's army found itself cut off, as the provinces rose against it, and the General surrendered at Bailén when he was confronted by the army of General Castaños. The débâcle of this defeat was made even more terrible by the fact that Dupont had permitted the inclusion in the French capitulation of the division under General Vedel – troops that had not even been involved in the defeat. In this sorry business there was one officer, the commander of the Sainte-Eglise battalion, who disobeyed Dupont's order to march himself and his men into captivity, saying that he was not bound to obey the orders of a general who was already a prisoner of war. Between 20,000 and 25,000 French troops were taken prisoner in that one incident.

Maurice de Tascher felt the full force of the shock of Dupont's defeat. He was lucky to escape with his life, and even luckier to escape the subsequent terrors of captivity. He had the good fortune to be counted among the few aides-de-camp who, with the senior officers, were allowed to return by ship to France. The rest of the unfortunate captives were imprisoned on hulks in the Bay of Cadiz, or were consigned to Cabrera, a small Balearic island, where most of them died of diarrhoea, dysentery and typhoid fever. Only about 2,500 men made it back to France in 1814.

Although de Tascher credits the kindness of General Dupont for his own deliverance, is it, perhaps, permissible to wonder if his good fortune was not entirely unconnected with his relationship to the Empress Josephine?

Napoleon's rage at this disaster was the more terrible as he had assumed the popular uprising in Spain was nothing that could not be dealt with by a few French battalions, and this ignominious check to his ambition was made worse by having been inflicted by an ex-ally for whom he had felt, and shown, contempt. The returning generals and senior officers were not given a hero's welcome when they landed in France, and the Emperor's anger was vented in full upon the unfortunate, dithering Dupont, who, disgraced, was imprisoned until 1814. De Tascher was plainly bewildered at the anger the capitulation at Bailén had provoked – even to the extent of 'prudently' leaving Paris for the country for a month.

His leave over, he is again on his way to join the army, gathering near Vienna to meet the Archduke Charles at Wagram, when, as he points out '400,000 men, who hate no one, await the signal to tear each other's throats out'. Nothing could more clearly define the stupidity and horror of the war. Heat, thirst and pandemonium are the overriding impressions of the terrible battle, in which 30,000 of the French were killed or wounded. Just before the battle, de Tascher was promoted to captain, and shortly afterwards, was awarded the Légion d'Honneur.

By the time de Tascher joins the Grand Army that gathered for the invasion of Russia, the effect of the endless drain upon the manpower of France is now even more apparent, so that recruitment of foreign nationals, collected from the subject nations of Europe, is imperative to achieve the approximate 600,000 men considered necessary to begin the campaign. The huge army crossed the Niemen in June 1812, and by 18 July, de Tascher is writing of 'hunger and extreme wretchedness. The horses are suffering terribly'. Even in these early days, his diary gives details of losses to enemy attacks, of the suffering of the sick and wounded, and above all, of the looting and burning that marked the passage of the army. He looks over his shoulder as he leaves Gjatzk and sees that it has been 'Utterly destroyed'. Unhappily, his brief notes allow for no full account of the Battle of Borodino, although he certainly took a very active part in it, as he speaks of his hope that he will be awarded an 'Officer's Cross'. A few days later he writes of 'utter wretchedness'. It is on 15 September that all his belongings, including his notes, are lost. The hoped-for triumph of the 'conquest' of Moscow, is a hollow one, as the army arrives in the sacked and burning town.

Of the terrible retreat from Moscow, which began on 19 October 1812, de Tascher writes briefly but vividly, for he was never able to amplify his jotted notes as he had intended, so that we are robbed of detail: but enough remains to depict the dreadful journey of the tragic wreck of the Grand Army as it struggled against cold, sickness and the endless attacks of circling Cossacks. The gap in his diary between 9 October and 20 November unfortunately covers the period during which, near Smolensk, he came across his brother, Eugène, wounded and suffering from frostbite in both feet. After this time, Maurice de Tascher continued the weary march on foot, so that his brother could be carried on his only remaining horse.

Strangely, but perhaps understandably, de Tascher makes no comment upon the departure from Smorgoni of the Emperor, who on 5 December, left in his coach with General Armand de Caulaincourt for Paris. The very presence of Napoleon had been enough to boost morale, and his departure had a serious effect upon the men. Although there was a pressing need for his presence in France, there must have been many who thought with Madame de Staël that for Napoleon 'men are despised tools, pieces on a chessboard'. Even more disastrously, Marshal Murat, whom he appointed Commander-in-Chief in his place, was not the right man for the job. He failed to hold Vilna, abandoning the sick and wounded to the depredations of the Cossacks, disease, cold and starvation. Although his physical courage and ability to inspire could never be doubted, Murat lacked the qualities needed to hold together the undisciplined mob into which the Grand Army had degenerated.

The final entries in Maurice de Tascher's notebook make painful reading. He writes in a few vivid phrases of his anxiety for his brother's sufferings, the misery of the terrible cold, his own illness and the horrible sight of men falling, dying in the snow while their former comrades, brutalized by wretchedness, plundered their bodies. The hope of respite from suffering was cruelly disappointed by the fall of Vilna and then of Kovno. Only at the end of December was Maurice able to take his brother into a hospital in Königsberg, but it was too late to save him, and de Tascher was forced to continue his weary journey alone. It was 23 January before he was himself compelled by fever, exhaustion and delirium to enter a hospital in Berlin, where he survived only long enough to see his brother Ferdinand for the last time on 26 January 1813. The following epitaph in the chapel of Pourvrai completes the unhappy story:

> Senator P-J-A. de Tascher and his wife C-F. Bigot de Chérelles, Dedicate this Chapel to God and this Memorial to their Sorrow. Eugène de Tascher, their third son, aged 20, an artillery officer on his first campaign, wounded in the foot near to Moscow who was found, unable to march further, by his brother, Maurice and having travelled on horseback, with both his feet frozen in a frost of 27°, died of exhaustion and distress when he reached the hospital of Königsberg on 25 December 1812.
>
> Maurice de Tascher, their second son, aged 26, a captain in the Horse Hussars, member of the Légion d'Honneur, in the course of his sixth campaign and during the retreat from Moscow at Smolensk, found his brother Eugène near to death. He put him on the only horse that remained to him and led him for 200 leagues, although he himself was ill and on foot. Failing to save his brother, Maurice, a victim of brotherly love, succumbed to weariness and wretchedness, falling at Marienwerder and at last dying at the Berlin hospital on 17 January 1813 in the arms of Ferdinand de Tascher, his elder brother who had hurried there in the hope of saving him.
>
> Ah, you who are the descendants of such wretched parents and you, the faithful, pray for them.

The information concerning the de Tascher family was obtained from the precise and well-documented work of Robert Balsan, a grandson by marriage of Benjamin Tascher, entitled, *History of the Tascher Family*.

Rosemary Brindle, 2006

Count Ferdinand de Tascher's Foreword

When he left our family home to start his military career, my brother, Maurice, adopted the custom, continued until his last days, of writing a daily account of his campaigns which became less detailed during the interludes of peace. He kept his memoirs to bring pleasure to his old age, as his readings had so often cheered the country evenings around our family hearth. In many of his notebooks the ill-starred author had written the quiet, hopeful epitaph: 'Forsan et hanc olim meminisse juvabit!' [*'Perhaps one day it will give us pleasure to recall even these things!' – Ed.*] But alas! who can rely on the future or on this fragile existence that God may take from us whenever he pleases, cutting short the struggles of life and the sorrows of old age? At the age of twenty-seven, the most sublime devotion led him to a tomb that had already opened to receive his younger brother, the companion of his sufferings. Maurice never enjoyed the fruits of his labours, but his family gained a precious heritage from it.

If there was a worthy custom that obliged each well-born individual to write down the various circumstances of his life, and if such writings were preserved like a sacred trust in each family; if, before embarking on and following in the footsteps of their fathers, young men could draw from these observations respect for religion, honour and love of duty, then there would no longer be seen, as is the case now, so many individuals dishonouring their names and their birth. (They would demonstrate no more) conduct unworthy of their forebears by taking up arms with the enemies of this ancient nobility that is the support of the monarchy; then the nobility of their spirit would be in accord with that of their birth. If such a custom was established, the fine maxim, expressed by our forebears when facing death, 'Remember whose son you are, and commit no disgrace,' would not have fallen into disuse.

Anxious to render into a single, compact form the various notebooks of which the journal of my brother is composed, I have been careful to transcribe them with the utmost exactness and by doing so, I have felt the sad pleasure of being drawn close to him who is no longer with us.

Disregarding the interval of about two years between the entry of Maurice into the Military School and the beginning of his first campaign, I have taken the notes from the date when, by crossing the Rhine, he for the first time left the country far from which he was doomed to die.

Count Ferdinand de Tascher

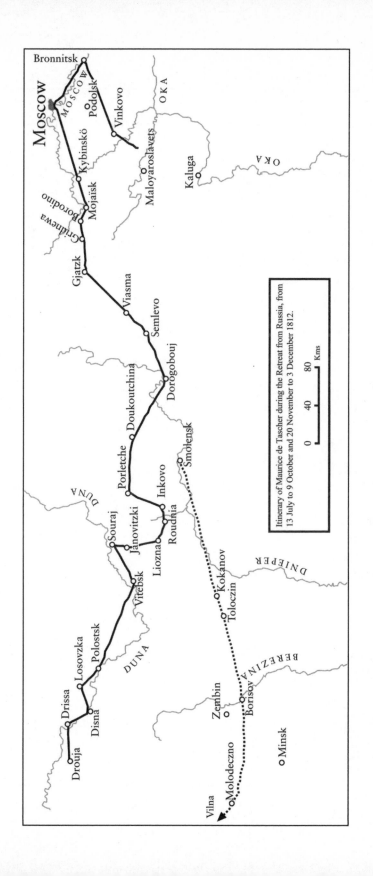

Itinerary of Maurice de Tascher during the Retreat from Russia, from 13 July to 9 October and 20 November to 3 December 1812.

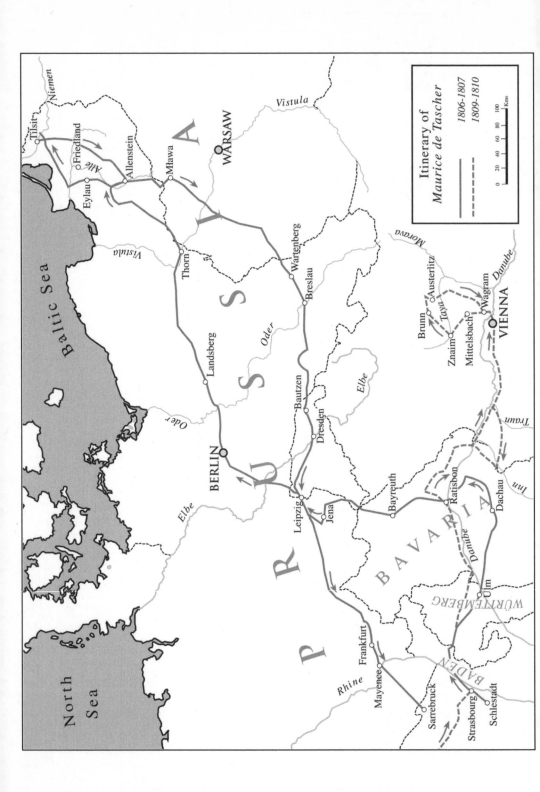

Chapter 1

Jena, Eylau and Friedland:
July 1806–December 1807

1806

21 July: Schlestadt. At last! Our welcome order to leave arrives, and at last, I shall leave Schlestadt without feeling either hatred or regret. I have been the dupe of a coquette for so long! Happily, long before my departure, I was able to prove to her that she could not make me do quite everything she wished.

23 July: When will the longed-for 24th arrive? I fear so much that some damned counter-order will keep us at Schlestadt.

24 July: Erstein. Farewell at last, to that damned place, across whose length and breadth I have so often trudged! Farewell glacis, where I have, many times, directed manoeuvres! Farewell! May it be long before I see you again, unless it should be with my regiment.

[*Editor's note: Students leaving the school at Fontainebleau were obliged to take a course at the depôt and pass through all the ranks before rejoining their regiments as sous-lieutenants. Maurice de Tascher's impatience was all the greater as his regiment was already on campaign.*]

25 July: Strasbourg. The detachment is now under the command of Captain Mareschal.

26 July: Monkensopt. Five leagues and I am no longer in France. This causes me a disturbing and extraordinary sensation; this is the country where I was born and that I love deeply and tenderly, but I leave it without regret, indeed with joy. Ah! The love of Glory … No, my ties to my country are not weakened, they grow even more sacred. Today, I leave my fatherland, for which I have, as yet, done nothing, but I am determined to return more worthy of her and of my brave compatriots. At six o'clock this morning we paraded at Strasbourg before General Rapp, chief aide-de-camp to the Emperor, then we marched off.

The entire road between Strasbourg and Kehl is bordered with Triumphal Arches, and with columns bearing inscriptions commemorating the victories of this campaign and the noteworthy words of the Emperor. The coldest military heart must have been stirred in passing these memorials. Some are still without dedication; we must hope that we are about to fill the vacant places.

One's heartbeat quickens as one crosses this bridge over the Rhine for the first time. It is easier to entrust these emotions to memory than to convey them faithfully in writing.

I have never yet been with the regiment; I am going on a campaign for the first time and a whole new career opens before me. I feel that I am only now beginning my life.

27 July: Rastadt. Instead of Bischofsheim, we went to Makensturm yesterday. Today, we were sent, instead of Rastadt, to Biegelsheim, a little village about 1½ leagues away, and saw the Vauban fort as we passed by. Since I have been in Germany I have had to admire the richness of the countryside. The roads are like public promenades, bordered with fine poplars. After leaving Strasbourg, we have continually skirted the Brisgau Mountains through areas of almost endless beauty. On reaching Rastadt we heard the cannon fire that celebrated the arrival of the hereditary prince of Baden. He is only twenty years old and is about to marry Stéphanie Beauharnais who is barely sixteen.

About eighteen months ago I saw this young lady, who was then lodging with Madame Campan. She had no presentiment, at that time, of the rôle that she was destined to play today. She was then so artless; a Ball was, to her, the height of pleasure while deprivation of some treat cast her into the depths of despair, but how delightful she was even then! A close relative of Stéphanie de Tascher, the two girls shared the same bedchamber. I was then on my way to my regiment at Lille and they thought my uniform was very handsome; 'How lucky you are, for you are free,' they said, 'I wish I was a hussar, too, so that I could travel.' If I see them again, here, I shall remind them of these innocent words.

[*Editor's note: Stéphanie's father was a first cousin of Alexandre de Beauharnais. She was adopted by Napoleon in 1806 and married the Prince of Baden in the same year. The Empress Josephine paid Stéphanie's fees at the school run at St-Germain-en-Laye by Madame Campan, who had been bedchamber woman to the late Queen Marie-Antoinette.*

Stéphanie de Tascher de la Pagerie (1788–1832) was a first cousin to the Empress Josephine. She was ordered by the Emperor to marry Prince Arenberg and later, the Marquis de Chaumont-Quitry, Prince Eugène's orderly officer.]

28 July: Ettlingen. As usual, instead of being allowed to remain at Ettlingen, our destination, we have been sent on to a miserable village, 2 leagues away. The scenery around Ettlingen is similar to that in the Vosges. On our way from Ettlingen to this village, I believed that we were travelling along the road from Saint-Marie-aux-Mines to Liepvre. Up to this time, I have not found the ladies

particularly seductive. They tell me that German ladies are very fond of the French, but I have not sought to verify this saying.

Something that seems very strange to me is that we pay nothing for our board and lodging. It is true that, so far, we have been very uncomfortable and it is fortunate that the countryside is full of game. As soon as we have arrived and all is in order, Captain Mareschal (who is extraordinarily skilful) and I seize the first guns that come to hand and then are off until nightfall. Yesterday I shot three partridge and found them very welcome today.

29–30 July: Pforzheim. Here we are, at last, in a town, and quite a pleasant one. I am billeted with a minister who has a very young wife. I am obliged to congratulate the virtue of my hosts. But, to the devil with the prudish lady and with the bed full of bugs . . .

31 July: Schweiberdingen. At three this morning we left Pforzheim to proceed to this village. Our halt was at Faengen; we have crossed the Baden states and are now entering Württemberg. The women here, dressed in black like those at Pforzheim, have a strange appearance. Like the men they have large hooks or buttons on their clothes, and their headgear is particularly eccentric. It is in the shape of a truncated cone that only covers a small part of the head; the hair is braided and interlaced at the end with ribbons that hang down almost to the ground. The men wear leather skullcaps that make them look very ugly, which they certainly do not need, as they are already ugly enough.

1 August: Altstadt. We should have been billeted at Cannstadt, a charming little village on the banks of the Neckar, but were sent much further on. Having passed a league and a half beyond Stuttgart, which lay, with the Black Forest, on our right, we went through Esslingen, a pretty town in delightful surroundings near the Neckar. I have seldom seen such pleasant places. The bridge at Esslingen is quite remarkable, but the mood of the town is not friendly towards the French; we only passed through it and went on to halt at Altstadt, a league further away.

2 August: Göppingen. A pretty little town, quite well-built. The Protestant ladies here can be distinguished at a glance from the Catholic women. The bosoms of the first are veiled only by a kerchief that is arranged à la Française to reveal their shape, but the breasts and corset of a Catholic lady are exactly like a pulpit and the corset is stoutly anchored by a hook on either side. At midnight, the Governor of Göppingen ordered us to billets at Westerstetten, in the mountains.

3 August: Westerstetten. This morning we were 11 leagues from Ulm. We have just covered ten of them and there are still seven left for tomorrow. We had left the main road near Göppingen and marched into the Devil's

mountains to get here. Who, except he, would have had the idea of putting a village there? It is a very unpleasant place, but never mind, we are getting several leagues nearer to the regiment and to war; this compensates for everything. One of our horses drowned itself in the middle of the village. The men always wear hideous leather skullcaps, but the women's clothes are truly peculiar; their very short petticoats are not without drawbacks when they bend over. They also wear a corset of the shape and thickness of a cuirass, garnished with hooks on either side, that is connected from top to bottom with a little interlaced chain. One has to wonder if their charms are comfortably contained within this flat, hard breastplate.

4–5 August: Gerlenhofen. Having travelled 2 leagues amongst the mountains and craggy rocks, through the wildest country, we found, on the other side of a mountain and after a long descent, a village set in the loveliest place. It lay amongst beautiful meadows, through which a wide stream wound, the mountains on either side, with castles and jagged rocks, formed the frame of this delightful picture. Beyond, were the gentle slopes of a hill, ending in an extensive plain; it was from here, on the summit of this hill, that Ulm could be seen. Is it possible for a French soldier to stifle his bitter disappointment when he is forced to say; 'I was not here a year ago!' What glorious memories are brought back to us by these walls, stained with our blood and crowned with laurels.

We passed through the town and are now billeted at Gerlenhofen. Twenty horses would barely fit into the hovel from which I write, and we have a hundred of them. There is no bread, no wine and no meat. The bedroom would be freezing if the proximity of the stable did not warm it a little. The place also contains the owner and his family. As for me, I have the best bed, I am in a wooden chicken coop; four hussars are stretched on a bed of straw on the ground. How I wish Mama could look in her mirror and see me now. She would say: 'Poor Maurice!' But how can I complain, when I see the plight of my unfortunate hosts?

I forgot to note that, at Ulm, we crossed the Danube – narrower here – and left Württemberg to enter Bavaria. I took advantage of our stay to go to visit Ulm and its surroundings with an officer who had been present at the battle. Everywhere, I saw the relics of the conflict. The outskirts were covered with rubble and most of the houses had been replastered and the windows replaced. The ruined villages still bore witness to the devastation of war. Truly, a soldier with any sensitivity needs to be quite intoxicated with dreams of glory, or the horrors inseparable from this lovely chimera would appal his soul. It was, above all, the wretched villages, pillaged in turn by both sides, which presented the most terrible spectacle. The forced gaiety, the timid eagerness of the miserable inhabitants, who saw themselves being drained of their last drops of blood, resembled the rictus grin [*a gaping or fixed grin – Ed.*] of a dying wretch. Ah, well! He who is most affected by such evils will, if he hears the sound of the trumpet, soon forget his weakness and hurry gladly to arms. But, even so, it is vital to experience the two sensations. Without the first, what would become of humanity? Without the second what would happen to one's country? Yes, let us fight, but let us make as few people miserable as possible!

6 August: Burgau. We marched up to the gates of Ulm, and then took the road to Gunzburg along the Danube. Instead of allowing us to halt we were sent on to Burgau, 2 leagues further, where we were billeted in a house that was still very prosperous thanks to the protection of General Murat.
[*Editor's note: Prince Joachim Murat (1767–1815) was Napoleon's brother-in-law, having married Caroline Bonaparte in 1800. He was also one of the Emperor's original marshals and Grand Duke of Berg.*]

7 August: Sommerhausen. We halted a league from this place in a little village that had been ravaged by both sides.

8–9 August: Friedburg. We only passed through Augsbourg and were halted at Friedburg. It was here that, six years ago, the regiment received a severe setback. The lieutenant colonel and twenty-four men were captured. There is an unfinished steeple here that can be seen from far away. The town stands on a hill, and those parts that face Augsbourg are high above the fields and fortified.

I took advantage of my stay here to see something of the large, handsome town of Augsbourg. It is very well-built; nearly all the houses, especially those in the main street, are carved and painted; some interesting pictures are to be seen on the walls of several houses. Houses occupied by Catholics display pictures and statues depicting the Holy Scriptures. I think there cannot be many towns where there are so many pictures of the Virgin to be found – and where there are so few in reality. Morals are incredibly loose; in this respect Augsbourg ranks higher than Ulm and is worthy to rival Munich. The ladies love the French with staggering determination. I am not referring to the brothels, one of which stands on every corner, but to the excess that reigns everywhere, and in nearly every class of society, the same facilities are offered to the French. The ladies in this town are usually very handsome, with good figures, however their brazen approach and looks tend to confuse every class with the lowest.

10 August: Adelshausen. It was my duty today to arrange the billeting. The extensive fir forests that bordered the road made it seem dark and dreary. Adelshausen is a tiny town, and we halted a league from it in a village dominated by a handsome castle.

11 August: Dachau. We halted 3 leagues away in the village of Hainhausen where there is a superb castle belonging to M. le *comte* de P——, who also

owns vast properties in Hungary near Pest and others, just as large, near Vienna. His wife, it would appear, is very pretty and even more flirtatious. She has separated from her husband, they say, so that she may more easily indulge her taste for the French; she lives at Landshut, where we shall have the honour of paying our respects to her.

The count showed us over his castle that, truly, is well worth seeing. He lent us guns and promised to take us out to shoot roebuck this evening.

Where can I hang myself? I, who ever since I have been in Germany, have killed with my first shot, I, who two days ago, killed three hares, a quail and a pigeon; Oh, misfortune! a roebuck practically ran across my belly; my heart thumped, I was afraid of missing, I urged myself to fire, and I missed – missed a roebuck! Where can I hang myself?

I have horrible lodgings with a priest, but I found a Bavarian lieutenant called Haan already there, he is a delightful man, very friendly and speaking good French, he has been awarded our Croix d'Honneur, and has been with Bernadotte for a long while.

[*Editor's note: Marshal Jean Baptiste Jules Bernadotte (1763–1844) was made Prince of Ponte Corvo following the Battle of Austerlitz. He was elected Crown Prince of Sweden in 1810, later ruling that country as Charles XIV.*]

12 August: Erding. I found Louis Tascher here. The two of us, comrades, friends and relations, were delighted to meet again, both of us so far from our fatherland. We gossiped endlessly of our days at the École Militaire. I asked for news of his brothers, Charles and Henry, who I had met in Paris a year earlier; the elder then a lieutenant in the Guard and the younger a *sous-lieutenant*; now, the first is a *chef d'escadron* [*a cavalry major – Ed.*] in the Imperial Guard and the other a captain in the Guard of the King of Naples, Joseph Bonaparte.

The women here are very pretty and reasonably free and easy. The well-bred ones are dressed in the French fashion, while those who, at home, we should call working girls, wear little bonnets covered with gold and silver, like those worn by Alsatians but, instead of an edging of lace, the two sides of the cap are rolled over the chignon, like two ears. This arrangement is the same as at Augsbourg, where a little rosette is also worn over the ear, which looks very attractive.

It was here that we were informed of a change of direction. Our entire column, until now under the command of M. Renousier, *chef de bataillon* [*an infantry major – Ed.*] of the 10th, has been disbanded. We are no longer going by way of Landshut; for we have to make a detour to Haidenburg, where our battalions are located; we halted for the night at Erding, 4 leagues from Freising.

[*Editor's note: Colonel Count Louis de Tascher de la Pagerie was a first cousin of the Empress Josephine, born in Martinique in 1787. He was a pupil at the École de*

Fontainebleau at the same time as his cousin Maurice. He was a sous-lieutenant *in the 4th of the Line in 1806, then an aide-de-camp of Prince Eugène with the rank of captain. He became* chef d'escadron *in 1809 and colonel in 1814.*]

13–14 August: Dorfen. We are remaining here because our horses are very tired and there are still 8 leagues for us to travel tomorrow.

I have been struck by the little caps worn by the peasant women; they are completely round and trimmed with beautiful black ermine. This headdress gives them a sort of primitive air that is very becoming. Others wear caps decorated with a coarse lace that does not look so attractive.

There is a place of pilgrimage here that is very popular. It is on a small hill near the village. There are 144 steps up to the church, and on each one, the pilgrims repeat an Ave. There are some who come here from far away, carrying with them all the food that is required for their journey, and who climb the hill on their knees. The wall bordering the steps is decorated with paintings depicting scenes from the Passion. At the top, there is a pleasant church, the walls of which bear messages attesting to the gratitude – or the credulity – of the pilgrims. There are several arches leading to many chapels in which life-size statues can be seen representing scenes of the Passion. Built into the walls of these chapels are little compartments, all filled with skulls; there is an altar surmounted with a statue, the pedestal of which is made of them. I detached and examined several of these skulls, each bearing an inscription, surrounded by a garland, giving the name and age of these relics of those who once lived.

15 August: Neumarkt. What a wearisome day! But at last it is over and there are only two more to pass before we rejoin the regiment. There is nothing of interest in this little town.

16 August: Hebertsfelden. All our billets are dispersed. Here we have found the gallant 36th of the Line, of which nearly all the officers are members of the Légion d'Honneur. So we shall meet our comrades tomorrow!

17–20 August: Haidenburg. After marching 6 leagues we reached the Haidenburg castle, where we found three battle squadrons, the fourth being detached 10 leagues away under the command of Colonel Beeker. Without yielding to an inappropriate diffidence, someone in my position could hardly avoid saying to himself: 'Here is a group of officers that I am about to join! I think of every one of them as a judge; each of them is bound to criticize me, I shall be held responsible for my every word and action and my only guide and adviser is the experience of nineteen years – not an adequate mentor!'

I am now in the 5th Company with M. Larchantel and La Ch——. If I had had the choice, I could not have done better. I am detached to Wing, a league and a half from Staff Headquarters. This was the first time I had experienced mounted manoeuvres, or even witnessed a regiment manoeuvring. What a great deal I have still to learn!

1 September: I am so happy, so overjoyed to be with the regiment at last that I sometimes say to myself: 'Can it be true that I am no longer at the depôt? Now, free to go wherever I please, I am at my post and sincerely hope that here I shall see closer action than in the recent campaign.'

3 September: At midnight, came the order to march off at four in the morning. I spent the whole night preparing myself, for anything can happen. Just as we were mounting our horses, the order was countermanded. The prospect of this change had already made my mouth water, for no matter for what billet I was destined, it would certainly be an improvement. I had been in this pigsty for fifteen days and had nothing to drink but beer; if I had had nothing to eat, it would have been all the same, for the little I received was capable of destroying my appetite for the whole period. There were only two forks in the house and I had taken them for my own use, but I returned them when I noticed that, apart from my mealtimes, they were used to support the candle. Everything was in keeping with that. The house was without chairs, chests or cupboards, all was confusion in my bedroom, where it was so damp and unwholesome that, in the course of a single night, iron grew rusty, and books, boots etc. were covered with mildew. Oh, what a filthy hole!

6 September: Pfarrkirchen. This time the order was not cancelled. I am making my first march with the regiment, and please God, it will not be the last. We have retired 6 leagues, and I am stationed in a farm a league from Pfarrkirchen.

8 September: Payerbach. Suddenly, an order comes without warning! At ten o'clock I was out hunting, anticipating nothing, then, at midday, I was on horseback with the company. Now we are in the same quarters that the regiment occupied three months ago; our company is in the village of Payerbach, and the 3rd is in the magnificent convent at Anspach.

9 September: Today, I visited the convent. What a contrast there is between its present desolation and its past magnificence! A brewer owns the main part of the abbey. At the side of a superb picture, a soldier has scrawled a caricature; cartridge pouches and rifles hang from the gilded mouldings, it is the same everywhere. I was not able to see the church, which is said to be one of the most beautiful in Germany. Even the farmhouse could pass for a castle, for the stables are vaulted and could accommodate sixty horses.

11 September: A day worth repeating! We were told that Marshal Soult was coming to conduct manoeuvres, and at the same time, were ordered to proceed to the Anspach plain. We mounted at once and reached the place at seven in the morning. His Excellency arrived at eight o'clock and carried out a rigorous

inspection, then the manoeuvres began. I commanded a platoon and was very much afraid of making a mistake, but happily suffered nothing worse than my fear. We continued to manoeuvre for six or seven hours, then we dismounted and all the officers of the corps reported to the Marshal, who asked a number of questions, all on the subject of the approaching war.

After we had separated and I had barely arrived at my billet, an instruction arrived to inform me that the Marshal was asking for me. I took the orderly's horse and hurried away. His Excellency honoured me with a most gracious reception; after questioning me about various matters, he asked me if I wanted anything or had any particular request to make. I replied that I had nothing to wish for apart from his continued kindness, and then took my leave. It was five o'clock and I had been in the saddle since eleven in the morning, so I was delighted to say farewell to Monseigneur and go to dinner.

15 September: The whole regiment was mustered, and in compliance with an order given to the entire army, those who, by reason of wounds, illness or other causes were not fit for combat, were detached. After this, the 4th Company was incorporated in the other three and prepared for battle.

16 September: Today, the NCOs and men of the 4th Company, who were to be reorganized, left for France, together with the officers of that company. The officers were plunged into despair. How happy I was to be out of that wretched company. At the same time, we learned that all the formations in France were to send detachments and that we should receive 125 men. Ah! Gentlemen of Prussia, we shall soon see you close at hand. We changed our quarters today, and left Payerbach for Birenbach on the other side of the river.

17 September: Birenbach. I have been detached a quarter of a league away from Birenbach, in a windmill, where the miller's wife, who is called Liselle, is very pretty.

26 September: I am passing peaceful days here in my windmill, where fishing and studying German, occupy the days so that I scarcely notice them as they quietly slip by. It has been so long since I last breathed the pure air of the countryside, that I enjoy it all the more. Whether I think of the days that have passed or try to imagine the future, I see nothing but bustle and strife. Now there are a few days of tranquillity, they will be brief so let us make the most of them!

27 September: Eggenfelden. I did not think, yesterday, as I wrote of the peace I was enjoying in my windmill that it was nearly at an end. Windmill, fields and study, all are nothing but a dream! Slumber is over, and it seems that it will be long before I can slumber again. As in a play, the curtain has come down, and when it is raised again, the images revealed to me will be of quite another hue.

For six months we have been in a state of uncertainty, would there be peace or war? Now all is settled. It is war. I received the order at midnight; this morning the regiment assembled at Pfarrkirchen, and we have arrived at Eggenfelden for the night. Braunau and Passau have been evacuated; the entire division is on the march, we go to Prussia. I am about to sleep on straw for the first time but I hope it will not be the last. My thoughts are in turmoil; at last I have a foot on the ladder of my career.

28 September: Landau. We halted 3 leagues away from this town, having covered 11 leagues today. Not bad for a start.

29 September: Straubing. Today, the Staff and the select few are lodged in the town, and we are 2 leagues on the other side. The countryside is beautiful, with superb plains; what wonderful cavalry charges could be made here.

30 September: Now, we have just crossed the Danube at Ratisbon. We are lodged a league and a half away in a village, all mixed together with the infantry, about forty or fifty to each house. The entire army is marching into Prussia.

I took advantage of being so near, to visit the beautiful, large town of Ratisbon. The ladies of this town are charming, but accustomed as we have been for so long to dirty peasants, any properly dressed woman is bound to attract our glances.

1 October: On 4 August I crossed the Danube at Ulm, and this morning, I recrossed it at Ratisbon. We covered 7 leagues today on our way to Amberg. At least, I shall be able to get my clothes off today. I am lodged in the castle at Pilsheim. The Baron and his noble lady being away, we were received by the amiable Eleanor d'Adrian – aged eighteen – charming and speaking French very well. If we had to stay in this neighbourhood, I should not be displeased to live in the castle. Poor Eleanor, I felt sorry for her; what a sad fate for a young lady to be compelled to do the honours of a castle for a dozen hussar officers, all intent on teasing her to make her say an unguarded word.

2 October: Haubach [*most likely Auerbach – Ed.*]. We passed through the little town of Amberg and have halted at Haubach. *Chasseurs*, hussars, dragoons, infantry, cavalry and artillery, the whole army has come together and is marching in battle order. We are barely 7 leagues away from the Prussians and shall certainly meet them tomorrow. Cartridges were distributed yesterday.

3 October: We have reached Turendorf, only a league from the Prussian frontier; all arms are loaded and everyone is on the alert, however the enemy has not yet been sighted.

4 October: It is to be hoped that we shall have a rest today; after such a rapid march, our horses need one. From my bivouac at nine o'clock, I received an

order to go out on reconnaissance, and with twenty men, went at once to a position on the frontier between Bavaria and Prussia, there I established my outpost in a wood, so that my sentinels were barely 40 feet from enemy territory.

Midnight. The first bivouac, the first outpost, are great events for a young soldier; what thoughts ran through my head in the course of this long night! What castles in Spain built and destroyed. Having (in imagination) crushed the Prussians, saved the army, captured flags and won all the medals of honour in the world, I woke, shivering, from my dream to refill my flask and eat my potatoes.

5 October: I was relieved at midday today, but as our company was the only one in the advanced village, we had all been on duty throughout the night.

6 October: There are a thousand conjectures; many do not believe in the war and think that the Prussians are again drawing us into trouble; others say that the Russians are coming to their assistance; everyone has an idea, or rather a nonsense, for no one knows anything.

7 October: Bayreuth. War! War! Here it is at last! We shall see them this evening. I snap my fingers at the depôt, now! How very happy I am to be out of it and how wretched I should feel if I were now in France and reading of our successes in the newspaper. Soult's entire division gathered this morning at Birenbach. With the Marshal at our head we marched off into Prussia. We marched for 5 leagues into the pretty town of Bayreuth; the enemy was no longer there, having withdrawn to the camp at Hof. The keys were brought to us, and the Staff took up quarters in the town. As for us, always having the great privilege of being the furthest forward and the nearest to the enemy, we went 3 leagues beyond the town, and bivouacked before Berneck village, in the mountains. We are posted at the entrance to the gorge by the river. So here I am, at the start of my military career! How many things remain for me to see before I reach the end of it, which, perhaps, may be very near?

8 October: It would appear that the enemy has retreated to concentrate his forces. That which is postponed is not lost; we have bivouacked 3 leagues from the camp at Hof, near Lichtenberg village. It is a wonderful night; our camp looks like a fairground, with all its campfires aligned. Battle standards, supplies of all kinds, hussars gathered round the fires, everything presents a war-like aspect suffused with a spirit at once joyful and brave. Everyone drinks and sings as they go about their duties; the atmosphere breathes of war, happiness and bustle, all at once. Only the French can dance and fight at the same time.

9 October: Hof. This time, on the left, cannon fire and shots can be distinctly heard.

Prince Murat's corps is there. Ah, well! Tomorrow it will be our turn and we shall see what happens. How mixed one's feelings are; thoughts pass so rapidly from one notion to another they are like the changing pictures in a magic lantern.

We have passed through the camp at Hof, it was empty; we are bivouacking before Plauen. The Tirailleurs du Pô [*i.e. Skirmishers from the River Po – Ed.*], who are in our brigade, are level with us; two villages are burning on either side. Wretched peasants! Everything speaks of desolation and havoc. Ah! Is this war?

10 October: We are moving further to the right to cut off the enemy. A corps of 6,000 Saxons is now 6 leagues to our rear. We have passed through the town of Plauen and are in Saxony. I had been on the flank from three in the morning until ten at night and have just set up an outpost in front of the little town of Reichenbach. We could hear loud cannon fire.

11 October: We have pulled back much further to the left today, to join up with the main army. We have been sent in a wide circle to the right, followed by Marshal Ney's corps.

We have passed through Greiz, a charming little town in neutral territory under the command of the Prince de Reuss. The place was burned down six years ago and has been rebuilt; to our eyes, weary of seeing nothing but desolation, there is comfort in the sight of a land that is cared for.

This evening, we saw an immense line of fire in front of us; the entire French Army lies before us. A quarter of an hour after our arrival, all the horses had been unbridled and nearly all the men were in the village collecting provisions. I was without my weapons and was distributing fodder from the top of a hayloft. Suddenly there was a cry 'To horse! To horse! The enemy is upon us'. My heart beat wildly until I reached my horse but it was wonderful to seize the bridle and find my sabre in my hands. We mount and rush forward! A false alarm!

12 October: Our corps, that of Marshal Soult, today joined up with those of Marshals Bernadotte and Murat near the little village of Géra. Marshal Ney's corps is a day's march away from us. I was sorry, when I recognized the white pelisses of the 5th Hussars, and to know that Sainvilliers [*the name by which Tascher called his friend Saint-Hilaire – Ed.*] was not among them.

The Emperor has just arrived with some of the Guard and made a proclamation to us. Now, at last, there is open warfare, we are in battle and the enemy is not far away. A few days from now there will be some news.

We went through the pretty little town of Géra and then through Grünenburg.

At last, we know the outcome of the cannonade we heard two days ago; the encounter took place near Saalfeld. The Saxons fought, and thirty-two guns were taken, this is the beginning of the campaign! Young Prince Ferdinand, brother of the King of Prussia, and one of the principal instigators of the war, was one of its first victims. A sergeant of the 10th Hussars named Guindé killed him. Why have we, ourselves, not been the first to see the enemy?

[*Editor's note: the sergeant's name was Guindet and his letters on this incident were published in the 'Carnet de la Sabretache' (1904). Prince Louis Ferdinand was felled on 10 October 1806, having refused to surrender, even though wounded.*]

13 October: We were still in our bivouac at eleven in the morning. Suddenly an order arrived; we returned through Géra, and after a march of 16 leagues, we reached the bank of the Saale at the Jena bridge at two the following morning. We dismounted to wait for the dawn. On our way we had passed through the infantry and the Imperial Guard; artillery arrived at speed from all sides. Now we could see all the enemy's firing line, less than half a league away from us. This was a significant moment in my life; I knew that, when daylight came a widespread, and undoubtedly terrible, battle would begin; perhaps, in a few hours … Heaven preserve us! All I know is that, for nothing in the world, would I wish to be at the depôt now.

Why are you not here, Sainvilliers? One is twice as brave when with a friend. Anyway, here's to tomorrow! Sainvilliers, if these are my last words, you know that I was thinking of you.

14 October: From the hospital at Jena. (*The following entry was written entirely with the left hand: F. de Tascher.*) They are still fighting, but I am not! Maimed at twenty! If only it had been in the final battle instead of the first! I do not regret the loss of my blood, I would be happy to see that shed, but I can no longer fight! This morning I had other hopes; but never mind. I do not regret this day and prefer the memories I have of it to the hand that it has cost me. Such hideous sights! I was wading in blood, surrounded by corpses; how dare I complain! They took my 'wooden hand' off today, and I shall take advantage of this to write, although very slowly and with pain. I now recount what happened:

A lively cannonade at dawn warned us that the Prussians were waiting for us. We mounted our horses, crossed the Jena bridge and moved to the right, marching about a league and a half from the foot of the hillside. Having reached a village, we cut to the left in a large fir wood, and climbed through it up the hill to reach our battle station. There was a thick fog now that was of use to us, as it concealed our movements from the enemy who were in an excellent position, for our various corps, converging from several directions, only arrived one after another. The left flank of our army rested on Weimar, and the right, containing Soult's corps (our own), was resting on the Jena hillside. Marshal

Davout was to the rear of the enemy army near Raumbourg; like our own, Marshal Ney's corps had marched throughout the night and did not arrive until about midday, as did the Cuirassier and Dragoon divisions. The 34th of the Line and the 17th Light, who had bivouacked with the Emperor on the hills and on the other side of the Saale, began the battle at dawn, but the combat did not become general until ten o'clock; it was decided by five in the evening.

To return to our regiment. We went through the forest, moving past the Prussian batteries, whose shot passed over our heads, and arrived at last on an open space that was already heaped with the dead. We were formed into squadrons and moved off at a trot. After a quarter of a league, shells and shot from the enemy infantry, wounding men and horses at every step, warned us that we were near. The sun, now dissipating the mist, revealed to us a magnificent infantry square that was flanked by a wood and supported by numerous and well-served artillery. Two regiments of the Saxon Red Dragoons, in close columns, drawn up by divisions, were on the right.

Marshal Soult instructed General Guillot to order us to charge immediately. The 1st Squadron charged in echelons. The Saxons came up to meet us in good order; they threw themselves upon the 1st and 2nd Squadrons, broke them up and returned to attack the 1st Squadron in the rear. At once, the Colonel [*Jean Baptiste de Deban du Laborde, colonel of the 8th Hussars 1805–9 – Ed.*] ordered: '1st Squadron to the left.' In our turn, we attacked them on the flank, and the struggle became general. At last, after losing more than a third of the regiment, we succeeded in pushing them in, and threw ourselves upon them in their square.

As for me, I saw no more of it; I was commanding the 3rd Platoon of the 1st Squadron and when the order 'squadron to the left' was given, and we turned, I found myself leading the struggle amongst the dragoons. At first, I was lucky; I had received a shot in my cloak and taken several sabre slashes without having been wounded. A single cut on the wrist had drawn blood, but just as I fought with a dragoon, two others attacked me on the left side and rear, one of them cut my wrist half through, and at the same time, the other caught me a blow with the flat of his sabre that was so violent that it dismounted me. I tried to seize my saddle but it slipped. Then, on foot and losing a great deal of blood and quite unable to hold my sabre, I was forced to go back. A short distance away, I came upon several officers of the 11th Chasseurs who, like myself, were wounded. The regimental surgeon stopped the bleeding from my injury.

At the edge of the wood I was delighted to find Monsieur Charroi, our surgeon, who slowly and with great care dressed my wound and fixed my hand on a wooden support. But he told me that, as the tendons of three fingers had been severed, it appeared that I should remain disabled.

My companions in misfortune and I wanted to go back to a large village that lay to our left, but it was in flames, so we took the road towards Jena. One of the districts of this town was also burning and the rest had been given over to pillage. We took shelter in the Black Bear Hotel, into which we gained entrance. We were soon distracted from our own wounds by news of greater disasters. We learned of the death of the gallant Captain Chardron who was mourned by all who had known him. We saw Le Blanc and Schouleur, officers of our regiment, carried in with grapeshot wounds, and finally, our colonel with a bullet in his thigh.

The 34th Regiment had lost thirty-six officers and more than 1,500 men, while the 16th and 17th Light had lost nearly as many. Marshal Davout's corps lost nearly 10,000 men. More than a month afterwards, the surgeons reckoned that there were 6,000 wounded in Hamburg. There was a time when Jena contained 6,600 casualties. Our regiment had thirteen men killed and eighty-three wounded, nearly half our original strength. I can never forget the horrible sight of the three men I saw killed with a single cannon-ball. I was near to one of them, both of his thighs were broken, he said: 'I am nearly finished, but, if only I could get up, I would shout, Vive l'Empereur!' I saw one wounded soldier cut his own throat ...

Those dying of tetanus presented a particularly dreadful sight. General Debilly and sixteen colonels paid with their lives for the honour of having taken part in the Battle of Jena; amongst them, Barbenègre of the 9th Hussars and Lamotte of the 36th of the Line, were especially mourned.

Habreman saved my life by dismounting in order to snatch me from the midst of the struggle. Of the many slashes that I had received, only two wounded me, but the blow on my neck had stunned me. I had two bullets in my fur-lined cloak. A Prussian aimed at me point-blank but a hussar named Boutri – who I did not see at all – deflected the shot. As I turned, and never having seen a shell before, I was interested when one fell nearby, thinking it was a cannon ball, but I had taken only ten paces when it exploded. The unhappy young Bernier was killed with a single sabre-cut that split his head open. He was an only son, well-born and wealthy, fate had bestowed everything upon him and nature had given him even more, for he was high-spirited and brave. He lived long in the memory of those who had known him. From the first, everyone was charmed by his kindness and gaiety, and the quality of his mind served to strengthen this initial attachment. This had been his first experience of battle and he died in the first charge. His poor mother!

[*Editor's note: French losses for the battles of Jena–Auerstädt have never been firmly established. Digby Smith's* Napoleonic Wars Data Book *puts Napoleon's Jena casualties at 5,700; as for Davout's Auerstädt casualties, the Marshal himself estimated them at 7,000.*]

15–19 October: A field hospital presents a dreadful sight while a battle rages! There are more than 3,600 wounded here, and there are not enough doctors, bandages or other necessities! The town is in flames on one side and abandoned to pillage on the other. Blood is running in the streets and a more horrible sight than the church cannot be imagined, for the dying are heaped upon the dead, stretched out pell-mell on the stones, while arms and legs pile up near the surgeon's table. What a sight for those who are waiting for their turn!

Together with my two companions in misfortune, I was directed to lodge with the Burgomaster. For three days there were six of us officers lying on straw in a little room that we were very fortunate to have. The doctor ordered a light diet for us, but this was not always adhered to. On the 18th our conditions became a little better; we – Curée and Schouleur and I – were accommodated with the lawyer Asferus. For the first time in a long while, I was able to be undressed and to lie down in a bed. Several wounded officers of the 34th are here with us. Adversity makes us resourceful; each helps his friend with whatever limb remains to him. Necessity enforces equality and fraternity, wherever possible, far better than any law.

On the 19th, impatience to send my news to my parents and to Sainvilliers, compelled me to write a few lines with my left hand. My unhappy parents! They are more to be pitied in their anxiety than I, with my wound; their love makes them suffer more than I. As for you, Sainvilliers, I am sure that you grieve that you are not here! I am wounded and in pain, it is true, but I suffer for my country and it was at the Battle of Jena that I received my injury; this thought comforts me.

When he saw me injured, my poor hussar wept that he could not follow me. To be wounded and have no one with you – that is hard! Our unfortunate horses are dying of hunger, and there is no one to look after them.

24 October: They say that the sight of so much misery hardens the heart and concentrates all feeling in upon itself; but the most deadened soul would be stirred by such dreadful sights; although convoys of wounded were evacuated daily, although carts full of the dead daily made their way to the cemetery, yet the hospitals, the churches, the houses remained overflowing with the wounded. I asked to visit the hospitals with the senior surgeon; in just one of them, fifteen or twenty individuals died every day from lack of care. Ten days had already elapsed since the battle, but many of the wounds had still not been dressed and several amputations were still not carried out. When these brave and unhappy soldiers did not die of their wounds or of hunger, the pestilential air they were forced to breathe was enough to kill them. Had I not every reason to bless providence for the bread, potatoes and bed that I enjoyed?

26 October: Today, I visited the field of battle. The more one studies the Prussian position, the more impregnable it appears to have been. Our triumph

must have been due to the Emperor's 'star', to the dashing bravery of the French and to the thick fog that prevailed. How terribly the soil is soaked with blood! And what a number of graves! All the dead have been buried, but six days after the battle, several wounded are still breathing on the ground on which they fell.

I recognized the corner of the wood where our wounds were dressed, the spot where the regiment charged, and where I fell, and the place where the brave Captain Chardron was even more tragically cut down. I saw where Didy was killed at my side, and where Gérard was captured and a moment later, attempting to escape, was cut to pieces.

1 November: I have taken Georges into my service; he had been with Captain Chardron for seven years.

9 November: We have, at last, left Jena, that place of misery and horror, to go to Leipzig; we take with us the regrets of the Asferus family, who had been saved from looting by our presence.

All our field hospital has moved off, composed as follows: Colonel Laborde and his wife, four officers, eight NCOs, twenty hussars, and of concern to us all, Monsieur Charroi, the senior surgeon. We reached Naumburg. There was no need to enquire where the hospitals are, for the clouds of ravens point it out. Their black legions wheel around and their hideous croaking seems to lay claim to their prey.

10 November: We slept at Weissenfeld after travelling 6 leagues.

11 November: We have reached the famous town of Leipzig. This is, for us, the Promised Land, for we have travelled for too long in the desert. This town is the main warehouse for the trade between the English and Germany, Poland and Russia, making it extremely rich and busy. Although it is surrounded with towers and moats, it has not been put into a state of defence for a long while. Some parts of the moats have been converted into delightful gardens and the whole of the town is surrounded with charming avenues that must be very pleasant in the summer. Leipzig University is one of the most famous in Germany and attracts many young people to this town. The fairs that are held at Christmas, at Easter and above all, at Michaelmas, bring together merchants from every corner of the commercial world.

18 November: There has been a month of absolute silence from my parents, causing me the greatest anxiety; I am no less anxious to have news of the regiment, to which, no doubt, all my letters have been sent. These things determine me to go to Potsdam for news, and stay there if I am well enough, if not I shall come back here. I therefore leave tomorrow, with a few of the regimental wounded.

20 November: Düben. The countryside is devastated and the most terrible wretchedness is seen everywhere.

21 November: Wittenberg. The remains of bivouacs, and traces of the Prussians' precipitous retreat can be seen all around. I saw where the town's big wooden bridge had been set on fire, but the French had not given them enough time to burn it and we are now fortifying the bridgehead.

22 November: Trebisen [*undoubtedly Treuenbrietzen – Ed.*]. This is only a large village, equally as devastated as Wittenberg.

23 November: Potsdam! What a contrast. When one thinks back to the time of Frederick the Great, one recalls Delille's verse:

> Potsdam, home of heroic victory,
> Potsdam, warlike and peaceful by turn.

This town is very well-built with wide, straight roads, magnificent houses and superb gardens; but today, there is a terrible difference to be seen. All outwardly speaks of luxury and royal splendour, yet signs of fear and desolation are everywhere apparent. The more grand and the more ornate this town seems superficially, the more its state of desertion and distress is intensified – it is like a town taken by assault. Traces of our bivouacs can be seen in the beautiful gardens, windows are broken and the sumptuous palaces and houses are filled with soldiers: horses, plunder and prisoners occupy the public buildings. All this is side by side with monuments to the victories and the glory of Frederick the Great. What a picture of human vicissitudes!

24 November: The Emperor reviewed the regiment at Berlin and made promotions to fill the vacant positions. Nearly all my comrades have been promoted a rank. He promoted one *chef d'escadron*, three captains, five lieutenants and five *sous-lieutenants*. I am perishing of hunger here, and because of my wounds, am not able to rejoin the army for a long while: I decide to return to Leipzig with the Colonel and Charroi.

25 November: Trebisen.

26 November: Wittenberg. Damned spot!

27 November: Düben. Even more damned spot!

28 November: Leipzig. I have been billeted with a good old lawyer in the Fleischergasse, and am able to enjoy eating with my hosts. The father and mother are elderly, and together with three daughters, one of them married, and a son, make up the household. This picture of domestic life, of the frankness and good-nature of the family home, remind my heart of the peaceful hours spent in the bosom of my own family, and recall memories of the happy hours, which never forgotten, have, of late, been less in my thoughts.

4 December: Today, it is twenty years since I came into the world, and as if to celebrate my birthday, the Colonel told me that General Guillot, who charged with our regiment at Jena, has recommended me for the Croix d'Honneur.

15 December: I am trying to profit from the idleness of a long convalescence by learning German. I could not have a kinder teacher than W—— [*Wilhelmine Lötze, the daughter of his hosts – Ed.*] but this does not help my progress a great deal as I find myself often thinking more of my teacher than of the lesson.

25 December: Christmas. The Catholic religion is only tolerated here. It was observed for the first time in public on the occasion of the burial of General Mâcon. There is only one, very small, Catholic chapel, whereas the Lutherans have several magnificent temples. The Nicolai-Kirche is a monument to behold. The entire building is simple, spacious, magnificent and worthy of the divine. Here, there are no statues, no bad pictures that, displayed with the best of intentions, nevertheless attract as much ridicule as piety. The women are always separated from the men here, and everyone seems to be inspired with a devotion that could serve as an example to every religion. The music, that is invariably excellent, occupies a large part of the service. In any case, where music is concerned, I prefer that of the church to that of the concert. A large number of young people and students, brought up by the state, have to come to sing in the church; this singing is in the common tongue and this, no doubt, enhances the noble sound of the chanting and the reverence of those taking part. The union of the voices and the sonorous tones of the organ that accompanies them, combine to form a delightful harmony, touching the heart and lifting the spirits in a way that is impossible to convey to those who have not heard it. After hearing such a service, I no longer wonder that everyone is devout and music loving.

1807

1 January: The whole town is illuminated. On this day are celebrated the peace that unites the two crowns, and the birthday of the Elector and his coronation as king. These same Saxons who, at Jena, made us purchase victory so dearly, will now fight under our banners. These same Saxons, who displayed such courage while fighting the French, of what will they not be capable as our rivals and companions in glory?

[*Editor's note: following the Battles of Jena–Auerstädt, Napoleon created the puppet kingdoms of Saxony, Bavaria and Württemberg.*]

15 January: In any gathering, any meeting, a Frenchman can easily distinguish the different national characteristics. I went skating yesterday; Germans love this activity. The ice was covered with skaters, most of them very skilful; there were, however, some beginners, inviting laughter at their expense. Used to the

gaiety and noisy happiness that enlivens our French skating and to the outbursts of loud laughter that greet the frequent tumbles of the maladroit, I was amazed at the calm and gravity of the Germans. When they walk, when they dance, when they skate, it is for the sole purpose of walking, dancing or skating, it is not for entertainment or for pleasure. Always intent upon what they are doing, they show the same seriousness that they display when working in their offices.

19 January: Our good, brave Colonel has had the ball that was lodged in his thigh for thirty-nine days removed, at last. Before the operation a probe penetrated the wound for 11½ inches; the ball had gone 7 inches into the wound then, instead of continuing in the same direction, had gone upwards into the buttocks for 5 or 6 inches. Monsieur Charroi covered himself with glory by this operation, which he performed in the presence of Messieurs Ecotte, Rose, Mullet, Erliets, Glarus and all the most accomplished members of the University. A wadding, that had been driven in with it, was removed with the ball, but unfortunately, some cloth from the breeches still remains in the wound and may, perhaps delay the healing that is so essential and so greatly hoped for by the whole regiment.

17 March: Part of the piece of cloth [that was] in the Colonel is out; now all that can be done is to wait. Schouleur left today to rejoin the regiment; I would have gone with him, except that the Colonel and Monsieur Charroi consistently opposed it. There are now only four of us wounded left in Jena.

18 March: A letter from my father, dated 18 February, tells me that I was promoted to lieutenant of the 12th Chasseurs and I am so overjoyed by the news that I still cannot believe it.

20 March: The widow of Lieutenant Colonel Porcher of the 24th of the Line, passed through today with the body of her husband, who had been one of the most handsome men in France. This story makes one shiver. Madame Porcher went everywhere with her husband, accompanying him until the fatal day of 8 February on which he was killed [*at the Battle of Eylau – Ed.*]. Throughout the evening and the following night, she ran from bivouac to bivouac, begging for news of her husband. All those she spoke to tried to pull the wool over her eyes or did not reply. At dawn she hurried, by herself, onto the battlefield. After many hours spent in this terrible quest, she at last found the bloody, mutilated corpse of her husband, completely naked. She took him in her arms and dragged him back to camp, had him embalmed and placed in a casket. She never left him for a moment, carrying back to his family (in Paris) this proof of her love and of the horrors of war.

21 March: The last piece of cloth that remained in the Colonel's thigh has now come out; I can now look forward to my departure that has been so many times delayed, in spite of my own wishes.

1 April: Today, I tell my hosts that I am leaving – a difficult situation. The result of an indiscretion committed at Easter.

6 April: I comply with a letter from my mother. Heart-rending situation with Mademoiselle L——. The surgeons are ordered to rejoin.

7 April: I leave with two other officers. Charroi still remains. Düben, Wittenberg, Trebisen. To Potsdam on the 10th.

11 April: I have visited Frederick's palace, the famous Sans-Souci. From one side the appearance is of many terraces made of stained-glass windows. There are interesting details – Frederick's apartments, the room in which he died, the gallery, his armchair, the tomb of his white horse and those of his dogs; Voltaire's room full of parrots and monkeys. Since his death nothing has been touched. Beautiful gardens and a new palace. Very bad statues; we have carried off the best of them. I look at the Potsdam Palace. The King and Queen's apartments. The great salon in which Frederick sometimes held a review. His study, his tomb; Napoleon took away his sword and sash.

12 April: Dined with General Bourcier, Inspector of Cavalry, and again met the elder Potier, his aide-de-camp. Charroi has rejoined me.

13 April: To Berlin, 8 leagues. A magnificent journey; as we passed by I saw the famous marble palace. Berlin is a large and superb town; the roads are straight, some of them very wide and planted, like the Paris boulevards, with many rows of trees. The walks and public monuments are handsome, as is the courtyard, the castle and the fine bronze statue of the Elector on the bridge. The town appears somewhat deserted just at the moment. The upper-class area is fine and well-kept.

14 April: Passed through Dalwitz, travelled a double stage and slept at Munchberg. Poverty begins. Nevertheless, the route is well-provisioned; we have bread and half a pound of meat.

15 April: Custrin. This is a strong town on the Oder, well-fortified and surrounded by swamps. The fortifications could contain 10,000 men as well as their supplies. However, it would be possible for the town to be bombarded, as it has been by the Russians. The engineer officer in the town told us that 20 million cartridges had been sent to the *Grande Armée* in the course of four months.

16 April: Landsberg. A walled, but unfortified, town on the Wartha. We stayed until the 17th and saw, for the first time, the Polish militia in the service of France. The infantry wears square shakos and short blue coats with white lapels.

18 April: Driesen. A little town surrounded by marsh and floodwater. There are many Jews here.

19 April: Filehne. A big market town, full of Jews. The land is sandy and rocky. The inhabitants seem to me to be generally friendly.

20 April: Schönlanke. An even more impoverished town than the others.

22 April: The halt is at Grabione, a miserable village, 6 leagues from the previous one. All this country was Polish twenty-seven years ago; the inhabitants have preserved the language and the costume. They wear moustaches, and a sort of tight-fitting sheepskin hat on their heads with a long overcoat that almost drags on the ground and is belted. They occupy wretched, thatched cabins; we have pushed on to Wirsitz, a big town 4 leagues further on.

23 April: Nakel. This is a little town at the point where the canal joining the Oder and the Vistula begins. Frederick the Great set up a colony here. The colonists' houses are the only ones that are tiled; those of the native population are thatched.

24 April: Tzubing. To the right of Nakel we found, at Tzubing, a small regimental depôt. Here, I saw my faithful hussar, Carl, again and many others who had suffered frozen feet before Königsberg.

25 April: I finished my business with Gourlet.

26 April: Bromberg. A pretty, well-built town. Real poverty begins here; there are no storehouses.

27 April: From Bromberg to Fordon, 3 leagues. Fordon, a village, filled with Jews and smelling abominable, is situated on the bank of the Vistula that we crossed by ferry. We went on to Ostromerko and slept 2 leagues from Thorn. Today, at Ostromerko, Charroi and I separated. So now I am alone, crossing a ravaged countryside and not knowing where I can find my regiment. The innumerable corpses of horses, and the houses that had been stripped of thatch to feed them, tell me of the wretchedness that awaits me.

28 April: I travelled through Thorn, a big town on the Vistula that is heavily fortified. I slept at Crakoachim, 3 leagues from Gollub, at the home of Baron de Blumberg, whose son, captured at Lübeck, is a prisoner in France. Travelled 8 leagues.

29 April: Went through Gollub and slept at the miserable village of Lapinosee, a league from Strasbourg. Some of the army is here, I found the dragoons and covered 8 leagues.

30 April: I travelled through Strasbourg, over a horribly devastated country-side; all the houses are abandoned and the ground is covered with the corpses

of animals and with debris. I was, by a lucky chance, very comfortably lodged with a Captain Larcher of the 15th Light at Neumarkt. (Travelled 10 leagues).

1 May: I went through Löbau and slept in a village a league on the other side of it. (Travelled 5 leagues).

2 May: I reached the General Headquarters of Marshal Davout at Osterode. This is a pretty little village, very pleasant and well-built in the midst of wretchedness and terrible desolation. All along the way no food is to be found except by leaving the main route and going into the villages and even then there is hardly anything. Here, I learned where my new regiment might be found. I slept at Baucken Mühle, a pretty windmill standing at the head of a large lake in a valley between two forests. The place is wild and picturesque. Here I again breathed the air of the country, although it is still troubled by the chill breath of the war. (Travelled 12 leagues).

3 May: At last, I have come into harbour. I found the regiment spread out throughout four villages; the Staff at Jonkowo, 4 leagues from Allenstein, and 2 leagues from the Passarge, a little river that flows between the enemy and us.

6 May: On the 6th I received permission to go back to the 8th Hussars to arrange my affairs there.

7 May: Travelled through Schlit, and reached Liebstadt, which I found to be in flames. This is believed to be due to treachery. Only one house remained, all the rest were destroyed within three hours; it presented a picture of total desolation. I slept at Morungen, 4 leagues further on.

8 May: I left Saalfeld to my left, and after 8 leagues, reached Misswald, where I found the 8th Hussars, Charroi, Collins and several other friends. I devoted the following day to rest and to the pleasure of meeting old comrades once more.

10 May: I returned again to sleep in the little town of Morungen, went through Liebstadt on the 11th, where I saw Marshal Soult, and I slept at Schlit. There has been a great deal of fighting over all the country between this town and Allenstein; to which the bullets, the debris and the corpses that still cover this wretched land bear witness.

12 May: Returning again to Jonkowo, and failing to find the regiment still there, I went to Guisekendorf, a miserable village that has been almost entirely abandoned. It stands on the edge of a lake, half a league from Allenstein. The day was passed in fighting. Enemy cavalry appeared on the banks of the Passarge and attacked our outposts. There was firing all day long.

13 May: The enemy returned with artillery, and attempted, or seemed to attempt, to take Allenstein. There was cannon-shot and firing all day without any result other than wounded on both sides.

14 May: Everything is quiet, but we remain alert.

17 May: Duty at Guttstadt, under Marshal Ney.

22 May: The Colonel and the Staff left for Gilgenburg. We are no longer at Guisekendorf except for six officers and 100 men, who are to continue on duty at Guttstadt and Allenstein. The new route that we are following to Guttstadt, is along the Passarge, passing between our advance posts and those of the Russians.

1–4 June: False alarms. Everything quiet on the 4th.

6 June: At seven in the morning, 1,500 Cossacks crossed the river near a burned-out village and fell upon the infantry, pushing our forward posts back into the woods. At nine o'clock I went out on reconnaissance. The enemy had repaired the bridge at Bergfried, and his infantry and cavalry had crossed over and spread out between the III and VI Corps. At five in the evening the Marshal [*Soult – Ed.*] arrived, and sent an order to the divisions of Friant and Gudin and the light cavalry to come forward. Guttstadt seemed to us to be cut off, its communication with Schlit ruptured and the buildings on the riverside burned.

7 June: At eleven o'clock. The enemy seems to intend to hold his position. He holds the bridge at Bergfried in strength and has passed a large number of artillery across. Let us wait for the evening. The VI Corps seems to be surrounded; we hear bombardment and can see a great deal of smoke. All the camps near to Guttstadt seem to be burning. I was sent, at midnight, with thirty men to guard the line of the Alle, from the mill as far as Allenstein.

8 June: I drew back into a redoubt near Allenstein in the morning. The whole of III Corps retreated. I was to hold my position until eight in the evening, and then, myself, retreat if I had not been cut off. At eight in the evening the entire town and all the outposts were evacuated. I provided the rearguard, and withdrew to Ditterswald during the night; I found all the army corps assembled there.

9 June: I left at once, and went to the windmill, where I found General Lacour (he had come from the Siege of Gäeta) who, with two infantry regiments, was holding this heavily fortified position above a gorge in the middle of a wood. Here, we are waiting for the enemy.

At eight in the evening, no enemy having appeared, we withdraw on Osterode. The whole army is assembled there, and supplies for seven days are collected. The army marches all night and reaches the banks of the Passarge at dawn on the 10th.

At midday, all the infantry, carrying fascines, marches off to the music of the band, throws a bridge over the river and continues on to Guttstadt. I rejoin the regiment; we reach the walls of the town and bivouac on the right of the Alle with all the army, in battle order, along its bank. It was on this battlefield that the VI Corps, surrounded and cut off, had sustained the attack of 60,000 infantry and numberless cavalry. Marshal Ney had won glory, for he had lost no more than two or three thousand captured and some of his baggage.

[*Editor's note: fascines are bundles of sticks or branches, about 6 feet in length, tied together and used to line trenches or ditches. As for Gäeta – a formidable fortress on the west coast of Italy, defended by soldiers of the Kingdom of the Two Sicilies – it fell to a Franco-Neapolitan force on 18 July 1806, after a siege of some 142 days.*]

11 June: The army marches on Heilsberg. The brigade countermarches to the right, and occupies the bridge at Bergfried, over which the enemy had crossed. I rejoin General Marulaz, who takes me with him.

For five days, I had not closed my eyes. I was on horseback day and night and under orders. Biscuit and water were my only food. And all this as well as dysentery!

At two in the afternoon, the regiment was ordered to stay at the bridge until the Poles arrived, the remainder of the brigade (1st and 2nd Chasseurs) left to follow the army. We, too, left and bivouacked 3 leagues from Heilsberg, near to the Russian camp. There had been fighting all day, and cannon fire was still heard at eleven at night. The two armies face each other in battle order and the following day will certainly rank alongside those of Austerlitz and Jena. An examination of the state of the 8th Hussars: one *chef d'escadron* captured; General Guillot, the Major and the Sergeant Major, Amalric killed.

14 June: The Russian camps at Heilsberg are captured. We fought hard throughout the day and gained 4 or 5 leagues from the enemy; meanwhile, he retreats before us and does not seem anxious to engage in a full-scale battle today.

I saw Cossacks nearby for the first time; from two o'clock until nine in the evening we fired at each other and made several charges, but they were between 800 and 900 men against 200. We lost fifty men and horses. Colonel Asly was wounded. The General's horses and those of the aides-de-camp, as well as my modest accoutrements were captured by a Prussian patrol when they were only a hundred paces behind us.

13 June: The enemy abandoned all his positions and made off during the night. We followed, and marched all day in the direction of Eylau, sleeping 2 leagues away in a village where the ashes of Hautpoul and Corbineau remain.

14 June: We cross the famous battlefield of Eylau, where many brave Frenchmen lie, and see the cemetery that is so drenched in blood. Patience! Soon we shall avenge them, or follow them. We bivouacked 2 leagues from Königsberg, the steeples of which were in sight. Our orders being countermanded, we

march all night and reach Oderrangen, 6 leagues back, on the 15th, and return to Königsberg. We learn that the Emperor has utterly vanquished the enemy, who left 6,000 dead and 80 field guns on the battlefield [*i.e. of Friedland – Ed.*] Alas, where were we?!

15 June: We return to Oderrangen. The 12th rejoin us there; we went downriver and bivouacked in a village 4 leagues from Königsberg. Swam across the river at Tappiau. The IV Corps entered Königsberg this morning; we have pursued the enemy and taken a few prisoners. We bivouacked 3 leagues from Labiau.

17 June: We have contacted, attacked and routed the enemy and entered Labiau, after having put out the fire on the bridge. We crossed the Medlank [sic], chased the enemy for 5 leagues and took between 1,000 and 1,200 prisoners – infantry as well as cavalry.

Reaching Grosbaum, the enemy held us up for two hours at the entrance to the wood: we charged, took the position, and then returned to bivouac at the entrance of the wood. Malaise and Scoubar are dead.

18 June: We continued on our way; found the Emperor and all the army at Mehlauken. Bivouacked at Olrixen.

19 June: At Razgnit, a little town on the bank of the Memel, that was burned three weeks ago.

20 June: There is talk of peace. The Emperor and the General Staff are at Tilsit.

21 June: I am lodged with Monsieur de Sanden, the Grand Bailiff, at the castle of Toussainen.

22 June: The Emperor announces the peace in a proclamation.

24 June: The two Emperors meet on a raft in the middle of the River Memel [*German name for the River Niemen – Ed.*].

25 June: Emperor Alexander has taken up residence in this town.

26–28 June: There are reviews and manoeuvres. The King of Prussia has also arrived to take up residence at Tilsit. The III Corps performs manoeuvres before the three crowned heads.

1 July: I have again had the pleasure of witnessing a meeting of the three monarchs.

6 July: The Queen of Prussia arrives in Tilsit.

9 July: It is said that the Emperor has left for Königsberg.

10 July: I rejoin the company at Kussein.

20 July: Tilsit is evacuated, and the army corps sets out for Poland. The Emperor awards 320 Crosses to the III Corps.

23 July: At Insterburg, a pretty little town on the Pregel. The Prussians, in their arrogance and absurd vanity, follow us there.

24–26 July: At leisure. The Headquarters Staff is at Grosse Trumpen on the 26th.

27 July: I go to the charming town of Nordenburg and sleep in the handsome castle of Eglastein.

28 July: I remain at Nordenburg. The Count d'Eglastein is a pleasant man, but like all his compatriots, believes his country to be better than any other and is convinced that it has beaten the French. Here, the final meeting between the Emperor Alexander and Frederick William took place. Here, Alexander had publicly promised that he would rather lose all his land before he would allow him (Frederick William) to be forced to yield his.

29 July: Reached Barthen, a small town terribly ravaged by our infantry, where they had been ordered to seize everything. Remained here on the 30th. Went through Rössel to sleep at Sansdorf on the 31st.

1 August: Went through Bischofsburg, slept at Roclack on the banks of a lake. This countryside was the scene of the fighting in the summer where the two sides clashed, as can be seen from the surrounding devastation.

2 August: It is true that when forming the vanguard, the light cavalry acquires, at sword-point, some good things, but it has plenty of time to digest them when it becomes the rearguard. Covered 11 leagues and slept in a little town 3 leagues from Nordenburg.

3 August: The III Corps goes into temporary cantonments here. Marshal Davout is at Thorn, the Staff Headquarters of the 1st Division at Neidenburg, General Marulaz at Kleinstrauersee and the Colonel at Witzmandorf, and I am at Lipno with Baron Unruhe. We have fifty men at Allenstein patrolling the Alle, which the Prussians are forbidden to cross until the 16th. By 20 August we should have recrossed the Vistula.

7 August: Woe to all those French who desert or who lag behind. The Prussians are following close behind us; their pride, the defeat we have inflicted on them and our devastation of their countryside infuriates them beyond reason; the peasants kill all our stragglers. Near Osterode, huge ditches filled with murdered French have been found, as well as more corpses in a lake. A nobleman and twenty-five peasants have been shot after being convicted.

13 August: The infantry leaves.

15 August: Saint Napoleon, the birthday of the Emperor, celebrated with General Marulaz. There are details of Prince Constantine's brutality. All ranks, from field marshal down to *sous-lieutenant* and to the ordinary soldiers are subject to beatings. All the officers of Constantine's regiment have their teeth broken with the pommel of his sword.

[*Editor's note: Grand Duke Constantine (1779–1831), younger brother of Tsar Alexander I.*]

17 August: I leave Lipno and my skinny Baroness (Unruhe). I sleep at Usdau.

18 August: Travelled through Soldau, the last Prussian town. Crossed into Poland and lodged near the Mlawa. The villages are miserable and squalid, as are the peasants and serfs. The landlords are mean and filthy.

19–20 August: Near to Dobrzyn. Nearly all of Poland is full of Jews with their belted robes and long hair and beards. They are unable to obtain money to buy land and devote themselves to commerce, and to arts and crafts. Many of them sink into vagrancy and flood into the north of Germany.

21 August: Near Plock a pleasant town with a Polish garrison. I have found a dog, Wachtel, and shall bring her along with me.

22 August: I cross the Vistula by boat to Plock. It is with delight that I leave this land so soaked in blood and tears, where immortal laurels have been harvested from a heap of corpses. What contradictory emotions one feels; now we reach out to our fatherland, as if the brief crossing from one bank to another could wipe out the enormous gap that separates us from France, and now, as we look backwards to the far shore, we imagine the ghosts of our brave companions in arms, and bid them another farewell. I slept and stayed at Gostynin on 23rd.

24–27 August: I travel through Valy, near Kutno, Vitonia, see the fortress of Leczyca and the superb castle of Koskow.

28 August: At last! The end of my journey. The heat is extreme. Headquarters is at Sieradz, and I am at Volska Prierlinska. Now I can, once more, enjoy rest and the countryside.

1 September: I go to Bukoviess. As I did not take advantage of my leave to return to France while the fighting was going on, I claimed that permission today.

7 September: Bailly, returning from Warsaw, brought me Marshal Davout's permission to leave. As war with Austria is rumoured, I am leaving my horses, my baggage and my servant with the regiment, so that I can come back again as soon as needed.

8 September: Farewell damnable Poland! Farewell filthy barons and wicked landowners! Farewell to my big packhorse! I take my horses and reach Kempen, 20 leagues from Sieradz.

9 September: Wartenberg. A pretty little town. It is here that Poland ends and Silesia begins. The landscape changes completely. It is like leaving Tartary and moving into the Elysian Fields. Breslau is a magnificent, well-built town with a large population and in a fine position. The fortifications have been demolished.

10–11 September: I pass through Neumarkt and Görlitz into Saxony. The Silesian towns I have crossed were very attractive and well-built, the country fertile and pleasant with very good roads.

12 September: Lauban to Bautzen. There are Saxon troops and town governors everywhere. Schöfeld is only a staging post. The road to Dresden is in a bad state, through deep woods. After leaving Breslau, the mountain chain separating Saxony and Silesia from Bohemia, is to the right, and there are picturesque views.

13 September: I stayed here to see the town. A mass, attended by the King of Saxony, took place on Sunday. I saw the King and his family; his daughter, aged about twenty-five or twenty-six, is quite pretty, she is plump and appeared to be very bored; the Princess, cousin of our late Queen Marie-Antoinette, the Queen of Saxony, her brothers and family were also present. The King is already quite old with a continual tic of his head. He is very devout and his family attends mass faithfully every day. The music was wonderful, with superb Italian singing; reverence and decorum was observed in the church to the last detail. Dresden is a fine town with old churches and a beautiful tower and bridge. There are public squares and fountains, as well as a picture gallery that I was not able to see. The town has 50,000 inhabitants including about 6,000 Catholics, but seems a little empty. I saw the Saxon Guard; the troops are in magnificent uniforms, especially the cuirassiers, the Red Dragoons and the King's Guard. I enjoyed a pleasant walk around the town.

14 September: From Dresden to Meissen, hillsides covered with vines and granite rocks are to be seen. The Elbe is crossed by a covered bridge at Meissen where there is a strongly fortified castle. The garrison is composed of Saxon artillery in their fine uniforms with green coats, yellow breeches and gold braided hats. On to Leipzig.

15 September: Leipzig. I spent the day with Mme. Lötze and Wilhelmine, and felt, in this charming family, some of the happiness that would await me when I reached my own home.

16 September: Weissenfeld to Naumburg. At this town I left the road leading to Jena and passed, with a heavy heart, near these fields where so many of our brave comrades lie. I remembered them and felt fresh sorrow for young Bernier and courageous Chardron. Then on through Butelstet to Erfurt; this duchy may be the only part of Germany where there is a police force, and this consists of only one man. The river that flows through Erfurt makes it quite a pleasant town.

17 September: I reached Gotha at dawn; this attractive town belongs to the Duke of the same name. The town is dominated by the fine castle that it surrounds. There are public squares, gardens and fountains. Today, a festival was held to mark the start of the hunting season; on the first day anyone may join in the hunt, when the game is given to the town. The famous almanacs are published here.

18 September: Fulda, where I arrived at midnight, is remarkable for its abbey. I continued on to Frankfort, and I remained there on the 19th and 20th so that the Prince of Salm, with whom I had travelled since leaving Görlitz, could conduct some business. This is a large, wealthy and busy city on the River Main.

21 September: We leave for Mayence, where we were inspected at the town gates. There are 100,000 customs officers stationed along the Rhine. My travelling companion, who was present when the Austrians and Prussians besieged this town, showed me all the various military dispositions. It is easy to see the difference between the waters of the Main and that of the Rhine where they flow together.

I cannot express the joy I felt at eleven in the morning when I again saw France! How much more precious one's country becomes, when one has risked one's life and spilt one's blood in her cause! We only lingered in Mayence long enough to obtain post horses to ride to Paris.

22–23 September: Passed through Saabrucken and reached Metz at dawn. In this town I saw many Russian prisoners who were being put in uniform and formed into regiments. It was said that they were to be sent to the coast at Boulogne, and destined for an attack on England. It would not be possible to pass Epernay without celebrating the good wine of Champagne, so much better than Polish beer!

24 September: I arrived in Paris in the evening, but I did not find my parents there.

25–26 September: I visited some of my old acquaintances.

27 September: I left again, with my faithful Wachtel [*Tascher's dog – Ed.*].

28 September: I reached Mortagne at one o'clock, and set off, post-haste for Bellême, where I arrived at two and then on to Pourvrai at three o'clock. Today is one of the happiest of my life. I find all my family in good health. Every step I take brings back a crowd of childhood memories and reminders of past happiness.

1 October: I am revelling in a peace and happiness, that is even more enjoyable when I contrast it with the trouble and discomfort I have endured in the past two years. Here, love is repaid with love, tenderness with tenderness, and one need not fear false friends. Here, one breathes the untainted air of one's homeland, and only here can I feel truly alive; all that went before was but a dream, a delirium. In the maelstrom in which I lived for the past three years, I was perpetually in a throng of other people and seldom alone. Now, one is genuinely oneself and can speak from one's heart. When shall I live thus again? But no, I must turn my eyes away from these enchanting ideas; if I do not, I am sure that I shall no longer be able to maintain the vital resolution I need. One has no right to rest until one has laboured; one cannot, one should not, live for one's self, alone. O, my country!

13 October: I have received a letter from my regiment: I must leave so that I can make some small purchases for it.

14 October: Today is the anniversary of Jena. A day to be remembered forever! I left Pourvrai and my family this morning.

16 October: I arrived in Paris this morning

21 October: I saw Racine's *Iphigenie*, with Lafond in the rôle of Achille. I divide my admiration between the author and the actors.

25 October: I quickly dispatch the business for my regiment on 26th and leave for Lille on 27th.

29 October: I reached Lille at two in the morning. I have so many memories of this town that I feel myself two years younger. Wherever I go, I remember a moment from that delightful period that is only experienced once in a lifetime. There is a place where we played out the bloodiest of battles, where my youthful heart thrilled with thoughts of glory and longing for a fine cavalry charge, and where this sabre held in a trembling hand seemed impatient to strike. There is the room where my ailments were tended with such loving care. Here, this prison, this parade ground, where I mounted my first guards as a hussar and as a corporal.

I met the families Vernot, Datis and Bigot again, all of them heaped kindness upon me and I felt once more, when I embraced M. and Mme. Fosseaux, some of the sensations that my own family had woken in me. The good M. de

Fosseaux … But, alas! His charming wife could embrace me, could hear me, but could no longer see me. Blindness is a terrible affliction and how brave she is!

31 October: I left at four in the morning, passed through Douai and Cambrai, then took the post and reached Havrincourt in the evening.

1 November: I have had the happiness of embracing a dear sister who I had not seen for three years. When I left her she was a girl, now I find her a wife and mother. How quickly the stages of a life are passed, without our being aware of them!
[*Editor's note: a reference to Tascher's elder sister, Charlotte (1781–1852), wife of Marquis Henri de Cardevac d'Havrincourt.*]

14 November: Saint-Hubert's Hunt. I lead such a delightful life here. I rise at 10, breakfast at 11 and hunt until nightfall then, enjoy an excellent dinner, followed by music, chess and a comfortable evening at the fireside. Wonderful existence! How good all this feels by comparison with the cold of Poland, and how comfortable my bed when I recollect the discomfort of that campaign, and how delicious is the food, when I think of the misery and the hunger that we so often suffered.

15 November: Happy times always pass too quickly. My parents, now back in Paris, summon me to return there. When I arrived at Havrincourt, I met a brother-in-law who I barely knew and today, I parted from a friend and brother. Adversity and grief has given him a rather harsh exterior, but what a good heart this enclosed!

My dear sister took me as far as Cambrai to meet the public coach; we both felt great sorrow at this parting.

Cambrai, Saint-Quentin, Compiègne are the places where provisional regiments are being formed to go to Portugal. All available troops in France are on the way to that country, which will undoubtedly become the theatre of great events.
[*Editor's note: the weariness of the French Army after the recent campaign and the imminence of the Spanish campaign, made it necessary to form new regiments, mostly composed of conscripts. Over time, regular units were mixed into the new formations to supply the experience and training that were lacking in the 'provisionals'.*]

16 November: I reached Paris this evening and saw my parents again.

20 November: I am very busy in Paris and my days are usefully employed. At nine in the morning there is a physical training course at the French College with my brother; also with my brother, I attend the fencing master at ten o'clock. Then at eleven o'clock I am with the violin master at the opera, and at

two o'clock I have a German lesson. After dinner, comes a chess contest, very closely fought; I see very little company (at home), but pay many visits. It is the same at every house, except for those who have visiting days. The lady of the house is alone at half past seven, or goes out. There is actually very little society in Paris. The circle of the Tuileries and the theatres on one hand and on the other, distance and bad weather make it very difficult to meet any but one's near neighbours at home.

21 November: To see Sainvilliers again has been a great and longed for happiness. He is now a lieutenant in the 5th Hussars, and he is quite unchanged. How very fortunate I am to have such a friend! He came from Namur on his way to Portugal [*to join Junot's army of occupation – Ed.*] and had obtained permission to take a few days' leave on the way, to see his parents. There are so many things for two friends to talk about! We were together from six in the evening until four in the morning, when he left for Orléans from where he is to return to his regiment at Tours. To Portugal! There is talk of an expedition to Africa, others speak of Ireland, while some claim that it will be to Gibraltar. We shall see: there will always be some expedition; I pray I may be part of it!

On one hand there is inactivity in Poland, and on the other, an enterprise in which I shall be close to my best friend. There can be no doubt about it, my mind is made up.

4 December: I am twenty-one today; a year ago I was at Leipzig. Poor Wilhelmine! The *Geburstag* [*i.e. birthday – Ed.*] will not be the same for her this year. Ah! may next year's anniversary find you changed; may those that follow quite erase from your heart a memory that torments and destroys you and may crushed hope be replaced by peace and not by despair. Such hopes were vain, if indeed she held them! Ah! may I never awaken such hopes!

I am truly happy that I have nothing with which to reproach myself in her case. Another, in my place, might have taken advantage of her feelings and not repaid them with such sincere friendship. Poor Wilhelmine!

16 December: I am to go to Portugal. The Minister of War has granted my request, and I have today written to my poor Georges that he is to rejoin me with my horses.

Wilhelmine – the memory makes my heart bleed! But Sainvilliers! A campaign! All other thoughts will vanish in the heat of combat.

29 December: I left, today, for Orléans with Ferdinand, and saw my three brothers again. I am worried about Frédéric's health. I was overjoyed to greet my uncle de Tristan and my good aunt and to see my relations and friends once more.

[*Editor's note: Louis-Frédéric de Tascher (1795–1808), Maurice's second youngest brother.*]

30 December: There are those whose lack of feeling, apathy, envy and egotism are quite disgusting; who, feeling no sense of duty to their native land, are irritated when they see that others do not share their views. Those who, always seeking profit and yet more profit, have replaced the word 'honour' with the word 'profit', for honour is, to them, a word without meaning. Money and profit is, forever, upon one side of the scales and honour on the other. One would gladly renounce such a town for the sake of one's country, were it not for the fact that it contains many friends and beloved relations.

[*Editor's note: old and powerful prejudices against all those who supported the government, or wore its uniform, had caused Maurice to receive a cold and disdainful welcome from many of his acquaintance, and even from his family. This had sickened him, and it is to this feeling that the anger expressed in this entry is attributable.*]

Chapter 2

Spain: January–June 1808

1808

1 January: I left Orléans on the 2nd, reaching Paris in the evening of the 3rd. On the 10th there was great anxiety for Frédéric, who had suddenly fallen ill; on the same day my orders came from the Minister to go to Portugal when my leave ended on 26 January. I am still dividing my time between exercise, fencing practice, music and German, for I see very little company and take less pleasure in high society and balls with every day that passes.

19–20 January: I have been looking at some of the many improvements that have been made to the capital in the course of the past few years. The Louvre has been finished; new quays have been built and also the bridges of Austerlitz and Jena, which will remind our children of our victories. There is a column in the Place Vendôme *ex æe capto* [*a reference to the fact that the bronze column was made from 1,200 melted cannon, captured from the enemy – Ed.*] and a road has been opened from it to the garden of the Tuileries. There is an enormous project for a temple of victory to be built to the glory of the French armies. The names of those wounded at the battles of Jena, Eylau and Friedland are to be inscribed on marble plaques in letters of silver, and those of the dead in letters of gold.

23 January: I went, for the first time to the great masked ball at the opera: *The Adventure of the Black Domino.*

24 January: The result of the 'Adventure': a letter, a stupid début, an embarrassing meeting.

28 January: My leave expires today, and I went to obtain my movement order, but as there is no fighting, I am able to spend another twenty days here, and then travel post.

1 February: Today is the first day on which the public is able to see David's painting of the coronation. The beauty and grace of the Empress Josephine is admired beyond anything, as is the impression of the whole picture.

3 February: Frédéric is extremely ill and has been brought here from Orléans by my kind aunt and her son.

8 February: I went to the Riding School at Versailles, to see Bizemont, Gondrecourt and the officer of the 10th Dragoons who, at Lapinosee in Poland, so generously shared his bread and straw with me. I visited the gardens and felt a mixture of admiration and sorrow when I looked upon the magnificence of Louis XIV that is, today, gloomy, silent and scorned. Versailles needs a court to breathe life into it, and a soul to animate its splendid body.

13 February: Time rushes past, but the day of my departure remains the same. I must be at Bayonne on 28th. Today is the marriage, of Mlle. Stéphanie Tascher – now a Princess – to the Prince of Arenberg. They are to occupy the mansion opposite to ours.

18 February: By this evening, I shall have left behind me all that I hold most dear in the world. Who knows for how long it will be or, indeed, who I shall see again? I have never before felt so sad at a parting; Frédéric is dangerously ill and Wilhelmine is dying, I have no news of my servant or of my horses. I am setting off alone for an army in which I do not know a soul, and I am leaving my beloved family behind me. It is at times like this that one is briefly aware of the shining illusion that surrounds the iron yoke that we bear. But we need this illusion, for one must arm oneself in courage or sink into nothingness.

19 February: I slept at Blois, where one can see the place where the Duke of Guise was assassinated and even the trace of his blood that the guide to the place is careful to renew from time to time by slaughtering a chicken. The bridge is handsome but the town is badly built and the roads descend in steps. It is possible to spit in your neighbour's pot from a window across the street. It was a strange sensation to meet a detachment of the 8th Hussars commanded by Captains Subra and La Bourdonnais.

20 February: We pass through Amboise and Tours to dine at Poitiers; a big and ugly town, one of the few in France that are so badly built. The roads are uneven, twisting and deserted. Travelled all night.

22 February: Vivone, Ruffec, Mansle, Angoulême. There is a high and a low town here, both of them equally badly built. There are ancient fortifications and in front of the town, a pretty rotunda, from which there is an extensive view of the River Charente winding at the foot of the walls; but the surrounding countryside, covered with vines and with trees, looks deserted. Again, I travel all night.

23 February: The route that has so far been very good becomes very bad near Saint-André. But the countryside grows more attractive near Cubzac. The confluence of the Garonne and the Dordogne, the start of the bec d'Ambés and Médoc [*the name of the point of confluence of the two rivers – Ed.*] – the country venerated by wine-drinkers – can be seen from the road. Cubzac is 6 leagues

from Bordeaux and the imposing ruins of the castle of the Lords of Montauban
– the so-called Four Sons of Aymon.

[*Editor's note: a reference to the story of Charlemagne's struggle against four brothers, sons of the Duke Aymes, renowned in chivalric song and story.*]

24 February: I crossed the Dordogne by ferry at dawn, and travelled 6 leagues
on foot to Bordeaux, the better to enjoy this lovely countryside, which is dotted
with pretty country houses. When I reached La Bastide, I was struck with
admiration at the view of the Bordeaux anchorage. The quays are magnificent,
bordered, as they are for a distance of 2 leagues, with fine houses. I crossed the
famous Garonne, a river hardly less celebrated than the Styx. There is a fine
triumphal arch, erected for the Emperor who is expected any day. Prince
Murat passed through tonight. There are dark clouds over Spain.

I travelled all through the town and saw the ruins of the Gallien Palace.
These ruins, that should inspire so much interest, are cluttered with miserable
hovels. There are superb boulevards lined with trees, and I also saw the
Château Trompette that was built by Louis XI, at the expense of the rebellious
citizens.

25 February: I left for Bayonne at six in the morning. There are seventy-five
post stages between Paris and Bordeaux, and thirty-three from Bordeaux to
Bayonne. I dined at Castres, on the lovely banks of the Garonne, adorned with
rocks, trees and fine houses. The fabulous desert countryside of the Landes
begins at Langon. I slept at Bazas.

26 February: We are surrounded by sand in this arid desert; its capital is
Roquefort – not the town made famous by its cheese. The peasants travel
everywhere, very fast, on stilts that are tied to their legs; their clothes are made
of black sheepskins, with the fleece on the outside; they wear little, flat, plate-
like hats that seem held in equilibrium on the top of their heads, like the
primitive dress of Robinson Crusoe. They have cloaks with brown hoods. The
women are pretty, shapely and slender, almost all of them are brunettes. From
here, we can see the Pyrenees, although we are still 48 leagues away.

Mont-de-Marsan is a charming little town, such as one would hardly expect
to find in the middle of the Landes. Everywhere, along the road since leaving
Paris, there have been pyramids, triumphal arches and guards of honour
awaiting the arrival of the Emperor. Mont-de-Marsan also has a guard of
honour, mounted on stilts.

27 February: I dined at Tartas on the Midouze, where the ruins of an old castle
built by Henri IV stand, and then passed near to Dax, where the steam from
the hot spring can be seen from a quarter of a league away. The heat of the
spring is so great that one cannot place a hand in it. The pool is about 30 feet

across. I have been told that there is a fine hospital at Dax. I slept at Saint-Joux, still surrounded by sand and woods.

28 February: The inhabitants of this part of the world stare at strangers, following them with their eyes with a look of amazement and stupefaction that, together with their clothing gives them, at first, the appearance of savages seeing Europeans for the first time. They have the reputation, however, of being very zealous and anxious to be of service. On holidays, the men and the women gather in groups separately and their diversion is to drink, sometimes to the point of drunkenness. The wine is heavy, practically black in colour and very strong. A great deal of corn is grown here and the *galettes* [*a sort of pancake – Ed.*] that are made from it are much favoured. There is a strange way of travelling on horseback in this area; it is called 'cacolier'. The horse carries two platforms, balanced across its back, and two people, of more or less equal weight, travel seated one on each side.

There is no road at all through this sandy desert. However, a few leagues before Bayonne is seen the remains of a wide road that was built for the Count d'Artois when he was on his way to besiege Gibraltar. There is another way to travel from Bordeaux to Bayonne, even worse than this one. We journey through the Grand Landes; there is one stretch of 14 leagues where there is not one house or tree to be seen. About 4 or 5 leagues before Bayonne there is a big lake that extends as far as the sea, and is said to be full of fish. Around it there are many cork trees; this is a type of oak with a bark that can be taken off every two or three years and is very profitable for the owner.

At midday, I arrive at Bayonne, a town in a fine position on the coast at the foot of the Pyrenees. There are wonderful views and a handsome wooden bridge. The anchorage at Bayonne is unsafe, for a wide sandbar makes the entrance to it both difficult and dangerous. I saw the sea again with the same feelings of surprise and admiration that I experienced the first time. I explored the dockyard at Bayonne, and examined every part of a seventy-eight gun warship. The *Dordogne* and the *Gironde* were in the shipyard. There is a tower at the entrance to the anchorage, from which signals can be made to shipping.

1 March: Prince Murat is here, and the Governor of the town gave a ball for him, to which I went. The capture of Pamplona is becoming generally known. The town was taken by surprise, during a distribution of bread, by French soldiers pretending to have a snowball fight.

2 March: Irun. I arrive at Lent and in Spain on the same day. Nothing was ever more precise. I left Bayonne with Monsieur Violas, we dined at Saint-Jean-de-Luz and there, finding no horses available, harnessed oxen to the coach.

Urrugne, is a village across the Pyrenees, in the Basque country. The men are magnificent, tall and well-made and have the reputation of making excellent infantry. The women are delightful, elegant with dark eyes and hair, lively and coquettish. I saw a sight of unequalled beauty when we first entered the mountains. Just before Irun there is a wooden bridge between France and Spain. This bridge is nearly surrounded by snow-covered mountains, half-concealed in cloud, on one side there is the broad sweep of the sea, while, on the other, the village of Irun can be seen in the distance. The last rays of the dying sun set the sea aflame and coloured the clouds and snowy mountains so that the whole picture was such as no art could hope to achieve. I slept at Irun and obtained an order for transport from the Spanish quartermaster.

3 March: I dined at Hernani, 3 leagues inside Spain, which is a dirty, badly built little town. The Spaniards are revoltingly dirty; in this country, which appears to be two centuries behind us, none of the conveniences of life are known. We are still travelling in the mountains, by the side of a torrent made up of the streams that rush into it on every side, plunging over the rocks to form cascades. The women seem to attach great importance, not to the cleanliness, but to the length of their hair; nearly all of them have dark locks, falling in a plait right down their backs. The men of every rank, in the heat as well as in the cold, are muffled to the nose in a cloak; black is worn by the upper classes and brown by the lower orders. It is the characteristic national dress.

3 March: Talosa is a pretty little town in the midst of the mountains, a wild and picturesque spot, surrounded by boulders, by the side of a delightful river. I notice that, from the palace down to the humble cottage, all the houses have balconies. The water throughout Spain is very good.

4 March: At Villareal we are still among snow-covered mountains that are scattered with a great number of boulders of marble and of slate. It would seem, however, that the inhabitants make no use of these at all, for only tiles are to be seen. Varied pictures, both wonderful and imposing, are formed by the torrents that leap down amongst the rocks and by the effect of sun and cloud on the mountains. But in this little town, where the streets are narrow and ill-paved, everything speaks of misery and squalor. The unbelievable number of convents and churches and of monks and priests has already struck me, and I think that I discern an outward affectation of religiosity concealing an inner contempt for its laws and ethos. The clergy are horribly corrupt. The women here are enveloped in large shawls, worn over the head and falling to their feet; this is as customary as are the cloaks worn by the men. The shawls worn by rich women are made of silk trimmed with cut velvet.

The roads, everywhere in Spain are admirable and perfectly maintained; in some places, especially in the mountains, the work undertaken must have been prodigious. The road itself is made of cobbles and is bordered by a pavement of dressed stone for foot travellers. The edges of the road are marked, and where the terrain permits, there are ditches and trees.

5 March: to Mondragon. This little town has a handsome town hall. We are still among the mountains. Nature all around us has a severe and terrible aspect. On leaving Mondragon, a high mountain must be crossed, beyond which the road is more level as far as Vittoria, one league distant. The eye, wearied at the sight of beauty so savage and huge, is grateful to rest upon a gentler more cultivated countryside. I reached Vittoria as night fell.

6 March: Miranda. I travelled through Vittoria this morning. There is a fine square, well-built and surrounded by arcades, as are several other squares and some of the roads. Although one sees some handsome buildings, most of the streets are narrow and dirty.

I travelled post as far as Irun and in a coach drawn by oxen as far as Vittoria, but when I reached Vittoria, everything failed me, and I was only able to obtain a mule. So, here I am, alone and completely isolated in a country whose language I cannot speak and where the French are regarded by some with dread, by others with horror and by all with distrust. At Miranda de Ebro I finally emerged from the mountains. There is nothing noteworthy about the town except a quite handsome bridge over the Ebro, which is not very wide at this point, and a half-ruined old castle. Among the ruins of the latter I saw a moat entirely filled with bones. I was delighted to meet La Bretonnière, an officer of the 3rd Cuirassiers, here.

7 March: Pancorbo. My baggage, which I left behind at Vittoria, has not arrived and this placed me in a difficult situation and prevented me from covering more than one stage. The road from Miranda to Pancorbo is, in places, cut through rock and affords views of great beauty. Enormous crags rise sheer from the road and appear, hanging overhead, as if they are about to fall and crush the traveller. Pancorbo itself is nothing but a wretched village between two high rocks, of which the one to the left is surmounted by a fort armed with twenty-seven cannon. I climbed to the top of the one on the right. Happily, my baggage has caught up with me.

8 March: Briviesca [*25 miles/40 km north-east of Burgos – Ed.*]. I had already travelled from Pancorbo to Briviesca with La Bretonnière, where, with great regret, I parted from him. I admit that I hesitated. By staying with him, apart from the pleasure of his company, I also avoided many discomforts, inconveniences and dangers; but the voice of duty ordered me to reach my destination as soon as possible and to ignore all else. So I resisted the entreaties of La Bretonnière. All the [army] corps are on the move.

The Prince Murat and the Emperor are expected every day; the Imperial Guard left Bayonne on the 4th. The Spaniards are intrigued and anxious in the extreme, wearying themselves with conjectures about our plans, of which we know no more than they. Everyone has his own idea; one notion sends us to Africa, another to Ireland and yet another to Gibraltar. The Spaniards fear for their country. Everyone speculates, but no one knows anything.

At noon, I left Briviesca alone, for Monasterio, mounted on a vicious mule and without a bridle, saddle or stirrups, sitting astride it on a straw mattress with my feet on folded sackcloth and guiding my mount by means of an iron chain attached to a halter. What a faithful copy I present of the Knight of the Sorrowful Countenance!

Monasterio is a miserable little village set in an almost uninhabited country-side, in which it is possible to travel for 5 or 6 leagues without setting eyes on even a hamlet. During this tedious journey there is not a farm, not a country house, few or no trees or fields, and all around lies a stony desert, arid, un-cultivated and mountainous. I am beneath a lovely sky but crossing a wretched land!

9 March: I reached the fine, big city of Burgos at noon. There is a well-built square with arcades around it, as are most squares in Spain, and a handsome quay running along the small River Arlanzon that flows past the town. Adjoining the quay there is an attractive portico with four stone statues and on the square, a bronze statue of Charles III. A well-fortified citadel commands the town.

Burgos Cathedral is said to be one of the most beautiful in Spain; but it is a gothic sort of beauty, in bad taste; the nave is surrounded by a bronzed and gilt screen of considerable magnificence. The carving on the pillars outlining the nave is so overburdened with ornamentation that it becomes absurd, and the eye grows bewildered by a mass of detail that was certainly not inspired by good taste. This highly decorated nave is somewhat similar to the exterior of the one at Chartres. As one walks around the church one sees many chapels, and all are embellished with the same grandeur and in the same bad taste. All the sculpture and paintings in this church are detestable. Not knowing the language, I have been unable to ask any of the questions about the things that interest me in this town.

11 March: Villodrigo. I left Celada del Camino, a miserable village, at dawn, as badly equipped as ever. The Spaniards show themselves to be more and more ill disposed towards us, and they voice their dislike energetically. The other day, when I found myself in a smoke-filled house, although I did not complain, my gestures made it clear that my eyes were irritated by it; 'if the smoke in our country offends you, why don't you stay at home?' a Spaniard asked me sternly.

The weather is terrible: hail, rain, wind and bitter cold, from which I have suffered greatly in my present way of travelling. The legions of infantry, all made up of young men of about seventeen, have left many of their number along the way, dead of cold and wretchedness. I tried to save one of them (Guillaume Contzin), but he died in my arms as I tried to move him. I reached Valladolid at nightfall.

[*Editor's note: the army of General Dupont was composed almost entirely of the barely trained conscripts called up in anticipation of 1808. They were quite incapable of resisting the rigours of a very hard campaign. This was one of the causes of the disaster at Bailén.*]

12 March: Valladolid. Here I find the Commander-in-Chief, Dupont [*Pierre-Antoine Dupont de l'Etang (1765–1840) was considered at that time to be the best divisional general in the army – Ed.*], Frésia, the general commanding our division, and an officer of my regiment. Now, at last, I am at the end of my troubles. In all my life, I have never been as miserable as when I was travelling alone through this dismal country. I have had, also, the happiness of meeting again the aide-de-camp Captain Boutier, who was in hiding at Orléans for a long while for having engaged in *chouannerie* [*name given to followers of the Royalist partisan Jean Chouan – Ed.*] and Captain Gaillard, a friend of Collins.

Valladolid is a big, badly built town; the square and the town hall are quite attractive. The cathedral is large, rich, and in similar style to the one at Burgos. The wide parade ground is outside the town, and it is here that the troops manoeuvre. The Spanish regiment – the Queen's Cavalry – is here. For the last five days, rioting and brawling have started between the French soldiers on the one hand, and the inhabitants and the Spanish soldiers on the other.

13 March: Medina. I find that the 2nd Provisional Regiment is here (Major Bureau and Captain Besson). Today, there were extensive manoeuvres at Valladolid and a firing exercise that cost the life of General Mahler, who was killed by the ramrod of a gun.

14–15 March: In the time of Charles V, Medina contained 80,000 inhabitants but now has barely 5,000. The castle and fortifications are in ruins and many houses are deserted. I am told that this is the result of a siege. The huge number of priests here, as in other Spanish villages, is one of the causes of depopulation. There are seventeen convents in Medina. The Inquisition still rules, but it is hardly more than a haunting memory; the people are much more superstitious than religious and violate the rules of religion, especially those that decree fasting.

The Spaniards possess all the most dangerous philosophical works; these poisonous ideas begin to insinuate themselves amongst them and the leaders dare to hope for revolution. None of the arts is encouraged here, even the towns provide nothing of this sort, and the smallest amenities of life are unknown. Most of the houses have neither windows nor chimneystacks, while, for part of the winter, one is forced to warm oneself in the rooms around a copper basin supported upon a wooden tripod. At nine in the evening, the order to leave is given. General Frésia and the rest of the division arrive.

16 March: We leave Medina. The entire army corps, artillery, cavalry and infantry are together, as if to meet the enemy. We have just received an ambiguous proclamation, one that, without declaring war, orders bivouacs, sentries and forward posts etc. into position and advises us to be wary of the populace. As a result, we bivouac in Olmedo, with sentries posted and we anticipate a fight tomorrow.

17 March: The Commanding General has arrived; the army corps has gathered, vigilance is maintained, with sentries and outposts. The whole day is passed in great uncertainty.

18 March: As we did yesterday, we continue our march towards Madrid, living as if we were in enemy territory. We halted at Martinmunoz and bivouacked.

19 March: There has been another ambiguous proclamation, this time to forbid looting. One does not know what to think or to believe. Matters should not be like this in the country of our allies and we can see no enemies. We are exhausted, the weather is horrible and we are lost; we spend a very unpleasant night.

20 March: We are stationary. There is talk of a big uprising in Madrid. Spanish women are reputed to be passionate, but this does not diminish their good sense. I have seen much evidence of virtue – at least, outwardly. To attempt to embrace a woman in public is to inflict on her the worst possible insult. It is quite unforgivable and she will punish it severely and at once. Many of the French, used to the informality of the Germans, have learned, by means of a brisk slap, that they are now in another country. I have heard that the successful lover here is the most unfortunate in the world, for the women are jealous, demanding and cruel to the last degree. The greatest kindness that a fair one can show her knight is, they say, to search his hair for the little natives of the country.

21 March: On leaving Espinar, we crossed the mountains that are now covered with snow and ice. We were extremely cold, but then we came down into a pleasant valley and followed the road towards Madrid, arriving refreshed at Guadarrama. We continued on our way, but having received a countermanding order, we bivouacked at Villalba, a small village to the left, in the midst of rocks. Here we learn that there had been a disturbance and a bloody revolt in Madrid. The result of this is that the Prince of the Peace has been arrested and shackled. It is rumoured that he wanted to oppose our march, dethrone the King and put himself in the King's place.

[*Editor's note: Dom Manuel Godoy, a favourite of Queen Louise, wife of Charles IV. Feeling himself to be in danger, he had determined to flee to Mexico with the King and Queen, but the people rose up against them. Charles IV, in order to protect his Minister, was forced to abdicate in favour of his son, Ferdinand VII, who he loathed, but he cancelled the abdication as soon as the rioting was crushed.*]

23 March: Prince Murat, with the Imperial Guard and 30,000 men, enters Madrid. By means of a sudden revolution the Prince of Asturia (later Ferdinand VII) is crowned King in place of his father, who retreats, it is said, to Toledo. We have left Villalba and have come to Gualapagar, 4 leagues from Madrid.

24 March: No movement. General Moncey's corps and the Headquarters of Generals Dupont and Frésia are in Madrid.

25 March: A court martial takes place, in which I defended and saved a *chasseur* of the 20th Regiment named Gérard. I receive a letter from my brother Ferdinand, to tell me that there is dreadful anxiety about Frédéric. There is also a letter from Mademoiselle Lötze to say that, although she did not see him, my servant passed through Leipzig on 17 February.

I took advantage of our stay here to visit the Escorial Castle. But of greater interest is the large church, containing a vault that serves as a sepulchre for the kings of Spain. To one side, outside the choir, is the door leading to this vault. I went, by torchlight, down the highly polished marble staircase. Halfway down, there is a door leading to what is known as the place of putrefaction (*pourissoir*). It is here that the bodies of the sovereigns are left until corruption has detached the flesh from the bones; they are then gathered up to be placed in the room of tombs. This room is octagonal and situated beneath the main altar. Opposite the door is an altar on which the last funeral rites are celebrated. The whole room is of marble and the slab, against which the golden figure of Christ rests, is of a particularly rare and precious variety. The other walls of the room each contain four marble tombs, placed one above the other and standing on gilded copper feet. What thoughts arise on the hollowness of human life and the immortality of the soul! What a sight to consider! On one side we see the long line of kings and the magnificence of their history, and on the other, the narrow grave, the little space that holds their ashes.

The convent of the Escurial is immensely rich. There are 200 monks here and only those with great titles are admitted. The Prior, a man of great virtue and learning, was kind enough to accompany me on my tour. Near the palace is a little village that is the Versailles of Spain. Oh, Charles Quint [*i.e. Holy Roman Emperor Charles V, who, as Charles I, was also King of Spain – Ed.*], if only a spark of your genius could rise from your cold ashes! But no, it died with you, shut up in your tomb, and your successor has not the power to revive it.

What would you say if you could see the successor of the king you captured at Pavia advancing into Spain? [*Francis I was taken prisoner by Charles V of Spain at the Battle of Pavia in 1525 – Ed.*]

27 March: I am to go to Las Rosas, a roadside village 2 leagues from Madrid, for which I set out immediately, reaching it in the evening.

28 March: I spend the day looking round Madrid and at midnight, return to join the regiment at Las Rosas.

29 March: All of us go back to Madrid, the *chasseurs* are in the Las Rapies barracks and I am at the home of the Spanish Colonel Miguel de Alcazar in Calle de Toledo, near Sebada Square.

31 March: We are hardly able to look around, for we are so crushed beneath our duties and wearied by distributing supplies over a wide area.

I have learned the details of the revolution that has just taken place. The Prince of the Peace (Godoy) had grabbed for himself all the power, all the money – and all the hatred, for he is universally feared and disliked. Any favour that did not emanate from him was sure to be dishonoured. No one received any pay. In the King's house I have seen servants practically in rags, who had not been paid their wages for six years.

Made fearful by the approach of the French, he (Godoy) wished to seize the King, escort him to a seaport, and then leave with him for England. When a rumour of this plan became known, it was the signal for a revolt, which began in Aranjuez on the 16th and 17th, and in Madrid on the 17th and 18th. The peasants, for 7 or 8 leagues around, cut down trees and blocked the roads with them. The Guards stopped the coaches and the mob moved towards the palace of the Prince of the Peace. Only two officers made any attempt at resistance, firing a pistol shot in the air. The Prince hoped to calm the discontent and avert a riot by pretending to remove one of the principal causes of it. He caused all kinds of valuables to be thrown from the palace windows, including chests full of gold. It was too late, the anger was overwhelming. Far from feeling grateful for this forced restitution, the people at once set fire to everything that had been thrown out, even the gold and silver money that no one dared to touch. Finally, he, together with his brother, was seized by the populace and would have been torn in pieces if the Prince of Asturia (Ferdinand) and the Guards had not saved his life by telling the people that important state secrets must be wrested from him; after which, he would be handed over to justice. The brother had been very ill-used. He himself had been hit by a stone that nearly removed one of his eyes, and received a blow in the chest from the butt of a gun that caused him at once to vomit blood. At this very moment, the two of them are held prisoner, only 3 leagues from here. The Grand Council of Castile is convened and Charles IV has resigned his throne in favour of his son, now

Ferdinand VII. This is not, however, yet recognized by the councils of the other Spanish courts, or by the French authorities.

Our life in the middle of this capital and our relations with the Spanish authorities are bizarre in the extreme. Everyone is regarded with the utmost mistrust, and ways and means by which to obtain all supplies, billets etc. have to be sought. All requests must be made to the *Alcaldes* [*civic dignitaries or judicial officers – Ed.*] as in the small Spanish villages. The lower classes regard us with irritation and hatred.

1 April: Madrid is a large and well–built city that contains 200,000 people and an incredible number of churches, convents and monks of every order. The Inquisition is nothing more than an empty threat, which perhaps, today, is of more utility than menace. At any event, it does not influence morals at all, but is only an article of faith.

In court circles, and among the upper class of society, the women are very flirtatious and the husbands are jealous. The working class is corrupt, but the middle class has kept many of its moral values. Pride is the outstanding trait in the Spanish character, but they are polite, humane and generous, and some-times so informal that one hardly knows if their manners incline more to arrogance or to familiarity. They are, fortunately, abstemious. The wines are very good and strong. The working class are easily exasperated, dangerous and cruel, being capable of the worst excesses when they are aroused. The Spaniards nearly always carry a dagger or long knife, with which they commit murder very skilfully.

2 April: This morning, two French soldiers who had stolen a sheep were paraded publicly and were to be shot, but the people gathered together to pay for the loss, and came near to a riot to obtain pardon for them, which was granted.

At four o'clock, there was an uprising to throw the French out of the town, all the French and Spanish troops were under arms and we mounted our horses. In an instant, all the shops were closed and the roads filled with the enraged populace. Many of the crowd were armed with long knives and were yelling that all French throats should be cut. Finally the calm and discipline of our generals, a proclamation from the King, and above all the presence of the Duke of Infantado [sic], calmed the mob. The people are waiting impatiently for our departure; a promise made to them has been broken, for we had only asked to be allowed to pass through the city. The King issued a proclamation to the effect that we should only be present for two days, and the inhabitants, seeing that they had been lied to, became anxious and did not know what to believe.

I have been assigned the duties of staff officer, which are very difficult in this provisional regiment. I feel exhausted and never have a moment to myself.

3 April: We have received an order to maintain half the regimental infantry and half the cavalry under arms, night and day; the cavalry are to be ready to mount and the artillery to be ready for instant action. Patrol after patrol.

I have a letter from Ferdinand [*telling of the death of Frédéric, their twelve-year-old brother – Ed.*] and one from my mother, poor mother! And poor Frédéric! You are not the one most to be pitied. How heavy is the iron yoke that oppresses me! I am not able to leave at once, to dry the tears of my mother or, at least, to share her sorrow. I am condemned to repress tears in the lonely solitude I inhabit, for there is no one in whom to confide my misery. There is no one here to share my sorrow; and I am never able to be alone to weep. I am forced to spend my time on a thousand details that are repulsive to a mind consumed with grief! What has become of my courage?

3 April: At least I have the comfort of being lodged with kindly people; they are like the Lötze family. I am with the widow, Madame Clara Bamehhi, whose daughter, married to a Spanish colonel three months ago, also lives here. It is like being with my own family, but I cannot take a great deal of advantage of it, for I have barely an hour, always unpredictable, in which to have my meals.

7 April: I should like to make a few observations about Madrid, but my duties allow me no time. The Les Rapies quarter, where the *chasseurs* are stationed, is the one where the population is most ill disposed, so that I have to maintain a constant watchfulness.

The Lifeguards look very handsome. They are all of officer rank, with epaulettes, embroidered hat and a blue pouch trimmed with silver plaques. The Spanish infantry, especially the grenadiers, is magnificent. The grenadier's hats are different from the others; they have a sort of flat, yellow cloth tail on which is embroidered the arms of Castile. The regiment of Walloon Guards is remarkable for its fine uniform. Several cavalry regiments wear yellow, but this branch seems to me to be inferior to the others. Then there are the hussars, but they are very badly equipped and have an uncouth and absurd appearance – at least in our eyes – for everything depends upon convention. They have hoods and saddles like those of the dragoons, and their carbines are suspended from the saddle by a hook.

9 April: At precisely midday, the King sits down at table. The palace is open, and any officer may enter freely. Yesterday I took advantage of this opportunity to see the King, his court, his generals and his ministers. The King does not look very distinguished; he must be between twenty-three and twenty-five years old [*Ferdinand VII (1784–1822) was twenty-four at the time – Ed.*].

The apartments and the staircases of the palace are beautifully adorned with sculptures and frescos; the rooms are filled with pictures, particularly in the King's dining room, where the ceiling is decorated with an Olympian scene.

With regard to the pictures, it seemed to me that more attention had been paid to quantity rather than quality. The magnificent Ambassador's room contains innumerable mirrors, lustres and many busts and statues, of which several are extremely fine.

We were ordered to leave this morning, and mounted our horses at four o'clock, but remained at the Prado until nine and from there returned to quarters. There is a big parade tomorrow, and after the parade we leave for Aranjuez. I shall deeply regret my comfortable billet. The Colonel and his lady have heaped kindness upon me. Madame Dolorès, married only three months ago, displayed a touching naivety in showing her delight in pure and happy love. Carmen, aged fourteen, seemed the very picture of innocence. When I came back from my wearying duties, I could not remain unmoved by such a guileless and happy scene.

Actors in the plays I have seen, appear to me to be much less good than ours; the music is quite good; but as for the plays, I do not understand the language, but as far as I can tell, there seems to be little plot and they often lower the dignity of the stage.

I have been too busy here to form an opinion of the society. The ladies of the court seem generally to follow the example of the Queen, as demonstrated in her relations with the Prince of the Peace. There seems to be great comfort and a friendly good nature in every home. The women are unselfish, generous and inclined to love, both physically and morally; though they are extremely jealous to the point of sometimes running great risks because of their fickleness. They are also tender, loyal and inclined to form many attachments.

10 April: Valdemoro. A grand parade was held on the Prado this morning, before Prince Murat, for which nearly all the army corps were combined. The object was to show the Spaniards how massive was the force paraded in front of them. After the review, we left for Valdmoro, 4 leagues from Madrid on the Toledo road.

11 April: Aranjuez. The hussars have just left Aranjuez. I saw Potier with a detachment of the 8th once more and also Sainvilliers. I am amply repaid for my labours and no longer regret having come here.

12 April: Nine months ago, I was bathing in the waters of the Memel; today, I braved the waves of the Tagus that flows round the gardens of Aranjuez.

This castle, where the kings of Spain live in the summer, is a truly royal house. The surroundings are well-cultivated and there are many roads that, forming a star, meet in a superb square embellished with arcades and fountains. All the roads are perfectly straight, as are all the houses – most of them have one storey only. The palace is to the left of the square; and on this side is a beautiful garden with ornamental basins and statues. A branch of the Tagus, flowing through a canal of freestone, encircles this area; another branch separates the garden from the road and winds round the park to form a magnificent waterfall in front of the palace. I have seldom seen a more enchanting spectacle: all is delightful, offering the happiest blend of architecture, verdure and water.

13 April: We sleep at Ocana, a little town 3 leagues from Aranjuez, built on a hill amongst arid rocks.

14 April: There was a riot in the square this evening. Two *chasseurs* were severely wounded, and there is talk of slaughtering us all, no less. The government had the utmost trouble in calming the people. Spanish troops – Royal Carabinières and hussars – who, in this difficult situation have been interposed between their own citizens and us, have behaved with all possible discretion and generosity. The Spanish people, more than those anywhere else, are swift to anger, cruel, given to excess and they no longer know when they have gone too far.

15 April: Good Friday. This holy religion, so pure and so exalted, all of whose ceremonies should inspire awe at the majesty of the object of their worship, is here disfigured by superstition and fanaticism. The processions are nothing but masquerades at which one would laugh, if one did not groan. Beneath the cloak of austerity and virtue, the convents conceal thousands of idlers, ignoramuses and libertines. The churches are filled with a profusion of frivolous treasures, extravagant and absurd trivia, the cost of which could have fed the innumerable poor, and with bizarre bad taste that now affronts the dignity of religion. One church, amongst others, is so gilded from floor to ceiling, that a hospital could have been built from the money spent on the gilding alone. Another contains a life-size Passion scene, sculptured in wood, of a grotesque appearance, as is usual in this country (I remember particularly the face and costume of one of Our Lord's tormentors) and these absurd statues are solemnly carried in procession! God, I know, sees only the intention, and this is pure among the worshipping people; but is the intention as pure among those who, with the ability to remedy and direct the religion of the people, still permit them to kneel before superstition? Or do they fear that, if eyes are opened, they might see too much?

16 April: Our dealings with the Spaniards are always the same. Are these people insolent and cruel? No! They are proud, vindictive and patriotic, and they are oppressed.

17 April: Easter Day.

20 April: The generals have received a letter from Prince Murat, to the effect that Ferdinand VII has not accepted the crown that was only briefly, and

against his wishes, bestowed on him, and has returned it to his father. Charles IV has reassumed the reins of government.

21 April: The Emperor left Paris on the 2nd and reached Bordeaux on the 5th. He is expected in Madrid, and it is said that he conferred with the Spanish King on the bridge at Irun.

24 April: It seems that we are to stay here longer.

25 April: We get the order to leave at midnight and take the road to Cadiz. After crossing an immense plain, cultivated and planted with many olive trees, we reach Cetza. This is a village set in an arid country bestrewn with rocks. We learn that there has been a revolt at Toledo, where the French were refused entry and where the inhabitants have hanged their *Alcade* in effigy, because he wanted to obey the orders of the King.

26 April: We left (Cetza) at four in the morning and at eleven o'clock, the whole division had gathered before Toledo, where we remained until five in the evening at the foot of the walls. After this we were allowed to enter the town peacefully, nobody seemed to be anxious to stop us.

27 April: When we had crossed the sands surrounding it, we came upon Toledo, where it extended over a little valley and the two adjoining hills. A short distance from the town, the countryside became more cheerful; the banks of the Tagus, flowing beneath its walls, are enlivened with weeping willows, poplars and olives. The eye, wearied by the sad monotony of a plain empty of all save menacing rocks, rests with pleasure on the fresh verdure, in happy contrast with the arid boulders surrounding it. Yet, as one approaches the town, it can be seen that what at first sight looks like three towns is only one; but it is strange that it could have been built in such a place. Ugly wooden houses that give an unpleasant impression surround the town square of Toledo. The roads are narrow, crooked, badly paved and uneven, so that it is difficult for horses or carriages to move around. But when, at last, one has contrived to find the cathedral one is rewarded. This church is said to be the most beautiful in Spain. The archbishop is always a cardinal, a grandee of Spain, and is usually of royal blood. At the moment it is a Bourbon cardinal. What mixed emotions are aroused by that fatal name. The present holder of the name seems so unworthy that he brings sad disgrace on his lineage. His sister, wife of the Prince of the Peace, who lives in Toledo, has earned for herself as much regard and respect as her husband has deserved hatred and fury.

Eleven o'clock. I have just witnessed the famous Toledo procession. A Virgin, covered with gold drops and weighed down with jewels, was seated on an altar encased in gold that seemed to move of itself around the church in the midst of innumerable priests. There must, of course, have been several people concealed inside, who were either carrying the statue or pushing it on wheels. I do not know to what extent the people connect the idea of a miracle to this mysterious progress. The four priests walking near the altar wore copes of incredible magnificence. To the left and to the right of the statue walk two clerics, whose only duty is to grasp the rosaries that the people hold out to them, in order to touch them to the altar and return them. They need to have nimble hands to perform this task, for they are subjected to inordinate work. I must not end my description of the cathedral without mentioning the exceptional beauty of the chimes; there are thirteen bells, one of which has a circumference of 30 feet. At midnight comes the order to leave.

28 April: Ajofrin. This is a village 4 leagues from Toledo near the Cadiz road. For a league we followed the course of the Tagus, that flowed at our feet between two rocky ranges of hills, and then marched for 2 leagues on the crest of a chain of mountains. Finally, the countryside opened before us into a fertile plain, still bestrewn with rocks, but showing us the fine large village of Ajofrin.

A significant robbery has taken place at Toledo at the barracks occupied by the *chasseurs* of the 1st Regiment. The value of it is estimated at between 10,000 and 12,000 francs. Several of the culprits are already found. A terrible example must be made of them, in order to halt the excesses committed daily by our *chasseurs*, whose audacity now holds nothing sacred. They have displayed such criminal determination, and have been so united in concealing their crimes from us, that it is very difficult to detect the guilty. These wretches possess to a high degree the defects of our old soldiers without having a single one of their good qualities. Now blood must be shed; a hideous necessity!

30 April: The two majors have proposed that I should take charge of this matter, but I refused the painful and sensitive task. I would rather defend the innocent.

1 May: A divisional order has appointed me Recorder [*i.e. magistrate or judge – Ed.*] There is no way to escape!

4 May: It is eight o'clock in the morning. I have hardly eaten or slept for four days! What a terrible duty, and in the end, who are the guilty men and who the innocent? I shall remember yesterday evening all my life, when the court that I had requested, was convened. The discussions, the sentence! I have never experienced such disturbed feelings and have never before had to consider so grave a matter; for it is to hold in one's hands the very thread of a human life! At last, I put my signature to two death sentences. I leave the prison where I have just carried out my last, cruellest duty. I have just told them of the sentence of death – in one hour the wretches will be no more.

At midday, comes an order to delay; as no one was prepared to undertake their defence, I carried out this duty myself and had my speech read out.

At eight in the evening, the rumour went around that on 2 May, there had been an uprising and a terrible massacre in Madrid.

5 May: We learn the details of the massacre. It seems that, within one hour, the revolt had spread. All the French who were isolated were slaughtered. It was necessary to give the infantry the order to march, and the cuirassiers charged, cannon were placed in position to aim at all the roads leading to the Prado. There was dreadful carnage at the Porte del Sol; peasants had assembled there in force to seize our guns and were only dispersed by a hail of bullets. We lost about 2,000 men and several officers. The slaughter was even greater at Burgos, where Marshal Bessières was compelled to deploy his entire army corps. This Sicilian Vespers were to be carried out, at the same hour, on the same day, throughout Spain.

[*Editor's note: reference to a massacre of the French in Sicily on Easter Monday 1282, during the Sicilian uprising against Charles I of Anjou.*]

6 May: A sudden proclamation, dated the 3rd, is received from Prince Murat. The town of Madrid is disarmed, all gatherings of more than eight people must be dispersed by gunfire, and every village in which a Frenchman has been killed is to be burned. More than 200 men, captured with weapons in their hands, have been shot on the Prado, two priests and four women were among them; several houses have been pillaged and their occupants put to the sword. I tremble for my hostesses, for it seems the quarter in which they live has seen terrible carnage. Peasants coming in from the countryside to the aid of the townsfolk have been charged by the cuirassiers.

9 May: There is a rumour of the marriage of Ferdinand VII to a niece of the Emperor [*a daughter of Napoleon's brother Lucien – Ed.*]. It is certain that the old King, the new King and all the Royal Family are at Bayonne, where the Emperor Napoleon is also. What a puzzle!

[*Editor's note: General Savary, who was to replace Murat, had been able to induce Charles IV and Ferdinand VII to go to Bayonne to ask Napoleon for arbitration in their family quarrels. Napoleon made both of them abdicate in his favour and placed them under house arrest. The Spanish people were not impressed by what they called the 'trickery of Bayonne' and the exiled Ferdinand became their idol.*]

10 May: Another proclamation from Prince Murat, entirely different from the first.

11 May: It is certain that the revolt of the 2nd spread to several other areas and that, at Vittoria as well as in other places, sick Frenchmen were slaughtered in the hospitals. I tremble lest my own servant has fallen victim to his fidelity and affection for me. He left Poland on 24 January, reached Paris on 22 March, and left Orléans on 22 April.

12 May: All now seems to be quiet, but it is like standing on a volcano. Are we on another Eve of Saint Bartholomew? [*A reference to the massacre of Protestants on the eve of Saint Bartholomew's Day in 1572 – Ed.*]

13 May: Counts, marquises and generals – in a word most of the grandees of Spain – are hurrying endlessly through Burgos to Bayonne. It is said that the Emperor has made Ferdinand VII the gift of a crown worth 8 million francs, and many horses etc. However, it is a fact that our gazettes do not accord him the title of 'King'. Before him, on his journey into France, the entire route was filled with detachments of French soldiers. When the King was at Valladolid, General Savary, the Emperor's aide-de-camp, went to see him and said: 'Sire, we must leave,' 'Why do you speak to me thus?' replied Ferdinand. 'Is it not said that I am your prisoner!' 'No, Sire, but these are the orders of my master, and they must be obeyed.'

We have received the order to leave and are to go to Ioncica, a pretty little village a league from Ajofrin.

15 May: A letter is received from the Minister to the effect that, while granting the pay of a staff officer to lieutenants who are performing that duty, it also orders that, when the provisional regiments are dissolved, such lieutenants are to return to their corps in the ranks that they formerly occupied. So now I have the salary of a captain, while still being a lieutenant. I have been sent to Toledo on this matter. Cleanliness, so unusual beneath the same roof as destitution, is hard to find in this town.

All over Spain, the houses are built with a view to preserving warmth as much as possible, and this is true of Toledo. I visited the cathedral again, and went into a room where there are the pictures of the Infantes, the Cardinals and Archbishops who have been appointed to Toledo. Many of them must owe their depiction to the imagination of the painter, but those of the last century were painted from life. There are many bizarre and badly executed pictures high up on the walls; among them is a Last Judgement that would be highly indecent if it were close enough to enable the observer to distinguish the sexes in the crowd of nude figures. The ceiling of the room is magnificent, for the square wooden panelling is gilded all over.

16 May: We are ordered to leave for Cadiz the day after tomorrow. I had been hoping to see my servant again soon; I was counting the days, and now there will be a new distance interposed between us. What will happen to this unhappy fellow? Will he become a victim of his faithfulness? I fear the dagger, for him, as much as disease beneath this brazen sky. As for myself, I go wherever I am sent; but for him I can only view with dread his journey from Bayonne to Cadiz, after that from Paris to Bayonne.

17 May: Today comes a counter-order that seems only to be a postponement; there is a reason for this. Prince Murat, appointed President of the Grand Council of Castille, lived at the King's palace. On the 15th he wanted to leave, but between 7,000 and 8,000 of the inhabitants gathered to prevent this. Not wanting to renew the bloody scenes of 2 May he sent an order to the IV Corps to advance and to the II Corps to delay their departure. It seems that the astonishing revolution now taking place in Spain will occur more peacefully than had been thought at first; all the Spanish troops and nearly all the grandees have been won over in advance, while the others have already been secured. French and Spanish soldiers mount the guard at the doors of Prince Murat's palace jointly, and there is talk of the two sides combining.

19 May: Returning to Toledo, I was curious enough to visit the dreadful tomb in which can be seen the horrible skeleton of a man and those of about fifty cats, who entombed with him, had been first the executioners and then the victims of this terrible torture.

20 May: The Spanish passion for bullfighting is so excessive that, in the absence of this spectacle, they rush avidly to anything that is at all similar. Butchers, before killing their victims, enjoy a little game of teasing them in a hundred ways, goading them with cloaks, letting their dogs tear at them. Sometimes, however, they display both humanity and skill, striking a spot just behind the head of the animal with a sort of short sword, so that the blow passes between two vertebrae, severs the spinal cord, and the creature drops dead.

21 May: At noon, the Major suggested I should go to Madrid. The drawbacks to this are considerable should the regiment leave for Cadiz; but Pinto is on the way there, and Sainvilliers is at Pinto! I leave, and shall sleep at Toledo.

22 May: I travelled by the side of the Tagus from Toledo to Aranjuez, leaving Villasesquilla on my right. For 2 leagues before reaching Aranjuez the road was delightful, ending at last in a superb avenue, a fitting introduction to a Royal palace.

It is now public knowledge here, and one is able to read about the voluntary abdication at Bayonne of Charles IV in favour of the Emperor; Ferdinand VII, King of Spain has also abdicated ...

A Grand Council is to gather at Bayonne; some say that Joseph will quit the throne of Naples to assume that of Spain, others say that Lucien will do so. Here in Madrid, the citizens do not express their anger in violence; their grim demeanour and an occasional word are the only indications. Many people disappear, and it is said that there are assemblies in Catalonia and Andalusia, in Valencia and Murcia. We shall have news of this soon, I think.

[*Editor's note: Joseph (1768–1844) was Napoleon's elder brother, Lucien (1775–1840) his younger brother.*]

23 May: The hussars have left Pinto and are at Madrid. So tonight I shall embrace Sainvilliers! How long the road seems! The wretched leagues stretch before me! At last I arrive in Madrid and greet my friend.

24 May: My business, or rather that of the regiment, will keep me here until the 28th. These four days will count among the happiest of my life, and this is due to our friendship.

25 May: While my registers are being printed and the stamps engraved, and during the times when Sainvilliers is on guard duty, I shall try to record some details of the events that took place in Madrid.

Distrust and hatred had, for a long time, concealed the treacherous intentions of the Spaniards. Many people were calling aloud for a new Saint Bartholomew's eve. A number of priests openly preached that it was time to ring in another Sicilian Vespers. At last the volcano erupted on 2 May. Many people suffered, and as always in such circumstances, there were many acts of ferocity, as well as acts of patriotism.

An elderly Spaniard left his home, killed three Frenchmen who were alone, then quietly allowed himself to be arrested and led off to his death, making no effort to escape, saying: 'I die happy; if every Spaniard copies me our country will be saved!' There were several houses in which the French who were in them were shut up, unharmed, in order, they were told, to save their lives and to prevent them from killing Spaniards. In many other houses the French were slaughtered or robbed. Only three houses were looted. In one, where the body of a Guards officer had rested peacefully until then, the Mameluks [*Caucasian warriors taken into French service following Napoleon's Egyptian campaign – Ed.*] rushed in and sabred everyone who was there, men, women and children. On this day, these outlandish individuals demonstrated their usual bravery, as well as a ferocity worthy of their origin. One of them protested to us, complaining bitterly of his troubles: 'We went into a Convent,' said this barbarian 'where there were sixty monks, and we were only able to kill thirty-two.' The Mameluks inspire such dread in the Spaniards that, if one is seen at the far end of the road, they think they see the devil and hurry past on the other side.

On the day after the uprising, the Prado became the scene of bloody executions. All those who, on the previous day, had been found carrying any type of weapon, even a knife (it is true that they had behaved towards us in a cowardly and cruel fashion) were pitilessly shot. There were many women among them, and these were no less guilty. Of course, there were also several innocent people who, through chance or curiosity, were caught up in the disorder and confused with the guilty. Among the latter were two unfortunate barbers and several others who were carrying the tools of their trade, such as razors and knives etc.

This disastrous period inflamed mutual distrust to the last degree. The Spaniards were convinced that the French troops waited only for the signal to burn down the town or give it over to pillage; while our soldiers, as they passed near one of the natives, believed they felt cold steel in their backs. The streets were deserted, and each day, many inhabitants vanished. I, myself, noticed that nearly all the houses were empty of servants; even those who remained were removed, forcibly, by their relations, who came from the neighbouring villages to find them. Spaniards often asked me if it was true that burning the town was still being considered, but I was happy to find that the attitude of my old hosts towards me did not change; they showed me the same kindness as ever. Poor little Carmen and Dolorès, how frightened you must have been! How many proofs of your continuing friendship you were generous enough to give. Tonight, it seemed that a revolt was starting, crowds gathered beneath our very windows. I remember, as I shall always remember, the sight of Dolorès bringing me the Colonel's sword, handing it to me and saying: 'Here is my husband's sword, may it protect you and not shed the blood of my country-men!'

To give some idea of the general mistrust: the other day a horse escaped and galloped at top speed through the streets; at once, doors closed, shops were barricaded, everyone gathered together, screaming and fled, not knowing where or why.

26 May: My faithful Georges will arrive here in eight days' time, but I fear that my regiment has left Ioncica and is marching quickly towards Cadiz, where the English are bombarding the town. When shall I be able to rejoin them? Shall I pretend to be ill, just for eight days? Sainvilliers would be very happy, but duty calls! I must go, the regiment's business will be finished on the 28th and I shall leave the same day.

28 May: I have just avoided spending a night under the stars. I was billeted with the officers of my old and dear regiment, who are in part of what was once the palace of the Prince of the Peace. This palace, with its beautiful furnish-ings, mirrors, pictures and carpets is worthy of a sovereign, and at another time, I should have taken note of all of this; I should have admired, above all, the beauty of the many marble tables, which are decorated with exquisite mosaics: but now, worried, hungry and exhausted, all these things passed before my eyes without making the least impression on me.

At last, day broke. I met Sainvilliers again, but for such a short time; the hours flew past and then I had to leave him and the town. I grasped him in my arms and bade him farewell once again, followed him with my eyes, turning to see him once more and at last, lost sight of him. Many times, on this fine road between Madrid and Valdemoro, I looked back at the town I was leaving and reflected: he is there. Only he can fill the emptiness I feel in his absence. Finally

I am in Valdemoro and I can no longer see Madrid so, tomorrow I shall not look back.

29 May: Aranjuez. As I cannot travel alone to rejoin my regiment, which is several days' march ahead of me, I have been able to join a column of 500 *chasseurs* (3rd Provisional Regiment), who are about to reinforce the brigade and are also heading towards Cadiz.

1 June: Temblique. The Spaniards call the region between the Tagus and the mountains bordering Andalusia by the name of the Mancha. So now we are deep in the Mancha, home of the great Don Quixote, patron saint of adventurers. This may, perhaps, not be the only resemblance between him and us. Besides, I think we have less to do to disenchant the Spaniards than he had to achieve to disillusion Dulcinea. It is only in our own eyes that we wield the sword of Amadis [*legendary knight errant of Spanish romance who possessed qualities of courtly love and gallantry – Ed.*], one has only to look at our knights errant for the spell to be broken. In the present, new romance, the principal actor, the unfortunate population, is pushed to one side. And we, who play the rôle of Sancho Panza, we get the thrashing.

2–3 June: Madridejos. This reasonably large village has, like others in Spain, a square surrounded by arcades, but here the stone arches are surmounted by two other, wooden, galleries, intended to contain the numerous spectators who come to watch the bullfights, which the Spaniards love with a passion that amounts, almost, to frenzy.

Madridejos is surrounded by fertile country, with fine vegetable gardens that are irrigated by means of rivulets, kept supplied by waterwheels worked by mules; there are many leafy little woods of elms, whose shade is more than welcome in the hot season. These groves and vegetable gardens clearly prove that, if nature seems sterile and unrewarding in this country, it is less her fault than that of the people, who do not know how to play their part, or of the government that allows them to languish in laziness and ignorance. Madridejos also has a Prado, where the trees are very fine. I went to look at the church that stands at the end of the promenade. The walls of this church are covered with pictures, and with bunches of hair that have been placed there as votive offerings. All this may be very well, but there is also an infinity of heads, feet, hands, arms, legs and women's breasts all modelled in wax. I must respect the motives behind these acts of homage, for by this means the suffering soul is comforted and hope is restored in the unhappy hearts of the wretched; to acknowledge this is a sacred duty. But how can those who, by their position and wisdom, should direct the religion of the people, permit such activities and errors that are so likely to attract ridicule to that same religion? Of all the Christian states, Spain betrays the greatest childishness, hypocrisy and affectation and the least real religious feeling. All worship here consists of vain display, to which the Spaniards cling with fanatic zeal. The hands of the people, when not making the sign of the cross, are ever upon their daggers. All their rooms are filled with a profusion of crucifixes and images of saints and of the Virgin (above all, of Our Lady of the Seven Sorrows), and when they are about to perform some act such as the images would condemn, they draw a curtain or throw a veil over them, and think themselves free of sin. Here is a little story that illustrates this way of stifling their scruples.

At Madrid, an officer was taken to the home of a woman of doubtful virtue. After a few moments alone together, he wanted to take matters as far as they would naturally go; to his great surprise he met with a resistance that, in view of the individual concerned, was neither expected nor appropriate. Finally, he was taken by the neck, forced to his knees before a statue of the Virgin and made to recite an Ave Maria. The statue and the holy pictures that decorated the room were then veiled, when the lady in question resumed and fulfilled her previous rôle.

At Pinto, where the hussars were stationed, the women took the smallest pleasantry as an attempted rape, and treated the French as heretics and excommunicants. No town ever contained more Lucrecias [*Roman lady who claimed to have been violated by a son of Tarquin the Great – Ed.*]. The General ordered the regiment to attend mass. From that moment, the soldiers were regarded as brothers, and for the love of God, the former Lucrecias showed themselves to be easier to deal with.

Should the Angelus be about to ring at a moment when the Spaniards are about to indulge in some guilty pastime, they will halt their activities to recite the Angelus devotedly. At Miranda, in a café, I myself witnessed an occurrence like this.

4 June: Villa-Harta. This is a little town surrounded by marshes. Two brooks unite here to become one called the Giquela, which above Ciudad Real, combines with that of the Guadiana. A fine causeway on arches has been built here. These swamps make a stay in this town extremely unhealthy. Today, I noticed how swiftly and skilfully the natives clip their mules that are always kept shaved to the middle of their bodies with different designs on their rumps.

5 June: Manzanarès. This is a pretty little town in pleasant surroundings planted about with olive trees. The season here is so advanced that the harvesting of barley has already begun. The mood among the peasants is not good; they are very proud and insolent – ready at the least sign to seize their weapons. Captain Dubois was nearly killed by them today.

6 June: In a bivouac before Valdepenas. It is a year today since the Russians attacked us on the banks of the Passarge and this is a bloody anniversary here,

in Spain. At the same time, a year ago, when almost entirely surrounded by Cossacks, I saw death coming very close, but today, my God, I was not far from it. Going forward, with my *chasseur*, to about half a league from the town, I found the billets, but no one had been allowed to enter, and there were 200 dragoons in full retreat; they had expected to be slaughtered in the gorges above Santa-Cruz, where they had lost an officer and a sergeant major. I saw a line of peasants before the town, fully armed and in battle order, with sentinels and mounted leaders. When I asked to speak to their leader, the Spanish commander came forward. He arrogantly told me that he was prepared to give me supplies, but only on condition that we did not enter the town. Finally, he demanded that we lay down our arms. I received this suggestion as it deserved. Then he proposed that I should go alone into the town to speak to the *Alcalde*. I agreed, but my companion, more cautious than I, opposed this. I suggested, in my turn, that the Spanish commander should himself come to speak to the General, offering myself as hostage to his men, so that my life would be security for his. He refused.

At eight o'clock, General Liger-Belair arrived with a column of 500 men. The General went forward with Rob and me, demanding that they should surrender their arms and admit us to the town; this proposal was received with shouts of rage and they loaded their guns and prepared to fire upon us. The two parties separated. All the peasants vanished in a moment, rushed into the town and sounded the tocsin [*i.e. alarm bell – Ed.*]. We took up our positions for an attack. The General sent me to the rebels several times to try to bring them back, but it was useless. The 'charge' was sounded.

The dragoons were on the right, the 2nd Squadron, composed of the 2nd and 7th, charged on the left, with a platoon of the 11th on the main road. When the dragoons reached the entrance to the town, they found themselves confronted by barricades and were forced to turn back; the *chasseurs* went in by way of the two roads that the peasants had left open on purpose. As they entered the town, they discovered that carts, firmly connected to each other, blocked by means of ropes, all the roads leading to the centre. The ropes were stretched as far as the middle of the town, with the result that the riders, setting their horses forward at a gallop and blinded by smoke and dust, were nearly all thrown from their saddles. At this moment, a hail of shots, fired from all the houses, came at them from every side; while cobblestones, pots and articles of furniture rained down on their heads, while they were unable to offer any resistance or to defend themselves. As soon as one of the *chasseurs* was dismounted or wounded, the peasants dragged him into a house and there set about mutilating him with appalling ferocity and disgusting inventiveness. It was at this time, that the courageous Captain Dubois of the 7th, who had dismounted to remove a barrier, was shot through the body. The officer in command of a detachment of the 11th, having been knocked to the ground by a shot, was attacked with axes and daggers; five *chasseurs* of the 11th and nine or ten of the 7th suffered the same fate, and they died without having been able to deliver a single sabre stroke in return.

Now, a number of *chasseurs* and dragoons having dismounted, the General combined them with about thirty infantrymen, and ordered me to lead them into the town, occupy the houses and set fire to them; this was done. His aide-de-camp (M. de Saint-Quentin), attacked on foot at another place, as did M. de Mahon, an infantry officer, but the latter, having advanced too far, was captured. M. de Saint-Quentin, setting an example to his troops, received a shot through the shoulder. As for me, I was very happy to find that the balls treated me with respect and contented themselves with making holes in my uniform. As I encouraged my infantrymen to follow by riding forward, a shot fired from a window at almost point-blank range, cut through my coat and breeches at waist height, while another went through my saddle between my thighs.

The battle continued from nine in the morning until six in the evening. All the houses we entered were set on fire at once and their occupants killed; those who tried to escape into the countryside were cut down. Yet, as we had no infantry or artillery, the burning went on slowly, until nearly all our cartridges had been used up and many soldiers were wounded. The others, busy looting, thought more of pillage than of burning; they were worn out, exhausted, hot and hungry. The excellent wine they had found in the houses had made them incapable of fighting.

At last, the General suggested that I should again go to the rebels and offer them pardon on the same terms as this morning. This was a proposal that could not be refused, even though it might lead to certain death. I agreed, putting forward an idea, which was at once approved. I was accompanied by two peasants that I, with difficulty, rescued from the rage of our soldiers; but our situations were soon reversed. They led me through side streets, and I suddenly found myself near the walls of a church in a square that none of us had previously reached. At first it seemed deserted, but a moment later a window opened, there was a shout, and at once, all the balconies, the streets, the church and the bell-tower were filled with men, women and children, while 300 guns were aimed at me. My two companions bawled to the people to be calm and pressed against me to cover my body with theirs. I crossed my arms, tried to look unruffled, and aware that only the appearance of calm could save my life, waited to learn my fate.

The square, deserted a little while ago, was now filled with a crowd of people whose posture and looks presented striking contrasts. Some of them, covered in blood, shaking with rage and black with powder, thrust their guns forward towards my chest, yelling with hatred and swearing that no Frenchman should enter their town, that I was to die at once. Others – and these were the family men and the elderly – interposed themselves and turned the guns away, tried to quiet the mob and to protect me; at the same time, the women, on their knees, came close to kiss my arms, hands and uniform, showing me their infants, while begging aloud for pardon. I calmly watched this scene, in a situation when a ball fired by one of the enraged men, could have prevented me from watching anything for much longer. The *Alcalde*, no doubt, feared that this might happen, for I felt myself lifted up, and without my feet touching the ground, was transported into a house; there the women's prayers, the tears of the girls and the cries of the babies redoubled, as did the yells of several peasants, still clamouring for my death.

All this time, the gunfire and burning continued, so that I could not make myself heard. To give the Spaniards time to calm down, I had water, wine and bread brought to me, and ate for a quarter of an hour, while I tried to reassure them of our good intentions. I satisfied the *Alcalde* that he should surrender his weapons to us, provide us with food, and that all hostilities should cease. I left, at last, accompanied by a crowd of them and returned to the General with the *Alcalde* and several notables, for whose safety I had given my word. I went back many times to collect the weapons, and little by little, all became calm.

We bivouacked within a cannon shot of the town, the fires continued to rage, but the peasants were trying to put them out.

7 June: Manzanarés. Although poetry and the arts celebrate the seductive charms of victory with pomp and splendour, they fail to depict the true picture. Victory is a Goddess greedy for death; her laurel is a branch dripping blood and soaked in tears.

I was sent, this morning, into Valdepenas town. I saw again the horror of burned houses, the slain bodies of women, babies and animals under the debris, peasants and soldiers and horses strewn here and there in the streets . . . and a band of villains, not natives of this village who are the (secondary) cause of all these atrocities!

We held the same position until midday, and then we withdrew into Manzanarés. Enraged men from two neighbouring villages, together with some other scoundrels from nearby, attacked the hospital, killing and mutilating all the sick and seizing 200 French guns. The infantry officer commanding the hospital was cut into four pieces and put into a cauldron. My pen refuses to write of other horrors. The hospital is swimming in blood!

8 June: Here we have found and released several Frenchmen who had been between life and death for forty-eight hours. General Roize, who arrived here with a handful of men, is also in an alarming situation, and our position is no less so. The day at Valdepenas cost us dearly and exhausted our ammunition; as we are now surrounded on all sides, it is impossible for us to advance or to

retreat. If we leave this town, we cannot hope to return to it except by fighting; all our communications with General Dupont and with Madrid have been cut. Frightening news reaches us from all sides, it seems certain that what we experienced at Manzanarés also took place at Valladolid, at Villa-Harta, in fact everywhere where we are not strong.

General Belair has sent a courier to General Dupont at Madrid; it was he who had sent help to us at Valdepenas.

9 June: We learn that 200 Frenchmen, captured – either while escorting a convoy or in other circumstances – are at Santa-Cruz under threat of death; their rescue by main force would cause the knife to be plunged into their throats. Negotiations are opened to attempt to save them. The priests, who have protected them, act as our mediators. The inhabitants of Manzanarés, are now in a state of mortal terror, being convinced that we only await reinforcements to burn their town. The mountains and ravines are filled with powerful bands, commanded and bribed by English agents, and by smugglers. The commander at Valdepenas wrote to the authorities here, on the day of the battle, that he was going to kill all the Frenchmen who confronted him and would afterwards come and perform the same service for those here.

We are awaiting an attack tonight. The townsmen have already sent their wives, their children and their valuables away. Many of the houses are empty.

Still in the same position and taking the same precautions, with the same fear on all sides. A Spanish officer passed through today, dispatched as a courier to General Dupont. All isolated Frenchmen have been killed. Has my poor Georges also become a victim of his faithfulness?

10 June: No help has arrived for us. The courier we sent to Madrid has not been killed but was stopped and robbed at Madridejos.

11 June: Captain Dubois, who was wounded at Valdepenas, died. The funeral ceremony was moving and the General delivered the funeral oration. We are in a critical situation, surrounded on all sides and without cartridges, artillery or infantry.

12–13 June: We are still in the same situation, on the alert every night, but as no one in Madrid is aware of our position, no help arrives. We have stayed here until now because the townspeople of Santa-Cruz continue to give us the hope that they will hand over their prisoners. We have met them every night, but always in vain. At last, we shall leave tomorrow and retreat to Madridejos.

Midnight. Some 115 French prisoners arrived unexpectedly from Santa-Cruz. Among them is Monsieur Le Roi, his wife and daughter. The Chief Administrator, Don Juan of Madenez, sent 200 men of the Queen's Regiment (cavalry) to escort them as prisoners of war to Ciudad Réal; but the inhabitants of Santa-Cruz, terrified by the burning of Valdepenas, refused to hand them over, replying that they preferred to hold them as hostages. Finally, today, they agreed to give them up and brought them to us on condition that the past would be forgotten.

The ration convoy and its escort had been captured in a strange way. When they arrived, (at Santa-Cruz) the French were received calmly. They were assigned billets, where they left their weapons, as usual, when they went to obtain their rations of bread. At once the cry went up 'Attack the mad dogs!' and all the houses were closed; the soldiers tried to rush back to their weapons but in vain, for the doors were shut in their faces, and at the same time, they were fired upon from every window. After half of them were killed, the rest were captured.

14 June: A bivouac at Villa-Harta. There is terror everywhere; many people have abandoned their houses. It is said openly that Joseph, King of Naples, arrived in Bayonne on the 7th. The mask has been torn away! Joseph Bonaparte is about to be proclaimed King of Spain in Madrid. Meanwhile, the fire of revolution is raging in Andalusia, Valencia, Murcia and in all the central provinces, fuelled by the Juntas in Ciudad Réal, Seville and Granada. Wherever the French are not present in large numbers they are killed, all too often with the cruelty of the Moors inflamed by the terrible vengeance of the Spaniards. They seek to destroy us!

The lists of conscripts have been issued in the name of Ferdinand VII. [?]

15 June: Madridejos. Terror and flight are almost universal. There has been some heroic conduct on the part of monks and some of the leading citizens who have, by their determination, saved the lives of several French officers who had been arrested by the people. The courier who was originally sent from Valdepenas, has been rescued a second time and dispatched once more to Madrid from Manzanarés. The humanity and discipline shown by General Liger-Belair has succeeded beyond expectation.

16 June: At last we are liberated by the arrival of Generals Poinceau and Coussard. There is talk of the sickness of mind and body of the Prince Murat, and his heedlessness. There is great disquiet in Madrid as to our fate and that of General Dupont, from whom no news has been received [*Dupont had crossed the Sierra Morena and taken up position near Bailén – Ed.*].

17 June: We were preparing to continue our march to Madrid, but we were ordered to wait here for the arrival of Vedel's division. We evacuated our wounded to Aranjuez.

20 June: General Liger-Belair made a celebration of the dispatch to General Dupont of his brave *chasseurs*, of whose actions he had given a glowing account.

An order from Prince Murat instructed them to take up position on the Burgos road and wait there for the arrival of King Joseph. They had already waited there for the Emperor – perhaps this time their wait will not be in vain. The threats and harsh actions of General Poinceau are having a most undesirable effect. The terror of the inhabitants increases, as does their exodus, so that before long we shall find the towns deserted; murders multiply; it is impossible, without risking one's life, to move a step away from the detachment. A Swiss regiment arrived yesterday. A grenadier was asleep by the wayside and a harvest worker found him and smashed his head in with a rock. The lack of discipline of our troops continues to infuriate the peasants, who descended from the Moors, retain all the savagery of their ancestors. It is much easier to inflame their anger than it is to intimidate them. Fanaticism becomes involved, and the cursed brilliance of its infernal torch serves further to delude people already enraged by the losses they have suffered, and by the violation of promises made to them. The conciliatory methods employed by General Belair had already succeeded in returning most of the emigrants to their homes; and had encouraged the principal citizens to form themselves into patrols, even to the point where a corps of 500 gentlemen offered themselves as an escort in pacifying La Mancha. Some bad behaviour, and a few houses pillaged by the soldiers, has destroyed, in two hours, the fruit of fifteen days of hard work, negotiations and discipline. Our commander himself has thrown in the towel. And so now it is everyone for himself; the sacred cause of patriotism and good government is sacrificed to each individual's personal interests.

General Vedel's division arrives, and we are ordered to leave tomorrow.
[*Editor's note: General Dominique Honoré Antoine Marie Count of Vedel (1771–1848) had achieved the first part of his mission – the junction with General Liger-Belair, with whom he was now to attempting to force a crossing of Despena-Perros to join up with General Dupont.*]

21 June: I am still acting as his aide-de-camp to General Liger-Belair. This morning we are marching with Vedel's division, having been ordered to force the crossing of the Sierra Morena, secure the route, and make contact with General Dupont, who until receipt of further orders, is not to advance further. Frère's division, two days' march behind us, should contact General Vedel at Madrid. We bivouacked at Villa-Harta.

22 June: Manzanarés. We remain here on the 23rd. The soldiers of the Paris Guard and the 5th Legion found the bodies of the unfortunate French strewn around the hospital, and were unable to control their rage; they were excited more by the thirst for pillage than by pity for their comrades. They shouted aloud their demands to loot the town. Priests and some of the leading citizens, who by their heroic devotion had saved many French lives at the risk of their own, and who had cared for and treated our wounded, were insulted. It would

not have taken much for them to become victims of these maniacs. Finally, to attain their goal, these impudent villains shouted, 'To arms!' yelling that the enemy was coming, and they even fired a few shots. Horses were mounted and battle formation assumed, but even as the good soldiers were hurrying into position, the bandits rushed into the houses and began looting, so that, before the false alarm had been recognized for what it was, half the town had been sacked.

24 June: Valdepenas. Yesterday's looting has produced the most terrible result. A peasant, fleeing from Manzanarés, has spread the news that the French were slaughtering everyone. Most of the citizens have vanished. But I have been kindly welcomed by those who have recognized me, and above all by the old *Alcalde*, who saved my life. General Belair, the cause of the burning of their town [*sic*] was received here with delight. They call him our general [*sic*] and their confidence in him knows no bounds. The looting continues.

25 June: We are in Santa-Cruz. Thanks to the pardon granted for the handing over of prisoners, sentries have been posted in on all the roads to prevent looting, but the great number of stragglers has made this precaution inadequate. Nearly a third of the strength of every corps is straggling along behind it. We march off every day at one in the morning, but often, not everyone has arrived by seven in the evening. We arrive at El Viso, a village at the foot of the gorges [*the Gorges of Despena-Perros – Ed.*].

I have seldom seen a sight more dreadful than the one that met my eyes when we reached this town! It was completely deserted! The most terrible affray inspired less terror in me than this solitude and horrible quiet. I found, in the ancient château, three women of between seventy and eighty years old and their brother aged eighty, the only living beings in this town, which only yesterday had been vibrant with three or four thousand inhabitants. How tragic their departure must have been! It is dreadful to contemplate the shrieks of the women and children, the groans of the sick dragged from their deathbeds, and of the aged, torn from their native town. How they must have cursed us, in the midst of their lamentations! Wretched are the French who now inspire such horror!

The doors of the houses had to be broken down to gain entry, and soon the need to find food, the impulse to loot – and the greed for gold – had effaced the feeling of horror and painful soul-searching that no one could have avoided. As for me, every step I took, everything I saw, filled me with sorrow and terror. How they must loathe us! Good God, what curses must be called down upon our heads! What a scene of desolation, these empty houses and these starving domestic animals presented; even as our greedy soldiers shared the spoils amongst themselves! This is the invasion of Rome by the Gauls!

This morning, M. le Chevalier de la Roque suddenly disappeared. He is a Spanish officer of the American Regiment [?] who was born in France and is on attachment to General Vedel; he had gone ahead to arrange billets, but only his horse has been found here. Has he been murdered? Or has he been captured?

It will be a long while before I forget the old man I found in the castle, or the explanation he gave for not fleeing with his countrymen: 'Although you are French,' he said, 'I thought you would be men; anyway, my life is nearly over and I have nothing that anyone can take from me.'

What are we doing here? Tomorrow, there will be a fight and the passage of these terrible gorges will be forced. I shall do my duty, but it becomes more and more painful for me.

26 June: We have reached Venta de Cardenas without seeing a single person. Across the bridge just outside the gate, the road on the left is bordered by terrifying precipices, and on the right, by steep rocks, ascending to menacing heights. General Poinceau advanced alone with only four dragoons. A sudden burst of gunfire killed three of them and also killed the General's horse. We prepared to attack. A Swiss battalion was placed on the heights to the left, and six companies of infantry on the right; two light artillery pieces and a battalion of grenadiers took up position on the road, ahead of the rest of the division.

After a battle lasting three or four hours among the mountains, we found ourselves in command of the gorge, and reached Paso del Perro; this gorge must be at least 2 leagues long, and in many places there is a sheer drop of terrifying depth among the rocks.

When we had advanced a league into the narrow pass, we found an emplacement, armed with two cannon, which had been cut into the rock; a quarter of a league further on there was a stronger position, this time with six cannon. Our infantry, acting with a determination and speed that was worthy of old, established regiments, had captured both of these. Throughout the length of the pass, there were a hundred positions in which 200 men of the enemy, if properly led and supplied with food, could have confronted and held 50,000 attackers. A precipice bordered the route almost continuously, and if the road had been destroyed for a few yards, it would have been possible, in an hour or two, to render it impracticable for artillery and cavalry, and very difficult for the infantry. All the inhabitants of the provinces through which we have marched were convinced that we should never emerge from these gorges – and they had told us so.

In the rear of the second emplacement, were the barracks, the powder and ammunition. Before taking this position, we had seen, through a telescope, the figure of a priest in his vestments exhorting the fighters. The numbers of his listeners grew less as our gunfire advanced: at last, the orator fled like the others. One lonely peasant – a superb man – did not move from his place and stood alone, firing continuously, to confront our regiments. He was killed where he stood.

Missals, chalices, Hosts and sacred vessels were found behind the battery among the weapons. Mass had been said daily in this place. Love of religion and love of country struggled with all their strength against ambition, and certainly, ours was not the noblest rôle! What will be the outcome? A great mistake was made in attacking the centre before having outflanked the wings. If the flanks had been turned, the enemy would have been unable to save himself by flight.

We bivouacked at Santa Elena, a pretty village that had been a German colony; it was completely deserted, for there was no water. A false alarm was raised, caused by a detachment of General Dupont's men.

27 June: La Carolina. As we emerged from the horrible rocks of the Sierra, the superb and scorching hot Andalusia was spread before us, its hillsides covered with ripening grain and its plains thick with olive groves; aloes bordered the fields of palms, oranges and lemons, pomegranates and figs; there were valleys deliciously shaded by poplars, tall oleanders and passion flowers. All these trees and plants to which, in our climate, nature is but a cruel stepmother, and without great care, enjoy only a languishing existence, here burst exuberantly from the ground. We reached La Carolina along a delightful road bordered with palms and aloes, almost all of them in flower; they had trunks that were 25 to 30 feet tall and leaves 5 or 6 feet long.

La Carolina is a lovely town, neatly built and surrounded with beautiful gardens. Although it is in the middle of Andalusia, this town, a German colony, preserves its foreign air; except for the heat of the sun I could believe myself to be in a village in Saxony or Bavaria.

We did not find a living soul in La Carolina, and all the houses were closed, but within an hour, everything had been overrun and looted. It was here that General René had been arrested, cut into four pieces and thrown into boiling oil. His aide-de-camp, Labroue, was hacked in two, as was War Commissioner, Vaugier.

28 June: We remain here. Fanaticism lights all its torches against us. A hymn to the Virgin seemed to me to call down curses and death upon the vile French. It begins thus:

> Spirit of the Mother of God
> We offer you our souls.
> If the French offend thee
> Yet Spain adores thee, etc . . .

There are processions of fanatics. We hear that Frère's division, which is following us to maintain communication between Vedel and Madrid, has just been ordered to march on Valencia.

The administration of La Carolina, Santa Elena, Venta de Cardenas and Paso del Perro, was set up by the last Spanish minister, who struggled against the decadence of Spain and attempted to bring abandoned territory under cultivation, above all, that of the Sierra Morena.

29 June: Bailén. This is a fine countryside and an attractive town where we, at last, find some inhabitants; the first we have seen for four days. We expect to be attacked by a corps of English and Spaniards arriving from Granada.

Chapter 3

Captivity and Freedom:
June–October 1808

1808

30 June: Andujar. It was with regret that I left General Liger-Belair and Vedel's division, in order to rejoin my own regiment, which with the whole of General Dupont's corps, was at that time occupying Andujar and the Guadalquivir line.

When, on 7 June, General Dupont arrived at the Alcolea bridge, a league from Cordova, he found the enemy was already there. After firing outside the gates for a long while, he had formed an attacking column. The Paris Guard carried the bridge and the redan [*a fortification forming a salient from the main wall – Ed.*] that defended it. As the gates were closed when he reached Cordova, he ordered them to be forced open with cannon fire, and finding that the inhabitants had been firing from the houses, the whole town was delivered up to the most dreadful devastation for six days. The Archbishop's palace was robbed of millions. The cathedral and its sacred vessels were not spared: this caused the Spaniards to view us with horror for, they claimed openly that they would prefer us to violate their wives rather than their churches! Eventually, both of these barbaric acts took place. The convents of nuns were forced to endure all the debauchery and outrages that the soldiers, into whose hands they were delivered, could invent. The property of the King was shown no more respect than that belonging to the churches or to private individuals. The superb stud farms of Cordova were destroyed in an hour – I believe that all the officers, and even the infantry soldiers mounted themselves on the royal horses. In spite of the huge bounties accorded to the senior officers (6,000 francs for a corps commander), the baggage wagons belonging to the generals still groaned beneath the weight of silver, sacred vessels and valuables of every sort. Officers and soldiers alike were covered in gold and plunder. It is hard to say whether we were more burdened with hatred or with riches.

After the affair at Cordova, the number of our enemies increased every hour; the commanding general withdrew to Andujar and stationed his division along the Guadalquivir. The advance posts are on the other side of the river, the enemy occupies the town of Arragonez half a league away, and the outposts and forward detachments exchange fire daily. The enemy army is under the orders of General Castaños, who commands the camp at Saint-Roch. He is supposed to have few troops of the line.

[*Editor's note: General Francisco Xavier Castaños (1756–1852) was one of Spain's principal commanders, having received military training in Germany before taking command of the Army of Andalusia.*]

1 July: General Vedel is still at Bailén.

2 July: General Chassagne attacked Cuenca. The town was taken and given over to pillage – 200 peasants died there. A Te Deum was sung!

3–10 July: Every day the arrival of reinforcements is announced, but we await them in vain. We are completely ignorant of the enemy's intentions. It is impossible for us to find one man willing to carry a letter for just a few leagues, even if offered 500 *louis*, whereas Castaños can command as many spies to help him as there are Spaniards, and every order we give is known to him half an hour later. No matter what reward we offer, no Spaniard can be found even to show us the way. We have nothing to expect but dagger blows. The moment a few peasants see a Frenchman alone, or with but a handful of companions, he is mutilated and killed. Work has started to strengthen the bridgehead at Andujar by means of a salient.

11 July: We are spread out, day and night, across the blazing sand, and breathing burning air, we all suffer to the limit of endurance; men and horses are dying. The regiments have barely half their strength effective and there are about a thousand men in hospital. Everyone suffers from diarrhoea, dysentery and fever. One loaf has to be divided between eight men, sometimes between thirty-two; every dwelling, every house has been abandoned and we are reduced to going out to cut wheat for ourselves and for our horses.

If only our cause were just, I should not grumble at privation or at this terrible heat!

13 July: The reinforcements, so long promised, have still not come; Prince Murat, who has left Madrid, has been replaced as Commander-in-Chief of the army by General Savary, Duke of Rovigo. It is said that the new Spanish king, Joseph [*Napoleon's elder brother* – *Ed.*], has arrived in Madrid. Some of the *Grande Armée* is, so they say, speeding to our assistance. Not before time, I think. We still know nothing of what the enemy is doing.

14 July: Two leagues away, on our left, there is a windmill, on which the division depends for its subsistence. This morning, between 500 and 600 enemy infantry and about 1,200 cavalry appeared. Our reconnaissance party lost fourteen men, who were taken prisoner during this encounter. It looks as if the enemy is preparing to attack this important point either tonight or in the morning.

Napoleon I (1769-1821), de facto master of Europe after his stunning victory at Austerlitz in 1805 (detail from a portrait by Ingres).

French infantry of the Line, circa 1808.

French hussars skirmishing (Edouard Detaille).

General Alexandre de Beauharnais (1760-94), Josephine's first husband, guillotined during the Terror of the French Revolution.

Josephine (1762-1814), a distant cousin of Maurice de Tascher. Born Marie-Joseph-Rose de Tascher de la Pagerie, Napoleon crowned her empress in 1804 and divorced her five years later.

General Rapp (1771-1821), Napoleon's principal aide-de-camp.

Marshal Bernadotte (1763-1844), the Prince of Ponte Corvo, who later became Crown Prince and then King of Sweden.

Marshal Murat (1767-1815), Grand Duke of Berg, later King of Naples, and Napoleon's brother-in-law.

Marshal Soult (1769-1851).

Spanish soldiers by Denis Dighton. Although individually brave, the Spanish Army had been run down by years of neglect and was no match for Napoleon's veterans.

Marshal Davout (1770-1823), Napoleon's 'Iron Marshal'.

Marshal Bessières (1768-1813).

French *chasseurs* ford a river (Chartier).

Marshal Berthier (1753-1815), Napoleon's
Chief of Staff.

Marshal Masséna (1758-1817).

Marshal Lannes (1769-1809), mortally wounded at the Battle of Aspern-Essling.

Marie-Louise of Austria (1791-1847), Napoleon's replacement for the infertile Josephine.

'War to the Knife' - Goya's depiction of the savage struggle between French regulars and Spanish partisans: the birth of guerrilla warfare.

French *chasseurs* in Russia at the start of the 1812 campaign (Edouard Detaille).

Tsar Alexander I (1777-1825), Napoleon's former protégé, whose stubborn refusal to parley probably saved Russia in 1812.

Barclay de Tolly (1761-1818), Commander of Russian forces at the start of hostilities. Wisely retreating before Napoleon's Grand Army, he was later sacked for not standing his ground.

General (later Field Marshal) Kutusov (1756-1813), replaced Barclay at the head of Alexander's army in time for the Battle of Borodino. Kutusov - the 'Fox of the North' - preferred to let 'General Winter' push the Grand Army out of Russia.

Marshal Ney (1769-1815), the hero of the great retreat, dubbed 'bravest of the brave' by Napoleon.

The Grand Army in retreat, Russia 1812.

15 July: At dawn, a powerful battle line could be seen, drawn up on the surrounding heights.

At nine o'clock the Spaniards brought their guns forward and began to fire upon the bridgehead. The shells forced us to abandon our bivouac. The town was also abandoned and the division was stationed in battle order at right angles to the Bailén road. There was a lively fight, sustained by the 3rd Legion, near the windmill. We held our ground and the Spaniards lost a large number of men. There is a great deal of anxiety as to the fate of Vedel's division, as the road to Bailén has been cut.

The enemy attacks from the mountains and is repulsed, but as he appears everywhere, and we have no knowledge of his objectives, it is not known whether this is a feint to threaten our rear, or if it is truly an attack on us. Tomorrow will, undoubtedly, decide our fate.

16 July: There is heavy cannon fire on the bridgehead and the enemy attempts to cross the river, his guns are dismounted and he draws back. He sets fire to the fields of wheat on our side of the river, to stop us reaching the water. It is a terrible sight to see this crop burned by its owners! How they must loathe us! Driven from the plain, the battle line is established on the hills, parallel to the road and the Guadalquivir, a quarter of a league from Andujar.

Vedel's division arrives at nine in the evening and General Dupont immediately sends it back to Bailén, from whence it came. General Vedel made a great mistake in abandoning his position at Bailén. Instead of sending the reinforcement for which General Dupont had asked, he himself came with his division, thereby exposing Gobert's division to a bloody battle in which that general died.

[*Editor's note: This unfortunate action on the part of Vedel left exposed the ford at Menjibar. Protected only by Liger-Belair with a single battalion, it was soon attacked by 12,000 Spaniards. Gobert's division, consisting of 900 infantry and 200 cavalry, counter-attacked with such ferocity that the Spaniards were forced to withdraw and this gave Vedel an opportunity to retake Bailén without meeting resistance. Instead of staying there, as he had been ordered, Vedel made another bad decision and followed the remainder of Gobert's division, which following the death of its commander, had retired into the mountains near La Carolina. This mistake, which caused Dupont to return to Bailén, could have had a fortunate outcome if, on the 19th, Vedel, marching towards the guns, had taken Reding in the rear and opened the road to Madrid to his Commander-in-Chief. Unfortunately, he took five hours to cover 7½ miles/12 km and arrived when the outcome of the day had been decided and Dupont's army was incapable of further effort.*]

17 July: There is very bad news of Gobert's division. It seems that he had attempted an aggressive battle against troops that were numerically greatly superior to his own. We know for certain that we have lost many men and that

the General has been killed or mortally wounded. We are still surrounded on all sides. The enemy has numerous detachments along the Bailén road and has captured many of ours. We hear that the passage, guarded by General Liger-Belair, has been forced; the numbers in the Spanish line facing us are perceptibly less.

18 July: The Spaniards positioned before Arragonez continue to lessen in number. At five o'clock, no one can be seen, and the three cannon shots we hear seem to be the last signal of their retreat. Montgardet is ordered to follow them and to try to discover the direction of their march. He fails.

At nine in the evening, the division marches off, abandoning more than 1,000 sick in Andujar, but dragging along with it a multitude of carts, coaches and wagons filled with gold, and more baggage than an army 30,000-strong would need.

19 July: At three in the morning, having crossed the bridge three-quarters of a league from Bailén, a few cannon shots and a hail of shells and bullets tell us that we are encountering the enemy. At first, very few troops are sent forward and only one battalion at a time. The *Chasseur* Brigade is sent off to the left, among the olive trees. The 1st Regiment charges at four o'clock. It throws the enemy cavalry into disorder and falls upon the remnants, but receiving no support from the infantry, is compelled to retire. The 2nd arrives at this moment, but all the enemy cavalry is waiting for it and occupies the position with superior forces. Nevertheless, we advance to the edge of a ravine, twenty paces from the Spanish cavalry, who – six times as strong as we – still do not dare to charge. The enemy's infantry advances and a hail of bullets compel us to abandon the position, leaving behind many of our *chasseurs*. The first thing I saw when I arrived on the battlefield was the body of Thierry, a *sous-lieutenant* of the 5th Chasseurs, stretched on the ground mortally wounded; a few paces further on I saw the unfortunate Caupenne, who, having left on the previous evening, found himself charging with the 1st Regiment. His ardour had impelled him alone into the midst of the enemy, receiving a sabre-cut across his body. I saw him by himself on the far side of the ravine, I saw him as he reeled in his saddle and then fell, one foot caught in his stirrup. Just as I attempted to hurry to his aid, my horse was killed under me and in the time it took for me to order a *chasseur* to dismount and give me his horse, the gallant Captain Besson hurried to our unhappy comrade, freed his foot from the stirrup and placed him on the saddle in front of him. But at that instant, the enemy advanced and pushed us back, forcing him to abandon the dying man.

We reformed our line of battle amongst the olives trees, where we remained for several hours in spite of the bullets and shells, always manoeuvring under cannon fire and at almost point-blank range of his infantry's muskets. The firing was so constant and so heavy that the older generals admitted that they had never seen anything like it. We held our line to the left of the road with a legion and Reding's Swiss, who fought energetically against Reding's Spanish Swiss [*two Swiss brigades under Reding the Elder fought on the French side, while other Swiss formations under Reding the Younger fought with Castaños for the Spaniards – Ed.*]. Our artillery, sustained by the bravery of its officers (Perdrau, General Faultrier, Foucaud, etc.), tried in vain to remain on the road. The enemy, having 24-pounder guns in position served by excellent gunners, inflicted damage on our guns with every shot. The French Swiss with the dragoons and a squadron of cuirassiers took up position to the left of the road. We continued to advance, slowly, then, at ten o'clock, two flags were brought in, one of them captured by a dragoon and the other by a cuirassier *sous-lieutenant*. There were shouted demands for a charge. At once, the Commander-in-Chief ordered a general attack along the entire line; we moved off and gathered amongst the ravines and ditches to confront a regiment of Spanish infantry; we charged forward. When about 20 paces from them, a final ravine halted us and we were compelled to wheel to our left, passing in front of the enemy bayonets. Besson fell at this moment, together with Leclerc and our bravest officers and non-commissioned officers. Just as the Major turned towards me to tell me to keep to his right, a bullet grazed my chest and passed through his body. But now, at last, we fell upon the flank of the infantry and began a dreadful massacre. I revenged the killing of my major upon the body of the enemy colonel, plunging my sabre into his chest; I retreated when I saw that there was no one with me except M—— and Labarrière.

After this general attack, in the course of which we pushed the enemy back at all points, we found that we had advanced no further than before. Behind the line we had thrust back, we saw another, outnumbering our division by five to one. All the hillsides were covered with troops with batteries in position everywhere, and formidable infantry squares. The heat was terrible and there was not a drop of water. Men were dropping, some dead and some of exhaustion, even as they cried out for water. Our horses, short of food for a month and having endured a march of 6 leagues, as well as a battle lasting ten hours, fell beneath us. We remained under the enemy fire until two in the afternoon. Shot and shell continued to rain down on us; it was so heavy that most of the trees were shattered, and over large areas, the grass and bushes were burning, set alight by the shells.

At two o'clock, General Dupré, whose brigade now consisted of no more than a squadron, received the order to attempt a last effort. He advanced at the head of the Marines of the Guard, much less in the hope of victory than in the certainty of dying honourably. In actual fact, no sooner had we shown our-selves on the hillside, than an infantry square, twelve or fifteen times stronger than we, began to rake this group of men with bullets, thinning the ranks with amazing speed. They spared us the trouble of marching up to the enemy for, before we could reach the valley, a large proportion of the officers and men were stretched upon the ground, and the rest forced to retreat to the hillside. The gallant General Dupré, at the end of a thirty-year-long career, in the course of which fortune had been as devoted to him as he himself was to honour, now saw himself betrayed by the first and dying faithful to the second. A musket ball passed through his body. I remained at the top of the hill for a long while with Labarrière and B——, the only officers of the regiment that were left. It was in vain that I wished to charge towards the road in order to rejoin Vedel's division, which could not be far away. But both men and horses refused to make this new attempt.

It was not the arrival at the bridge of the Spanish General La Pena – who was following us with 15,000 men and fresh troops – that was the death of our hopes, for we had none left. It only made us more keenly aware of the horror of our position.

The Commander-in-Chief then sent negotiators. As we awaited our fate, we stretched out on the burning soil, exhausted and consumed by hunger and thirst, the prospect of a terrible doom obsessed us, so that we envied the corpses surrounding us, for they had no knowledge of our wretchedness, and above all, knew nothing of the only thought that filled our minds: we are French, we are alive and we are not victorious!

When, at dawn, we had found the enemy near Bailén, the Commander-in-Chief had been delighted. He had believed that he had captured his prey, convinced that General Vedel, who was a short distance in the enemy's rear, was about to attack, thereby catching the enemy between two fields of fire. It was for this reason that he had not tried to seize the road by pressing home an attack; his sole aim until ten in the morning was to hold the enemy in check so that General Vedel had time to attack. But Vedel, instead of holding the position that had been assigned to him, had withdrawn several leagues to the rear. However, urged on by his generals, he set out to come to our aid, but when he reached Guarroman (3 leagues from the battlefield) he insisted on remaining there for five hours. His generals, who could hear the cannon fire, were in despair. Finally, Vedel did not take up his position to attack until about an hour after we had called for negotiations. When he saw that it was too late, he wanted to withdraw towards Madrid and had actually reached Santa-Cruz. Then, when he learned that no capitulation in which he was not included, would be accepted, he returned, and he and 9,000 men who had not fired a shot laid down their arms.

The enemy had been surprised to see us reach Bailén, for at that moment he had been preparing to attack us at Andujar. When the *chasseurs* first attacked him, none of his cavalry had mounted. We rode into his batteries, and if at that time our infantry had supported us, we should have captured his guns.

As for the Spaniards, General Castaños and the Madrid Junta admitted that General Reding [*General Teodoro Reding, in command of the Walloon Guards – Ed.*], at Bailén, was in command of 25,000 men. The General who was following us had 15,000 men, not including those spread out over the country to the right and left. In total the enemy had at least 45,000 men, while we had barely 5,000 combatants.

[*Editor's note: it seems likely that Castaños commanded some 34,000 men in 4 divisions, while Dupont's army had a strength of around 20,000 men: and yet, only some 25,000 Spaniards and 7,000 French took an active part in the battle. Tascher's figure of 5,000 French combatants can be explained by the fact that many of Dupont's troops were ineffective, due to fatigue and dysentery.*]

One hour after the negotiators had been sent, Vedel's division arrived and actually captured an enemy battalion. General Dupont asked his generals if a final effort could be made, but all except General Frésia replied that it was impossible, and General Frésia only offered a single *charge au pas*. The French cavalry, above all the *chasseurs*, had fought like lions. Of the eleven platoons that made up the brigade at the beginning of the affair, only three, with their strength reduced, still remained at two o'clock.

The Swiss regiments of Preuss and Reding (the Elder) were on our side and fought valiantly against the Swiss regiments on the Spanish side. The old Brigade General, Reding, distinguished himself. I was told that, after the battle, he embraced his cousin (who was fighting on the Spanish side). Monsieur de Coupigny, was one of the major-generals in the enemy army [*when they saw the day was lost, some 1,000 French Swiss went over to their compatriots on the Spanish side. General de Coupigny was a French* émigré *– Ed.*].

The Spanish infantry regiments of Malaga and Jérèz were, by their own admission, wiped out by our charge. The colonel of the former died by my hand. A lieutenant colonel of cuirassiers was slain by little La Moussaye, who alone seized him by the collar and killed him in front of his regiment. In the morning cavalry charge, three senior officers were killed by our *chasseurs* and one by Montgardet. It was the *chasseur* Garnier, from Orléans, who dismounted and gave me his horse when my own mount was killed. At the moment when I was killing the infantry colonel, a foot soldier pressed his musket against my chest, I used my sabre to deflect his gun, but it slipped down the weapon and cut off his fingers. When I was galloping among the olive trees, I saw an enemy infantryman lie down to take aim at me as I passed, but when I was level with him, I nailed him to the ground with my sabre. The regiment was fighting in front of a battery and I found myself, with Labarrière, between two olive trees and saw two field guns fired: a shot cut in two a *chasseur* of the 20th who was nearby. Thirst and the heat were so great that several officers and men dropped dead of dehydration.

Returning to the charge with Montgardet, we saw a partridge with a broken wing, presumably wounded by a stray bullet. At the time of the charge, Major Bureau took me on one side: 'One cannot tell,' he said to me, 'What is going to happen. Do not forget that I have a valuable money belt on my person; in any case, I depend on you; do not leave my side.' And I said to myself; 'Perhaps I am destined to rest here. Ah! Sainvilliers you know of whom my last thoughts will be! You know to whom I leave my cross and my sword!'

In the morning, Major Le Mire and I went forward alone to observe the enemy's movements. At a considerable distance away, I saw two peasants preparing to take aim at us. I said: 'Look out, Major, they have seen us and are kneeling, they are about to shoot.' They fired and one of the bullets tore through my cloak, which was slung over my shoulder, and the other went through the coat and shirt worn by Le Mire, grazing his stomach.

In the course of a fight that lasted twelve hours, while surrounded on all sides, we had not lost an inch of ground and had captured all the enemy positions as well as three flags. The Spanish artillery was excellent both in range and aim. It began by firing a little too high and then lowered its aiming point, and then did not waste a shot.

20 July: We are still where we were yesterday. Negotiations continue. Generals Chabert and Marescot have met General Castaños at Andujar. We expect that the peasants will come and rob us at any moment.

21 July: We remain in the same place. We are dying of hunger and thirst. We should have to travel a league in order to fetch a goatskin full of muddy water; the peasants continue to fire upon anyone who attempts to go in search of water or fodder.

22 July: In the morning. Our situation grows worse. General Castaños is unwilling to agree to any treaty in which Vedel's division is not included. Vedel is retreating towards Madrid; should he turn back? At any moment we may be plundered and handed over to the mercy of the peasants; what a fate! We have committed so many outrages against these same peasants that we cannot raise our heads and look them in the eye, for we have not even the consolation of knowing that other soldiers would respect our ill-fated bravery. Like Francis I we could say: 'All is lost'; but, unlike that valiant king, we could not add: 'all save honour!' Faith betrayed, Ferdinand a prisoner; Cordova! Cordova! Stolen gold! These are the shouts that make us hang our heads.

At nine in the evening we received reliable news of Vedel's division. It had not been contacted until just before it reached Santa-Cruz. Now it is returning and the surrender has been signed.

[*Editor's note: the terms of surrender accorded the honours of war to Dupont's army, which was to be repatriated by sea. The officers were to retain their swords and baggage and the soldiers their haversacks. The total number of prisoners would be about 17,000, including the men of Vedel's division.*]

23 July: Villanueva. This day has left an impression on my mind that will never be effaced in my lifetime. A terrible day, a day that made me almost regret that I had not allowed myself to be killed yesterday.

At four o'clock, we left our bivouac and marched, with all the honours of war into the midst of the Spanish Army, which was drawn up in two lines with flags flying and music playing. We marched in good order with drums beating; our guns leading each battalion. 400 paces from the enemy line, each soldier came forward to lay down his arms and each of the mounted troops handed over his horse. Even now, I grind my teeth with anger and stifle my tears of pride and rage. I can still hear – as I shall hear for the rest of my life – that loathsome music, every note of which makes me wince. I shall always see the contemptuous joy, and hear the murderous shouts of the peasants, indicating how gladly they would plunge their daggers into our throats. Once again, I see the glances in which combined hatred and contempt try to hide behind a veil of pride and generosity of spirit.

We have retraced our steps on the road to Andujar and recrossed the Guadalquivir ford, and halt to sleep at the little village of Villanueva. In justice to the Spanish officers, it must be said that the more the people showed their eagerness to let their horrid joy and bloodthirstiness erupt, the more the officers showed their coolness and their generosity.

24 July: Porcuna. We left at two in the morning and went through Arragonez. Six days ago we were there and free!

A regiment is being formed at Porcuna. These new soldiers, not yet in uniform, are armed only with daggers and bayonets, which they seem anxious to test on their prisoners. On every side, we hear shouts of, 'Death to the French. Death to Napoleon, cut off his head!' In order to avoid the consequences of these threats, we left only two hours after our arrival and went a league further on, to sleep.

25 July: Bujalance. Although we set out on the road at one in the morning, the number of wagons so encumbered our march that we did not arrive until just before midday. The heat is terrible. Nothing can give any idea of the dust that blinds us; every moment of the march is a moment of suffering. When we reached the halting place we found ourselves, once again, threatened with daggers amongst cries of, 'Cordova! Cut off their heads!' And our ears rang constantly with threats of death in many guises. We remain in bivouac.

26 July: Castro-del-Rio. This is an attractive town on the Guadalquivir, it is a fertile place with beautiful aloes, fig and palm trees. We have been assured that

tomorrow, a mob of armed peasants awaits us on the road, with the intention of cutting our throats. But our hosts regale us with similar information every day.

27 July: La Rambla. All along the 6 leagues of our journey we heard shouts threatening us with death; our cavalry escort (cavalrymen of Calatrava, 10th of the Line, in which each general has four or six men as servants) was very energetic in protecting us; they sabred the peasants who attacked us, for without their efforts, we should have fallen victim to them. The infantry, on the other hand, showed us much more ill will, and the moment a Frenchman lagged behind, it was the infantry of the escort who were the first to rob him, even, on occasion, to murder him.

We passed through Mandilla, a strongly fortified town and one that is violently opposed to the French. We bivouacked near La Rambla. The countryside is arid and mountainous with a large number of olive trees. The heat continues to be terrible.

28 July: Ecija. This is a well-built, large town. We bivouacked by a fine road on the bank of the Guadalquivir. I was not able to satisfy my curiosity by exploring the town. The guard, formed of the *bourgeoisie*, surrounded us on all sides. In any case, the Spaniards believe that spilling the blood of the French is an acceptable sacrifice to God. They have also been convinced that those who die fighting us are resurrected at once and transported to the place of their birth. There is scarcely a single day that is not marked by a murder. Today, an officer and an administrator were stabbed in the open street in the middle of the city. In every head, especially in those of the women, the torch of fanaticism is burning. I continue to be amazed at the fact that, when young girls of no more than ten or twelve years old pass near me, they pretend to stab me, indicating by their gestures that they would like to plunge a dagger into my throat. It is hard to reconcile the gentleness natural to their sex with the barbarity of their gestures. But hearing the constant shouts of 'Cordova!' I blush for my compatriots and lower my eyes, as I remember their behaviour and compare the Spanish cause with our own. The violation of churches, notably that of the cathedral of Cordova, the theft of sacred vessels and the excesses committed in the convents are the main reasons for the passions that have been inflamed against us. Our crimes are, as always, exaggerated so that we are looked upon as monsters, unworthy of pity. I receive a charming compliment from a young girl, who gallantly told me that my head would make a fine ornament in front of her door. Many of the houses near the bridge of Ecija are decorated with Moorish paintings.

29 July: Fuentes. We bivouacked near Fuentes, a pleasant town, unusual in that the surrounding countryside is covered with olive trees and farmhouses, unlike other towns that are surrounded by desert.

31 July: Utera. We are travelling in an arid, stony landscape and suffering a great deal from the terrible heat.

1 August: Las Cabezas. There are French and Spanish Commissioners ahead of us on the road, so we receive some supplies of bread and meat. Also, to make good some of the money we stole in Spain, we are made to pay two *douros*, worth two *pesetas*; we even have to pay for the water and fodder for our horses. It costs two *pesetas* to allow a horse to drink twice.

2 August: Lebrija. There is a ruinous fort in this attractive town. It seems that the townspeople are very ill-disposed towards us, for the Spanish infantry regiment that we charged and practically wiped out, came mostly from here.

3 August: Some 8,000 peasants, having armed themselves from the arsenal they raided, are marching to meet us with the intention of murdering us. As a result we have been halted here, and a regiment of the line has been sent to break up the mob. It begins to appear that an order from the Junta condemns to death all Spaniards who kill a Frenchman; but the whole country is in revolt. The Junta of one town issues a decree that contradicts the decree issued by the neighbouring Junta.

We were flattering ourselves that our troubles were about to end, and that we should arrive on the 4th at our destination, to embark at once, as laid down in the terms of capitulation; however it is said that the ships are not ready and that we are to be dispersed and lodged in the villages. The Commanding General opposes this and has just sent General Chabert to Seville to plead our cause.

4 August: Disarmed prisoners that we are, we still make the Spaniards tremble, for they fear that our wagons are filled with daggers. They have just ordered us to hand them over and have searched the baggage; not a single weapon has been found. A cunning proclamation is being reported amongst our soldiers, blaming the Emperor for all the troubles of the war and calling upon us to unite under the Spanish flag.

5–6 August: Nothing is happening. If the information spread by the Spaniards is true, it seems that General Junot, surrounded on all sides, harassed by 30,000 troops and without supplies, is on the point of surrendering unconditionally. Madrid was evacuated on 31 July and the King [*i.e. Joseph Bonaparte – Ed.*] was forced to flee on his horse, accompanied by General Grouchy; his baggage and his palace having been pillaged by the people. Columns of between 20,000 and 30,000 men are gathering on all sides, the army corps of General Moncey was defeated at Valencia and at Zaragoza. In this latter town, the gates had been opened to the French, but every house was barricaded and filled with armed men. The French were killed there without even being able to defend themselves. All the French forces seem to be concentrated at Burgos and across the Ebro.

[*Editor's note: General Jean Andoche Junot (1771–1813), campaigning in Portugal, was defeated by Wellington at Vimiero and forced to sign the surrender of Cintra. The English, however, would respect the clauses of the surrender and repatriate Junot's army ...*]

7 August: General Chabert has returned from Seville, where General Castaños received him in a friendly and generous manner; however he would not see him during the day and delayed the meeting until ten in the evening, as he did not dare to provoke the anger of the populace. This fury was so great that Messieurs Chabert and Daugier were attacked with stones as they travelled by coach to the Junta. At first they were lodged opposite a church, but swords were whetted and bloodthirsty verses sung beneath their windows. The vociferous protests of the priests and monks so endangered their lives that the Junta was obliged to move them to safety and to protect them. A captain-general received them with an armed guard, drums beating and a colour salute. It was thus that the proudest and most cruelly outraged nation demonstrated that it could still pay tribute to the bravery of the unfortunate.

A state of revolution exists and there are endless deliberations and delays by the Junta.

When our generals asked to be allowed to bid farewell to General Castaños, they were told that the Junta must consider the matter first. When General Chabert requested permission for us to leave, the English admiral's approval was needed and he has sent a sloop to the Admiralty for authorization. We await the reply and here we remain for the present.

During the uprising in Madrid, Monsieur de Solano was ordered by Prince Murat to march on the city with his troops. He hesitated, and kept Prince Murat's aide-de-camp with him for three days. On the third day, he dispatched an acquiescent reply, and this proved to be his own death sentence. Neither his kindness, nor his talents, nor even the love he bore for his native Cadiz could save him; in a moment, the battery placed in front of his house was turned upon it. A murderous mob marched towards him; he hid, and for a long while evaded the searchers. Finally, a painter, who had once worked for him, pointed out a dark closet that he had painted. Monsieur de Solano was found, dragged out into the road and slashed with a thousand cuts; his heart was torn from his body. His wife only contrived to escape over the rooftops. He had been loved in Cadiz, but as soon as he accepted the ribbon of the Légion d'Honneur, his friends started to turn their backs on him, and his reply to Prince Murat had doomed him. Information about Seville was learned from General Chabert, and that concerning Cadiz from the Spaniards.

8–11 August: We wait in uncertainty among the olive trees in our bivouac, where we suffer greatly.

12 August: At noon, a secret order to leave arrives, but this is only for the generals and their aides-de-camp. They set out at different times; all the wagons and carts meet at dusk on the road to Jerez. The morale of the regiments reflects the despondency of the soldiers and anger of the officers. We pass through Jerez at midnight. As far as I could see, the town is handsome and surrounded by a number of Moorish towers. I have never seen more beautiful vegetation than that of the countryside around this town. There are forests of orange and lemon trees, palms, figs and pomegranates, and thick hedges of aloes and cactus.

13 August: After a long, rapid march, the day at last dawned when we thought to see the end of our troubles. It was to be marked with abuse and fury. Port of Santa-Maria! [*The port of Cadiz – Ed.*] This name will, for many years, cause the French of our unhappy army corps to shudder. It will remain graven on our hearts forever; it will forever awaken indignation and stifle feelings of pity: 13 August 'thirteen' written in letters of fire on our wounded hearts!

We reached Santa-Maria at seven in the morning. The French officer in charge of billeting was attacked by the populace. He sought refuge with the governor and warned him of the disorder. This gentleman lavished reassurances upon him, but in place of the 800 men that he should have placed under arms, insisted on providing only twenty-five and sent us on our way, with the order to advance with confidence. We skirted the town and reached the port, followed and crushed by the rage and threats of a huge crowd of people, whose shouts resounded on all sides: 'Death to the French! Death to Dupont! Cordova! Cordova!' It is noticeable that it is women, especially those of the upper class, who, by their furious energy and fanaticism, continually urge the men to stab us, and make it quite clear to us that their only wish is to have a French head nailed to their front door.

All the time that we were waiting on the quayside for the boats, the fury of the populace increased. Finally, we were told to abandon our horses and baggage, thus leaving them open to plunder, and to embark immediately. The Commanding General, surrounded by his officers, who formed a bodyguard around him, jumped into a small boat, so escaping the threat of a thousand daggers. Now the anger of the people reached a height that seemed to know no bounds. In the midst of a hail of stones, and menaced on all sides by daggers, all of us were forced to leap into a boat as best we might, even while we saw, on the riverbank, those who had been less swift than we, buffeted and dragged away by the infuriated population. Men, women and soldiers engulfed the carts and wagons, seized our horses and flaunted our weapons and banners, while dividing up our spoils amongst themselves.

But the sight of the wagons, with their loads of sacred vessels, that had been the primary cause of the anger of the Spaniards, caused some among us to lower our eyes in shame and would have excused the people had their excesses not passed all normal bounds. For my own part, having left my horses and baggage with the faithful Strauss, my *chasseur*, who would have exposed himself to any danger to protect my property, I was able to slip away from the mob: without, however, managing to avoid all the stones and blows.

I contrived to join Generals Roize, Laplane, Daugier and Cevillard. A Spaniard with a stone in his hand gashed the face of the first, accusing him of the looting of Cordova (where he had never been), and with a blow to the head and a violent kick in the back, he hurled the second to the foot of the steps. I threw myself on top of him in the boat. My sabre had twice been torn from my hand and twice I had been lucky enough to seize it back. Feeling a blow, I gritted my teeth and wept with rage; I gripped my sabre and although burning with a desire to revenge myself on these bandits, I knew that if a drop of their blood were to be shed, it would be a death sentence for all the French.

Now in the boat, a Spaniard tried to grab from me a small case that contained my papers and some little items dear to my heart. I pushed him back twice and enraged, he seized a huge piece of wood and raising it, attempted to smash in my head. I was hemmed in on all sides and could not move, but fixed my eyes on the impending death blow: a young man dashed forward and gripped the plank by one end, while another interposed himself and begged for mercy (these were Dorilla, a secretary, and Gabalda, an aide-de-camp to General Laplane). Meanwhile, another villain took hold of my case. A moment later, his sabre was snatched from General Roize and a wretch turned to split my head open, but my coolness and composure checked his arm.

Once at sea, we believed ourselves saved. A boat containing the senior administrative official joined us. We had to allow him to search our pockets. This magistrate spoke good French and everything appeared to promise us safety and protection, he took all my money as well as my handkerchief, in which to wrap it, for as he said, he had to be sure that we had nothing that had belonged to a church. At last, he left us and as we traversed the superb anchorage of Cadiz, we lost sight of that horrible coast.

What a sight! On our right, the English squadron cruised before the port, enjoying the spectacle of our unhappiness and shame. On our left, was the squadron that had once been French (the *Algesiras*, the *Pluton*, the *Vengeur* and the *Cornélie*) and was now in the hands of the Spaniards and which, previously destined to carry us into battle and to victory, was now to serve as our prison.

After a crossing of 4 leagues, we joined the *Montagnez* and thought ourselves safe. The captain received us quite kindly. The dark anger and sulky silence of the sailors seemed to us less threatening than the yells of the citizens of Santa-Maria, which still rang in our ears. At nearly six o'clock in the evening and in the course of a very scanty meal, the crew, whose fervent anger had increased from minute to minute, came to the vessel's captain with shouted demands for our death. The captain, not daring either to refuse or to consent, avoided his responsibility by flight, and so rendered our situation even more dangerous (this event caused him to lose the command of his ship). Every sailor, every soldier, was armed and demanding our death. The frigate captain, faced with this danger, deceived the crew by letting us embark from both sides at the same time. It was now that a blow from an oar almost broke my finger and a Spanish soldier was stabbed by a dagger thrust intended for one of us. Our sabres had to be handed over to the frigate captain so that the sailors would not use them to kill us. We were obliged to leave our comrades and bid them what we thought would be a last farewell. The blackness of the night, the raging waves that crashed beneath our feet, the terrifying shouts for our death and these final farewells combined to intensify the horror of the scene.

After having sailed on for a short time, we came alongside an old dismasted hulk. We crashed into it and a gust of wind cast us into the sea. At last, after great efforts, we boarded the merchant ship *La Palmona*, where in spite of ourselves, we were forced by hunger, cold, destitution and our complete ignorance of the fate of our comrades, to confront the full horror of our situation. However, an ensign of the ship was about to leave for France in the company of Admiral Rosily and General de Marescot and I took advantage of this to write to my parents.

Before once again taking up the thread of these unhappy events, I shall recount some of the circumstances and details concerning the happenings of 13 August at Santa-Maria, the Battle of Bailén on 19 July, and an account of what had happened to the French fleet at Cadiz between 9 and 14 July.

All occurrences leading up to, and during, a revolution are characterized by tumult and confusion. This applied to the revolt at Cadiz even more than in any other. In fact, the prisons had been opened and 800 armed galley slaves were freed. It would have been almost impossible to return this criminal torrent to its confines, once it had been liberated. The clamour of the monks had turned these criminals into something resembling wild beasts, and the prestige and power of religion would be needed to reverse the process. The monks went through the streets with the Holy Sacrament in one hand and bestowing benedictions with the other, as they took back the weapons from these maniacs, who would not allow themselves to be disarmed save by these religious bearers of the Holy Sacrament. The madness was such that a rich Spaniard, known to be a supporter of Ferdinand VII, having been imprudent enough to leave his house without his official badge, was immediately and openly stabbed.

In all their activities and even in their games, the Spaniards had retained all the ferocity of the Saracens and Moors, but it was towards the French that their hatred and wish to inflict pain was demonstrated with a terrible violence. Even if the people of Castile had been quite friendly towards France, those of

Andalusia, Murcia and Granada had, from time immemorial, harboured a loathing for us that was perpetuated by the care with which it was imbued in their children from the earliest age. The first perception of us that they received was abhorrence, and in their early games they condemned us to torture. When they were unable to do this, one of their gentle sports consisted of making little wax figures called 'the French' and piercing them with a thousand pins. Such was the sort of treatment extended to our prisoners in many places. Fanaticism kept this attitude alive.

In the cathedral of Cordova there is a picture of the violation of the tomb of the Holy Bishop, and it is the French who are depicted as the violators (I have been told this by eyewitnesses). Whereas, on the other hand, the Spanish people have merited depiction in the brightest and most meticulous of colours. I speak of the greater part of the nation.

There is among them not one traitor, not one spy, not one man, who can be corrupted. General Dupont told me that he had offered nearly 10,000 francs to have a letter carried and met with a rebuff. A peasant would let himself be killed rather than be forced even to indicate a direction. There is not one who is not prepared to sacrifice his life and his wealth for his country and his religion. The history of their struggle against the Moors proves their determination and stubbornness. As to their frugality, we have observed it a thousand times; the bare minimum suffices to maintain life. In a country overflowing with strong wine, one never sees a drunken Spaniard. Their obedience to their king enabled them to bear all sorts of privations during the long association of Spain with France. As for their haughtiness and arrogance, foreigners find these defects unbearable. The Spaniards are able, strangely enough, to combine their dark and fierce energy with an apathy and laziness that ensures that our arms will always overcome theirs; for, when it is necessary to protect an important position, they begin to discuss the matter, so that we shall have long pre-empted the action they take.

The grandees and those Spaniards who have travelled abroad are aware of the state of decline into which their country has fallen. They long for a revolution and impatiently endure the dreadful governance of the clergy; they freely admit that the monks represent parasitic plants drawing to themselves and consuming all resources of the state. These innovators possess all the works of our philosophers, but they are careful to hide them beneath big statues of the Holy Virgin, for fear of the Inquisition. In any case, Ferdinand VII is only a puppet now, of whom they make use to conceal their plans and lead the people. The Seville Junta wishes to become a republic, and the monks know that if Joseph's party triumphs, then farewell to idleness and ignorance, power and wealth.

As for our fleet, at anchor in the roads with the Spanish fleet, it had found itself trapped without any possibility of escape, for the English commanded the entrance to the port. Fortunately a stay lasting three years had enabled the French sailors to learn the language and make friends in a town where there were many French people. Each one found himself protected by personal friendships from the feeling of hatred that swept over the nation, and their fate was far less painful than ours. Nevertheless, since the sacking of Cordova, of which they were certainly innocent, people distanced themselves from them, cursed them, and made their nationality into a crime. Now they prefer to remain on board their ships. But rage and hatred pursue them, and boats filled with infuriated individuals circle them continually, ready to seize their vessels. However, the composure of the old gunners, who with their fuses in their hands await only the signal to open fire, enforces respect. On 9 July matters began to heat up. At last, each French vessel found itself gripped, without any chance of raising anchor, between two enemy ships. The squadron acknowledged the impossibility of defending itself any longer and surrendered on 14 July. The officers were imprisoned in the Island [*presumably the island of Cabrera, notorious for the appalling conditions in which French prisoners were held, and where many of them died – Ed.*]; they had relied upon us to free them, but we only arrived in Cadiz in time to share their fate.

One of the setbacks that has caused us most harm in this unhappy land of Andalusia is the arrest of the two staff officers, Fénelon and Freral. Castaños learned of the situation in Madrid from the letters they were carrying; from then on he hoped to turn it to his advantage, there was no longer any question of letting us pass and we were forced to turn back.

Count de Tilly, once Minister of War, guided by the most inspired patriotism and fervour, replied hotly, when our generals assured him that this unequal struggle would bring down incalculable evils upon Spain and that there was no hope of success: 'And do you put no value upon the honour of dying, fighting for your country? We are sustained by the words of your Emperor to the Poles: No nation is ever conquered unless it wishes to be.'

A bizarre circumstance brought me dangerous attention during the pillage of Santa-Maria on 13 August, and it continued throughout the period of chaos without my knowledge. At Andujar I had bought some fine grey material, from which I had had breeches made. It was unfortunate that this same material was exactly that from which the clothes of the nuns of several convents were made, so that all through the turmoil of Santa-Maria, many Spaniards picked me out for their hatred, shouting: 'Kill him, kill him, he has violated the nuns! He is wearing the plunder!'

On board the *Montagnez*, when the crew mutinied, I again had the honour – one that I would gladly have foregone – of attracting the attention of the Spaniards, who were determined to throw me into the sea. Even on board the *Vencedor*, although it was fairly peaceful, the sailors were agitated to the point that the ship's lieutenant thought it right to tell me not to come out of my room again, or to change my clothes. But as I had no other breeches, I had to keep them on and they had to get used to it.

By inexplicable good fortune no one had died on 13 August. In view of the anger of the people, the violence they had shown and the excesses that we had suffered, it is remarkable that none of us died, although all of us had witnessed death close at hand. Quite apart from the rocks thrown at me, a deadly blow had twice seemed to hang over my head.

La Moussaye, pursued by a monk who was trying to kill him, was knocked over, and an oar raised to smash his head, when another furious individual threw himself upon him with a dagger in his hand upraised to stab him, the first man holding the oar struck, and split open the head of the other murderer. Brains flooded over La Moussaye, who got up, grabbed his haversack back again, and fled safe and sound.

His companion, Huguet, was less fortunate. Robbed and bruised by many blows, he took refuge in a rowing boat, where he underwent a new search. A pretty, well-dressed young woman carried insult and examination a step further: as he had still retained his watch, she took it, but at that moment a cabin boy grabbed it, and jumping into the sea, escaped. Then she seized his cross of the Légion d'Honneur, which a sailor also took hold of. At last, this female – or rather, this fury – determined to make up for this double loss of her prizes, lost control, ripped his clothes from his body and searched him everywhere. No modesty restrained her greedy hands; she explored his most secret places, and enraged at failing to find any of the hidden treasures of Plutus [*Greek god of wealth – Ed.*], she gripped the voluptuous parts that she was outraging, and with a violent jolt, brought the wretched officer to lie at her feet, as white as death. He remained like this for half an hour at the bottom of the boat.

An attractive female tapped on the shoulder of an officer, one who was usually quite conceited. He, thinking that good fortune had come his way as a result of his good looks and long blond moustaches, turned to her with a smile. The amiable female at once covered his eyes and face with spit. This fine fellow and many others had had the same experience.

The women in general showed themselves to be more relentless than the men; they screamed for our heads and demanded that the soldiers should kill us before their eyes. General Abbadie, Colonel Huchet and many others, had their uniforms cut to ribbons on their backs. Belts were cut off nearly all those who had them, and yet no one was seriously injured. Madame Le Roi, who was caring for an infant and a sick husband, was in an even more cruel situation than those of us, who had only ourselves to protect. Having been maltreated and robbed of everything, but not wishing to desert either her husband or her daughter, she was embarked alone and last of all. Her boat travelled all round the anchorage, calling in vain to every ship, but none would accept any more

French, finding those that they already had too many. After having wandered all night in this way, she returned to the shore, was handed over to the guard, and then taken to the prison and shut up. This was where I came upon her. Three days after we had been plundered, the frenzied populace gathered and went to the convent where she (Madame Le Roi) had been imprisoned (and where all of us subsequently were) with 2,000 other French. The people demanded entry for the purpose of murdering everyone. The guard, composed of troops of the line, prevented this and the mob then set fire to many parts of the convent, this continued for four hours and several attempts were made to break in. The terrible situation of the unarmed French prisoners can be imagined!

A Bishop's Cross taken from Major Estève's black servant, a pyx being used as a tobacco box by an officer, and above all, the sacred vessels, altar cloths and church property that was known to be in our wagons, had provided the first and strongest motives for the ransacking we suffered.

During the looting of our baggage, it was possible to estimate the degree of devotion of our servants to their masters. Most of them, when confronted with danger, thought only of themselves and their own property; others, both cowardly and faithless, were the first to steal and to show the Spaniards where money was hidden and share it with them. Some of the others (above all, my *chasseur*, Strauss), demonstrated both courage and fidelity. This faithful servant, rather than abandoning my horses and goods, refused to embark, and remained on horseback in spite of the stones hurled at him; he would have preferred to die rather than dismount, had he not been dragged to the ground with an iron hook. Bruised and wounded as he was, he still contrived to keep one of my horses, which he sold to a peasant for 40 francs. He was the only one who was able to sell a horse and although he would have been justified in regarding the money as his own, he told me of it and insisted on giving it to me. Also, he preserved and returned to me some of the items he had been able to hide (among others, a small purse of medals) but he had abandoned all his own property in order to save mine.

14 August: On board the *Paloma*. The day passes slowly on this wretched ship; we are always uncertain of our fate and are in a state of complete destitution. We gave a sailor some money to buy food for us. He took it and did not return. I try in vain to persuade the frigate captain to return my sword and my notes.

15 August: At eight in the morning, all the generals were summonsed, but they were not allowed to take with them a single aide-de-camp. We watched them leave for different ships. General Frésia showed a touching kindness. We learn that they are to be taken to Fort Saint-Sébastien at Cadiz. Then they come for us, too. Are they taking us back to the land? It would be better to drown us at once.

Thank God! We are now on a warship, on which the crew at least, is not composed of savages, thirsty for our blood. There are several men from Marseilles who welcomed us. Having been stationed at Brest, most of them realize that the French are not cannibals, as the general population is given to believe. They know that, among our numerous faults (at least in our foreign wars) cruelty is not included. The captain of this ship seems to be humane.

We were delighted to find some of our comrades again, even those of whom we were not particularly fond. General misfortune has made us love one another. The aides-de-camp of all our generals are gathered together on this ship (the *Vencedor*).

19 August: We are divided between two rooms, the captains are in that of the Staff Headquarters and the lieutenants are in the powder magazine. Nevertheless, it is almost impossible to enjoy a moment's peace; unhappiness has embittered everyone, and from morning to night our rooms are filled with unrest and disputes. I walk on the deck at night. It would be a great comfort to me if I had my notes. Even if I should perish, I must attempt to return to the *Montagnez* tomorrow for the sake of my sword! Must it be that I return to France without a weapon?

Ah! To return to France! Where is she, this beloved country? Unmindful of my own troubles, it is the thought of the misery of my parents that robs me of courage. They are undoubtedly weeping for my death. And my father, who at my earnest request asked for and obtained from the Minister, my posting to Spain, where my duty did not, in any way, demand my presence. Perhaps my father is blaming himself for my death!

20 August: At last a moment of enjoyment, of near happiness. The captain of the *Vencedor* has granted me the use of a small boat, and the help of a kindly sergeant, (Saint-Joseph) to accompany me. I approached the *Montagnez*. My companion would not allow me to go aboard with him, and held me back, because of the cries of rage that went up on every side at the sight of a French uniform; even the Spanish Sergeant himself was obliged to leave at once; nevertheless, he spoke to the captain of the frigate, reminding him of the promise he had given me to return my sword. Only my sabretache was returned, and he was told that my sword had been sent to the Admiral. I then watched my Sergeant climb hurriedly down (into the boat), but without my weapon. However, the journey had not been fruitless, for in my sabretache were various papers and this notebook. It seemed to me that by getting them back I had regained a year of my life.

21 August: I sent my good Sergeant back to the *Montagnez* with a letter for the frigate's captain. In it, I expressed very strongly the indignation of my offended honour, the value I should place on the return of my sword and my boundless

confidence in the word of a senior officer and the generosity of the Spaniards (something about which I actually felt very doubtful). If, in order to write persuasively, it was necessary to feel strongly, then nothing was lacking in my letter. A short time later, I saw Saint-Joseph return with my sword! Overwhelmed with joy, I embraced first my sword and then the Sergeant. I was delighted to recover my notes. If these pages, on which I had sketched my memories of Spain, had been lost to me, I should not have continued with this interrupted work. And this taste of happiness made me hope that I might be able to place these notes, in their turn, at my home, together with my recollections of Germany, as well as this new notebook, just brought to me from Cadiz, which was started under such gloomy omens, and of which the first few pages revive such painful memories. Yes! It contains many pages, and if I were not able to hope that the last lines would be written in France, I should hardly have had the courage to begin the first ones!

22 August: Swimming in the sea, and games of chess help to shorten the long hours each day: and they are indeed long for the prisoner, but how much longer they must seem for those who mourn his death!

23 August: Now, at last, a ray of hope. The Spaniards repeatedly tell us that our surrender was overwhelming, and demonstrate the truth of this every day. However, our generals have obtained permission to charter a ship; but, for the present, the English refuse permission for it to sail, though they have sent a schooner to obtain instructions on the matter from their government.

26 August: We are told that tomorrow we are to be disembarked at Santa-Maria. We can hardly bear to hear this name without trembling. Some of us believe that the small quantity of clothing we had been able to buy in Cadiz (which had not already been stolen from us by anyone who fancied it), would now be seized; others, more optimistic and credulous, think that their money and belongings will be returned to them. This hope is based on the excommunication that had been pronounced by the priests on those who retained French property. For myself, I shall postpone my judgement.

27 August: We disembark between two ranks of soldiers. Everything takes place in an orderly fashion and in silence. From afar, I see a convent, the barred windows of which are crowded with agitated figures, holding out their arms. These are my fellow-countrymen, these are Frenchmen! I meet again my faithful Strauss and wonder at his devotion. While their own servants had robbed some of the generals, my *chasseur* had risked his life and sacrificed everything he owned in the attempt to save a few items for me. Now I must again give up the sword that I had taken so much trouble to recover and to keep.

I take possession of a tiny room, 6 feet square, which I share with two of my companions. Nevertheless it is a pleasure to be able to lie down, even on the floor, and under a roof when for four months my only shelter has been the sky.

28 August: Some of the citizens of Santa-Maria have returned the stolen goods. Thanks to this restitution, I recover a cloak and some underwear; these have such value when one is naked and without a penny. I also recover the unfortunate Captain Dubois' sash, which I had picked up. But I must bid an eternal farewell to my books and all my letters.

1 September: If the mental picture of my unhappy parents and of my country did not continually assail my thoughts, I should find my prison less harsh and might enjoy some moments of peace.

2 September: 'The list has come!' 'Who wants to see the list?' 'Have you seen the list?' These are the words in every mouth, these are the questions heard every hour and every minute. And how could it be otherwise? Everyone knows that the generals are to charter a ship, and everyone also knows that not everyone can be carried on it. Each of us, by means of the flattering prism of hope, can see, in some vague future, the shore of France, his fatherland and his family; while each of us, looking through the bars that imprison – or protect – us, perceives only this hateful coast and hears the murderous cries of passers-by threatening him with death.

Our guards are armed with French weapons. An Andalusian peasant, dressed as an officer, mounts guard at our doorway wearing the sword of honour of a dragoon officer. Oh, you cowards! It was not on the field of battle that you won the arms you now dare to parade. Just let us out; we shall soon return to seek them, and then we shall discover if those who, like cowards, obtained them for use as a weapon or a decoration, know how to defend them honourably.

3 September: The officers gamble terribly – playing Red and Black and Thirty–Forty. Even officers who do not have as much as 1,200 francs in pay, dare to risk all of it on a single card! We allow too much of the money that escaped the greed of the Spaniards to be seen; this will provoke more looting.

4 September: Our departure is definitely fixed for tomorrow. Shall we really see France again in three weeks? This joyful prospect is so wonderful, so little hoped for, and so distant from our present situation, I dare not believe it or even think about it.

5 September: We leave the Augustinian convent at six in the morning, but no one slept last night; we go on board rowing boats, bid farewell to this detestable shore, swearing never to return except with fire and sword in our hands and we reach our little ship. It is a Sardinian vessel (the *Saint-Georges*).

But when we were all on board, it was impossible for every one to remain on deck, even standing up. There were 168 of us – including the crew and some passengers – in a space where fifty people would have felt themselves to be overcrowded. If only this ship would really take us to France, there was not one of us who would not have agreed to make the journey clinging, if necessary, to the rope ladders. But we had not yet left Spain, for the customs officers came to us, one by one, extending their search even beneath our shirts and into our boots. All French or Spanish money was confiscated; save from those who could trick the examiner or who were prepared to sacrifice part in order to keep the rest.

When this unpleasant inspection is at last finished, the anchor is raised at five in the evening. We pass the Diamond Rocks, and then we are at last in the open ocean and sailing to France. At ten in the evening, an English frigate, cruising before the anchorage, fires a shot at us. An officer comes in a boat to board us, and having seen our passport, signed and delivered by Admiral Collingwood, allows us to continue on our way.

I have retained three *quadruples* [*a Spanish coin – Ed.*], which I had sewn into my uniform on the battlefield of Bailén, and a fourth that I held in my mouth. Many of us have buttons decorating our coats and breeches, each one of which contains a gold piece.

6 September: We are passing an area that bears witness to the death of many brave Frenchmen, now by fate, intermingled with the gallant Spaniards. Patient, generous people, who dedicated themselves to France, your reward is here! How many are the corpses now covered by the tranquil waves! Their silence is of death; the eye strives to penetrate the mass of water, but this magnificent tomb has closed forever upon the victims it engulfed. We are now sailing over the spot where the famous Battle of Trafalgar took place, the battle in which the united French and Spanish fleets were destroyed. We double Cape Trafalgar. Nightfall surprises us in sight of the Mont-au-Singe, on the African Coast.

7 September: At nine in the morning, the wind died down and we are becalmed, remaining within sight of Mont-au-Singe. At eleven o'clock, the weather becomes very rough with a contrary wind and the ship pitches terribly. We remain at the entrance to the straits [*of Gibraltar – Ed.*] without being able to pass through. We tack endlessly from the coast of Spain to that of Africa, and after three hours of hard work and effort, find ourselves a little further back from the point at which we began the manoeuvre. Twice we have found ourselves almost within cannon shot of Tangiers. At five in the evening, the weather became so rough that we were obliged to seek an anchorage there. Spain and Africa are, indeed, a veritable Charybdis and Scylla for us; both of them offering us nothing but a cruel and hostile population. However, if we are

to run aground, there is not one of us who would not prefer to fall into the hands of the Moors, rather than under power of Spain once more.

8 September: A favourable wind is blowing and we raise the anchor. At ten in the morning we are level with Gibraltar. Unfortunately, a thick fog prevents me from seeing it.

9 September: The cool wind is blowing on our quarter, and our ship slices through the waves with a frightening speed. What a lovely sight, and what a wonderful way to travel! If only it could continue! We are doing 10 knots an hour; every moment, every hour brings us nearer to our homeland. Now we have reached Cape Gata, and we shall pass it tonight. Six days of a favourable wind and we shall be in France! O, unlikely happiness, and the hope that I dare not admit!

10 September: It did not last, that kindly hope. The wind slackened. We are in sight of Carthage; the port looks very fine. All the parts of the Spanish coasts that we have passed so far bristle with mountains and rocks and the soil looks arid and uncultivated.

11–12 September: The wind is still light, and impatience makes our slow progress intolerable. The blood courses through our veins, but the ship goes no more quickly. For forty-eight hours we have not been out of sight of an accursed jagged mountain called the Blow of Roland's Sword. However, we are now about to double Cape Palos, to the east of Carthage.

13 September: The wind improved and we saw the town of Alicante from afar. The rays of the setting sun showed us the Island of Formentera [*one of the Balearic Isles – Ed.*] like a dot above the waves. We also saw, perhaps with the eye of hope, Cape Martin appearing through the fog.

14 September: Now we are in the gulf of Valencia. We still see the unattractive arid coasts, bristling with rocks upon the horizon. The hillsides of Spain are exactly like the character of the inhabitants; it must have been nature's aim, in shaping both, to inspire loathing.

Savage Spaniards, we have not yet entirely escaped your bloody hands; a gust of wind could still cast us up on your coast; a corsair could encounter us and we have not so much as a pistol on board. This evening, we are level with Mount Colère, that forms a cape spiked with dreadful rocks and extends far out into the sea.

15 September: Now we are off Barcelona, and are overjoyed to see the French flag floating from the cathedral. But there is a large camp situated below the town near the coast. Are these our compatriots or are they enemies? At five in the evening, we encounter an English frigate, cruising before the town. It

signals us to approach and sends someone to inspect us. We had every opportunity to experience the courtesy of the English, who offered us anything they had on board and demonstrated the greatest respect and esteem for General Dupont, when they knew that he was on our ship. The English squadron, having departed Cadiz for Toulon a few days before us, had left this frigate to cruise before Barcelona. They tell us that the French General Duhesme was surrounded in Barcelona, and was defending himself bravely, firing many bombs into the camp of the Spaniards who were besieging him. The English paid frank and honest tribute to the courage of the French. I noticed and admired the magnificent condition of the English ships and the cleanliness of the sailors.

16 September: The weather has become completely unfavourable; since this morning we have been in sight of Cape Palamos, which is still between us and the Golfe du Lion. This proximity sharpens our impatience and renders our malcontents even more bitter.

17–19 September: The wind has been contrary for three days, keeping us in sight of this damned Cape, without giving us a chance to double it. We experience the torments of Tantalus. Our rotten water offends the nose and the taste; our food is nearly exhausted, and what food it is! We envy the ship's sailors their meagre nourishment; the food that sustains our miserable existence consists of muddy, horrible wine, a drop of rotten water, biscuit that is harder than our teeth, and rancid bacon. Sweet hope, our support in all our troubles, seems to have abandoned us at last.

The weather became rougher and rougher, pushing us a long way off course. We know that we are in the Golfe du Lion. But this morning we can no longer see land, and this greatly confuses our pilots, who usually remain in sight of the coast; neither they, nor our French sailors are able to tell us where, precisely, we are, nor exactly where the Cape lies. They are unable to agree on anything except that our frail ship is in danger. If we must die, why is it not on the battlefield with our weapons in our hands? But should our last hour await us here, God grant that we may be engulfed in sight of the coast of France and dying, cast our last glances on our native land!

20 September: At dawn, all were out upon the yards; I, however, was not, for I had been overtaken by the illness that I had been struggling against for two days and was stretched out between decks. Even the cry of 'France!' repeated a thousand times could not give me the strength to rise, for I was so overcome with exhaustion and still dared not admit the hope of happiness that was so ardently desired.

Finally, at about nine o'clock we can see land, like a mist on the horizon, of which we continually lose sight, even as we strain our eyes to see it. The wind was strong on the quarter, and our wishes sped (the ship) even faster. But before landing in France, mistress of Europe, we had to turn back once more and learn, at first-hand, that her power ended at the shoreline. We saw the English squadron in full sail (fourteen ships of the line and four frigates) and they signalled us to heave to. We had to furl our sails and go towards them; but the ship that was sent to meet us had the courtesy to spare us half the journey. When the name of General Dupont and the signature of the English admiral were seen, they overwhelmed us with courtesy. We soon went on our way, having admired the beauty of the sight presented by their squadron, sailing in two lines astern, and we contemplated the majesty of these floating citadels that could, in a moment, spew forth death and yet, despite their imposing size, were still the playthings of the sea they seemed to dominate.

It was five in the evening when we anchored, at last, on the French coast. We realized that we had gone a long way off course and instead of being near Marseilles, it was in the neighbourhood of Toulon that we had decided to drop anchor.

21 September: At last, this was truly the coast of France; and it was only fifteen days ago that we were in the hands of Spain and confined in the prisons of Cadiz! The thought of our comrades, abandoned by us to the threatening daggers, was cruel, but what boundless thanks we ourselves owed to Providence!

At dawn, we raised the anchor, and under the flags of Sardinia and France, sailed into the port of Toulon. We were all on deck, devouring the sight of the shore with our eyes and breathing deeply, and with delight, the pure air of France. We could not gaze enough at the men and women in the boats that quickly surrounded us, for their faces were not those of people thirsting for our blood. Our ears, for so long used to hearing imprecations and demands for our death, savoured the sound of our native tongue. But, as it so often happens, the longed for happiness fades as soon as achieved and ours did not remain untroubled for long. Admiral Ganteaume was at that time inspecting the squadron. Astonished and furious that the frigate *The Avant-Garde* had not stopped us, he ordered us to leave at once for Marseilles or for Ciotat [*capital of the Marseilles district or* arrondissement – *Ed.*]. On hearing the words 'Put back to sea,' a cry of anger left every mouth. A messenger was sent back to the Admiral, explaining our situation; meanwhile, to gain time, we remained at anchor. The order was given to put all the rowing boats into the sea to tow us out; already there were many of us who were prepared to jump into the sea and swim to shore. Happily, the negotiators had gained a lot of time, and they did not dare to hand us over to the English by driving us out of the port. It was thus that we were received by our homeland, after having shed our blood for her!

The cruel prospect, with which we had been confronted for so many hours, had diminished our happiness; and this was soon to be completely destroyed. In addition to the guard normally put onto ships awaiting quarantine, a local official was sent on board; a moment later a police officer arrived asking, mysteriously, to speak to the Colonel of the *gendarmerie*, Huchet. All this activity made us believe that there was, among us, not a guilty person, but a victim. We were soon aware that this was the person who, by his bravery, his military talent and his magnanimous conduct, should have been most protected from fate's injustice. But laurels, as we well knew, do not protect from lightning strikes.

[*Editor's note: if Dupont had committed tactical errors at Bailén, aggravated by the mistakes made by Vedel, the responsibility for his defeat must fall chiefly upon those who directed him into a country in revolt, whose strength they had underestimated. The Emperor's anger was terrible and in order to diminish the effect of this defeat upon morale, he crushed the unfortunate Dupont. The commission of inquiry dismissed the charge, but Napoleon, regretting that an example had not been made, had Dupont arrested once more in 1812 and dismissed by a Special Council. His arrest was made worse by his imprisonment in the fort at Joux and then at Dreux, from where in 1814, Talleyrand recalled him to the Ministry of War.*]

Isolated from France, and dead to our country for many months, we eagerly asked for newspapers, and the first words that met our eyes were those in which we were reproached – as if for a crime – for having failed, all of us, to die. And this was a French paper reproaching us in this dreadful and wounding manner! A few lines later, an accusation of stupidity and cowardice was made against the brave captain who, wounded as he was, had continued for eleven hours to fight a glorious battle against forces ten times greater than his own and forced the most eloquent testimony from his ferocious enemies, drunk though they were on power and vengeance.

We spent the night on board the ship, and our thoughts were so very different from those of the previous night. Our happiness at being in France, which had intoxicated us twenty-four hours earlier, had already faded. Each of us thought of Voltaire's verse:

> It is the cruel verdict of Destiny, the final judgement,
> I am a criminal if I failed to win.

22 September: At nine in the morning, the boats arrived to take us into quarantine. This is a fairly large building, divided into two groups of separate living quarters. One well-guarded enclosure gives onto a heather-covered hill, at the foot of which the house stands, with the waves breaking on the side facing Toulon. There are fifteen to eighteen officers in each room. It seems that they fear our liveliness, for with the exception of the few panes of glass that remain in the windows, there is nothing left to break: the four walls are

our furniture, and the floor provides both chair and bed. In addition, the sulphurous and repulsive smell of our rooms bears witness to the type of illnesses that had previously been suffered in them. Everything here, including the iron bars on the windows, reminds us of our prison in Santa-Maria, and the comparison, in more ways than one, is not to the advantage of that offered by our own country.

24 September: They finally brought each of us a mattress, and this was a great day for us all. As for me, it had been more than four months since I had taken my clothes off. Here, we lacked nearly all necessities, money above all. An unpleasant eating-house keeper came to visit us in our prison and offered to sell us anything at a very high price. Nothing could persuade him to be more reasonable; it is true that we had nothing to offer him. Not a chair, not a bench, not a table! Yet, accustomed for so long to every type of privation, even the simplest things were a source of pleasure to us; it was better to enjoy the little we had than to long for what we lacked.

26 September: As our basic needs were gradually satisfied, so our mental faculties were restored. Was it possible that we had been in Spain at the beginning of this month? Were we truly now in France, could it all be a dream? How happy we should have been, if it were not for the memory of our comrades who had been left behind, and even more, by the bitter contemplation of the purest virtue having been treated as a crime. What was the lesson to be drawn from this knowledge that every day, every hour, every moment filled my thoughts? I thought of the fate of Aristides, cast out of Athens [*Athenian politician ostracised by Themistocles in 482 BC – Ed.*].

30 September: My health is perfectly restored. My favourite recreation is climbing the hillside above the isolation hospital; there, alone, I am filled with the happiness of breathing the pure air of France; nevertheless, my happiness must be mixed with apprehension until the day comes when I can be reassured about the safety of those so dear to me. There has not been one word from them for nearly three months! And the last letters I received gave me cause to weep for the death of my beloved brother, as well as that of another relative (my cousin, Albert de Touanne), who was cut down in the flower of his youth and at the beginning of his military career.

1 October: Today the first fumigation takes place. This is a strict procedure that is always carried out before discharge. All the passengers are shut up in a room where a stinking drug is burned. The intention is to expose the plague or any other virus that may exist.

3 October: The instruction for our release has arrived; all of us will leave quarantine tomorrow; then we are to proceed to our homes to await the orders of the Minister. The second and last fumigation takes place.

4 October: At last it has come, this day that returns us to our country for, in quarantine, we could not believe ourselves truly to be in France.

At nine o'clock, the boats came to fetch us. I cannot express what I felt on setting foot on this shore, and in my heart I shall always remember the emotion of the moment. Every minute brings us a new joy, or a reawakening happiness. Yes, here is a French town, here are faces and voices that do not express anger and a thirst for vengeance. I wonder if my anxious parents know that I am here, so near to them. Tomorrow at this time, I shall be on my way, every moment bringing me nearer to Paris.

5 October. I took advantage of my short stay here to visit the fort at La Malgue, it is famous in artillery schools for the strength of its batteries, and famous among drinkers for the quality of the wine to which it gives its name. Although it would take twenty minutes by land, the sea-journey from Toulon to the fort is quite short. The fort stands on a hill, from where it dominates and defends the anchorage. Experts in the field claim that La Malgue fort is one of the finest constructions of the French school of fortifications and is a tribute to the genius of M. de Vauban [*Sebastien Le Prestre de Vauban (1633–1707), Commissioner General of Fortifications from 1678 – Ed.*]. The name of the La Malgue fort was changed to Fort Joubert, when the ashes of that General were placed there.

When I came out of the fort this morning, I saw a sight that moved me greatly: it was that of General Dupont being taken into it! I did not allow myself to dwell on my thoughts, they must remain in my heart; my heart that is so full of admiration and gratitude for him. I owe him more than my life, for I owe him my happiness as well. It is to him that I owe the fact that I am now back in my own country, and that I shall, in eight days' time, be in my parents' arms. Why must such happiness be denied to him, who is so good a husband and father? I cannot feel a moment of pleasure without thinking of him. There can be no joy that does not remind me of my debt to him, a debt that is owed, not just by me but also by my parents, my friends and all who feel for me. He has shielded me from such wretchedness! From so dreadful and slow a death, as that of my comrades who have remained in Spain, menaced by those who wish to revenge their defeat on their unarmed prisoners. Out of two *chasseur* regiments of 600 men, only six have returned. (Montgardet, Drouet, La Barrière, myself and two *chasseurs*, Ony and Castille.)

General Dupont, at the moment of departure from Lebrija, called the General of the division, Frésia, to him and said: 'There are three officers who have been of service to me, and to whose behaviour I owe a great deal. These are Montgardet, Drouet and Tascher; they must be saved, I shall take them with me.'

What fate awaits the French prisoners at Cadiz! This is the fate from which General Dupont rescued me! Up to the present time, out of the 20,000 men of which the army corps was composed, only 130 individuals have escaped slavery, and perhaps, death.

I go to join my parents, but my happiness is poisoned by the knowledge that, deprived of his liberty here, I leave the one to whom I owe my own.

At three in the afternoon, I am back in Toulon. I had not proceeded very far for, even as I got into the coach, I was arrested, and my permit to travel was withdrawn. The town is now my prison. We are confined to the port; all my companions have met with the same fate and orders have been given to arrest those who have already left.

6 October. The Commissioner of Police, M. Caillemer, gave me a kindly welcome and lent me money, of which I had great need. I am extremely grateful to M. Betin, his secretary, who was once an officer of the Horse *Chasseurs*. He was obliging enough to let me have his room and to lend me his belongings, for I lacked everything. So now, here I am, in a furnished room in the Rue Saint-Roche near the French port, at the house of Madame Massé, the wife of an artillery captain who has been a prisoner in England for four years. It is a wonderful feeling to have a moment of peace and solitude. There is no pleasure like that of being seated quietly at table, contemplating the prospect of an hour of leisure; then the even greater pleasure of thinking of the weariness and dangers suffered in the past three years! There was only one year separating Tilsit and Cadiz. How full of disturbance the past year has been, and I must wonder what troubles await me in the year that is just beginning? This moment of peace would be delicious, if only I were not so anxious about my family.

7 October: May God be thanked! Letters have come from Paris, at last. Today, for the first time, I can feel unmixed thankfulness at my return, something for which I had hardly dared to hope. My whole family is in good health. My faithful Georges, who had followed me to within 6 leagues of my position (I was then at Aranjuez), has been rescued by Sainvilliers and is now back in Paris. I feel a moment of regret for my faithful dog, Wachtel, for she is still in Spain. I brought her from the banks of the Memel, and she was linked with some happy memories.

10 October: Passing in front of the Hotel de Ville on the quay, I admired the caryatids that hold up the balcony, the work of the famous Pujet, they are among our finest works of sculpture. It is said, in connection with this work, that when the sculptors, summoned from Rome to work on the Louvre, disembarked in Toulon exactly opposite the Hotel de Ville, their eyes fell first upon this sculpture and they were stupefied: 'Was this made here?' they asked, and were told that it was. 'By a Frenchman?' and when they were told that this

was the case, they returned to their ship and re-embarked, saying that there was no need of them here.

One of the best things in this town is the large number of baths; they are well-constructed and the charge is modest (24 *sous*). The day after we left quarantine, we all went there, being anxious to enjoy a pleasure that we had so long desired. The baths at Toulon were like those in Paris, clean and elegant, and most of them were made out of blocks of white marble.

I have made contact with Commandant Thouin, and walk daily to the La Malgue fort, where I see our unfortunate general, and every day, feel more affection and admiration for him. All my days are so busy that time passes rapidly.

11 October. As Toulon is my prison until there are new orders, I want to see everything that is of interest here. The port is one of the finest in France. Nature provided it with nearly every advantage, and the fortifications that have been added, (Fort Malgue, Fort La Touch, Petit Gibraltar and the batteries) have rendered it impregnable. The harbour is funnel shaped, so that entry is made by a well-defended narrow passage. The roads are large enough to offer a good anchorage to the most numerous fleet. A chain of blue-misted mountains form an amphitheatre around the town, and their rocky crests, bristling with fortifications, are in sharp contrast with the ever-verdant land stretched at their feet. The foothills, clad with olive-groves, figs, vines and all the bounty of fruitful Provence, seem to soften the severity of the mountains, so that they appear to frame Toulon rather than to protect it. Fort Malgue is on the right of the entrance to the anchorage, while on the left, it is protected by a promontory dear to the hearts of sailors. It is here that the ashes of Admiral La Touche-Tréville were scattered. From this place the recollection of his glory seems still to protect our fleets and threaten the English. He is fortunate, for if he had become bowed beneath the weight of years and laurels, he might have lost the energy and all the passionate impetuosity of youth.

The remains of the fortifications built by the English during their blockade against the French Republicans can be seen on the hills behind the town. This is also the scene of Bonaparte's early activities; he was an artillery captain then, and it was here that he was promoted to lieutenant colonel.

On hills a short distance from Toulon are the ruins of a whole town, completely deserted.

I noticed that the anchorage at Toulon still contains seventeen warships; among them are a fine three-decker, *Majestueux*, commanded by the Vice Admiral Ganteaume, other three-deckers are the *Commerce de Paris* and the *Austerlitz*, newly-launched and still with no armament. Among the ships with two decks are the *Robuste*, one of the finest and best, the *Suffren* and the *Annibal*, the squadron also has five or six frigates. There are two Russian ships that manoeuvre under the command of the French admiral. The *Murion*, which brought Napoleon back from Egypt, now finely gilded, is enjoying an honourable retirement, and acting as a flagship.

19 October. We dine with the naval officers. Provence is well-provided with good cooks. They are very enthusiastic, and the fruits of nature abet their skills. Nevertheless, although I may appear to be unsophisticated, I have to say that I nearly always dislike their custom of replacing butter with oil.

What the people of Provence like, they like passionately; they would sell their last garment in order to eat a little bird; every class of person loves the hunt most of all, and all take part in it; from break of day, the sound of musket fire can be heard continually, as if the enemy was at the gate. And on what are they firing? On sparrows and tits! A great hunting party was made up for me, the other day. We left at four in the morning, travelled 2 leagues and returned, covered with glory, with firecrest and a goldfinch. All the gentlemen congratulated themselves on their luck.

20 October. I took advantage of the fine weather today, to go with M. Fleury, the Captain of a frigate, to inspect the anchorage and the finest of the ships. I examined the *Majestueux* and the *Commerce de Paris* in great detail. I admired everything about these floating citadels; they can accommodate up to 3,000 individuals with all their food and necessities, as well as more than 120 cannon. What a fearful and fascinating sight a naval battle must be! Certainly, a battleship must be one of the most ingenious and finest of man's works. From there I visited the *Robuste*, and I was struck, in all three of these ships, by the freshness, the luxury and the elegance of the Admiral's cabin. One would have thought oneself in the boudoir of some courtesan in Paris. Masses of flowers on the *Majestueux*. Our navy is in a deplorable condition. The sailors are in a state of utter destitution; they are kept in slavery; they are ignorant and hate their situation. Some of them have not set foot on dry land for two years and they long to desert. To make good their escape, they fling themselves overboard in bad weather.

The English squadron, made up of twelve ships and four frigates, completely blockades the port of Toulon, often venturing within range of our batteries, not a single French vessel can show itself at sea without running the danger of being captured at once.

While speaking of Toulon, the climate should be mentioned, for if one is not used to it, the frequent changes in the weather can be dangerous. The winds, *Sirocco* and *Mistral*, are unusually exhausting, even to those accustomed to them, for they bring with them a legion of ailments of the chest. In the autumn, winter and spring they freeze to the bone, and in summer are able to irritate and crush people physically and even mentally.

21 October: Today, I went with a senior engineer to examine the arsenal and its workshops. I admired the rope-walks, where the cables of our great vessels are laid out, and also the building where the sails are made. I was able to go into the model room, where a miniature of every battleship and piece of its equipment is made. There is no item belonging to a vessel of which there is no model. I also saw an ingenious invention – a device intended to lower a man to the seabed and enable him to work there: I thought that this invention was unlikely to succeed, for the water would inhibit the movements of a worker.

On entering the arsenal, the powerful noise of hammer blows is heard and the screech of the saw. There is frantic movement everywhere and the work and activity is, at first sight, admirable, as its goal is practical. But if one examines the significance of this busy scene, one is overcome with horror and pity. A pity that is painful to experience. Three or four thousand individuals are groaning there, scarcely clad, scarcely fed, chained together with heavy chains, bent beneath huge loads and endlessly subjected to the harshest work. Although the mark of infamy may be upon their hideous faces and recollection of their crimes may dilute pity yet, at the sight of these men, whose condition degrades humanity, the heart is more moved by their misery than by their offences. One asks oneself how men can reduce other men to such a state? It is terrible to think that, among these three or four thousand galley slaves, there must be several who are innocent and certainly even more whose crimes were insignificant. Besides, representatives of all classes of society are there. I saw, with horror, children of twelve or fourteen years of age. When I went into the *bagne [penal colony of forced labour camp – Ed.]* I saw a large number of galley slaves who would never leave the wooden beds to which they were chained: a considerable number of them die each year. In general, a man will hardly survive eight or ten years in the galley, and I cannot understand how they can survive a single year. They are better treated when they are ill than I would have expected, and the room that is used as a hospital is orderly and clean. Each patient lies on an iron bed (with a mattress) to which he is chained, and only death can release him from this dreadful bondage before his sentence expires. In the past, many escaped, but this rarely happens now, for an attempt to escape is penalized by an addition of twenty-four years to the sentence. Those who are nearing the end of their sentences are less distrusted, for they are unchained and allowed to go into the town, but nevertheless always wear an iron ring on their ankles. About 6,000 new galley slaves arrive each year, but barely 200 certificates of freedom are issued annually.

22 October: In a few hours Toulon, its rocks and harbour, its pleasures and pains will fade away and join past times in my memory. The slow hours in quarantine, the happy days bathed in the sunshine of my native land, will

vanish like fleeting shadows. I went out early this morning and when I returned, a police agent said to me: 'Sir, hurry! Sir, go to Headquarters. An order from the Minister has arrived; they have been looking for you for two hours.'

I was told to go at once to Maastricht. I hurried to the La Malgue fort, where I spent part of the day. Then, having bidden farewell to Commandant Thouin and his illustrious prisoner, I went on my way, unhappy and depressed. I left them, filled with sorrow and admiration, and with a powerful longing to be able to show my sincerely felt gratitude.

Returning to Toulon at night, by way of the Italian Gate, I packed in great haste and threw myself into the coach that hurried me towards Paris.

Chapter 4

Paris, Wagram and Znaim: October 1808–July 1809

1808

23 October: Marseilles. We left Toulon at three in the morning and travelled, until four in the afternoon, on a fine road; our eyes, so long starved of the sight of green fields, welcomed the lovely scenery spread out on either side. At last, we reached Marseilles and I started to look around, but the attraction of new sights failed to keep my heavy eyelids open; lack of sleep weighed them down.

24 October: I spent the whole day walking about and admiring the town. The fine houses, hotels and public buildings, as well as the broad well-kept streets, give Marseilles the opulent appearance and grandeur of a capital city. What must this town be like in the time of a prosperous peace? For even as it is now, one can hardly move about! Yet the townspeople consider the place to be quiet and deserted, the war having destroyed their commerce. In fact, the harbour is indeed filled with warships, rotting with inaction, for the English will not permit a single one to leave.

25 October: We spent the night at Aix, and the first rays of the sun found us in the midst of a delightful countryside. We shall never tire of gazing at this lovely and fertile land; but hillsides covered with olive trees brought back some unwelcome memories. However, the elegant figures of the ladies of Provence and the gaiety that animated their pretty faces soon chased away unhappy thoughts and assured us that we were no longer in Spain.

We travelled through Saint-Chamas to Orgon, where the Durance river winds through the smiling plain and dark crags can be seen in the distance. We reached Avignon at nightfall.

According to the well-known song, I expected to find a handsome bridge at Avignon. In fact, there are two of them. One fell in ruins a long while ago, and only two or three arches of it remain, while the foundations of the other, on which work is still being carried out, can scarcely be seen among the rushing waters of the Rhône. We left at nine in the evening in a rickety old coach.

27 October: The dreadful weather that is now following us prevents us from enjoying the beautiful countryside to the full.

At Avignon, we were cheated when we hired our vehicles, so that we now travel in dilapidated carriages, which do not keep out a single drop of rain. We change our coach every 4 leagues, and each new one that we get into is always worse than the one we left. At last, after twenty-four hours on the road, the worst carriage of all deposited us at Valence, cold, sore and hungry.

28 October: We abandoned our uncomfortable beds at the inn before dawn, and lacking any better carriage, were forced to resort to rickety old coaches. We think that, by speeding up the bumpy progress of our muddy vehicles, we shall the sooner see the dome of the Invalides. But 3 leagues from Valence, an unexpected obstacle brought us to a halt, and we had to join a line of sixty vehicles, berlines, coaches and carriages: all, like ourselves, forced to wait. The Isere, flooded and overflowing its banks everywhere, was sweeping along in its turbulent waters uprooted trees, beams and the remains of whole houses. This was the worst flood for seven years; there was no bridge! What could we do? Wait? Our impatience could hardly bear the idea. At last, after several hours of effort, we found a way to approach the ferry (it was thirty paces from the bank). Gripping our papers in our teeth, our swords suspended from our necks, and holding our portmanteaux – rendered very light, thanks to the Spaniards – aloft, we were carried on the backs of sailors, who waded in water up to their chests, to the ferry. We left the boat in the same way, an even more dangerous manoeuvre. Finally, three of us reached the far bank and waved in triumph at our comrades, who had remained behind; then, exhorting them to be patient, we went happily on our way.

A few hours later, we came in sight of the hillsides where the vines that provide the wines of Saint-Pèray and the Côte Rôtie grow [*one of the famous vineyards of the Côtes du Rhône – Ed.*]. Filled with reverence, we halted at each of these hills, so venerated by drinkers, and paid suitable homage to the wine and the land in which it grew. Like faithful pilgrims we halted at Saint-Vallier, to offer up another tribute, and as a result, spent the night there.

29 October: We left at dawn and travelled on the toll-road to Vienne; always finding delicious new charms on the banks of the Rhône, and leaving each delightful place with regret. I took advantage of the opportunity to see some of the sights of Vienne, a town rich in antiquities.

30 October: I abandoned the banks of the Rhône before dawn and embarked on the waters of the Saône. It is just as quick, and a great deal less tiring to travel post by water. So I went on board a barge that was filled with merchandise and about fifty passengers. A large, clean cabin, upholstered with velvet, is reserved exclusively for travellers going to Paris. Four post horses, always moving at a fast trot, are harnessed to our boat, and it seems to glide through the water. But if our sailors have an easy time of it, the postillions on the other hand need

great courage and skill. The flooded river conceals the neighbouring fields, so that the horses are almost swimming and the postillions are standing upright on their backs. To ensure that the current does not sweep them away in the deepest places, our ship sends a rowing boat out to guide the horses' heads.

As I travel out of Provence, I find that I leave springtime behind and am rushing swiftly into the icy arms of winter.

Halfway through our journey, our comfortable vessel was halted and we landed for a meal. It was pleasant and interesting to see the way in which the travellers are taken ashore and welcomed. These little riverside villages consist of hardly more than small inns, built in a row and existing only for the use of barge travellers. Each innkeeper wants to capture them all and for this purpose, tries to hire all the prettiest girls, who are like so many sirens. These girls stand in line when the passengers leave the barge, then fall upon them, seize them, quarrel over them, and at last carry them in triumph to one of the inns. If the modesty of their behaviour suffers a little in the course of this raid, it is rapidly recovered as soon as the threshold is crossed. It is true that these young women, like all of those in Lyon, are very pretty and with beautiful figures and they are perfectly aware of this fact, and increase their charms with every coquettish art. The ladies of Lyon are recognized everywhere by their hair-styles and above all, by their elegance. Our barge took us to Mâcon where we had supper and passed the night.

31 October: We left Mâcon to continue our journey at two in the morning, and found ourselves, at dawn, opposite the little village of Tournus, which had, just at that time, been the scene of a dreadful tragedy. Two young people had, for a long while, vainly begged their stubborn parents for permission to marry and had several times threatened to kill themselves if they could not devote their lives to each other. This threat was assumed to be only the rash words of lovers; the young man had then gone to Lyon and bought two pistols, powder and balls there. On his return, he and his mistress again made their demand to be allowed to marry, and repeated their threat to kill themselves if they were refused once more. They were given the same answer! It was yesterday that, having spent the night together and written their farewells and their wills and made a last request to be buried in the same tomb, they blew their brains out. The girl had died first; she was found lying half on the bed, still holding the pistol. Her lover, having gazed for a moment upon the tragic sight, covered her face with a kerchief, and killed himself at her feet. As they had passed the night together, a prurient curiosity had caused the girl's body to be examined, and this disgusting examination proved that this victim of love had sacrificed her life but had not, at least, sacrificed her virtue.

We dined at Chalon where, disembarking from the barge, we took a coach that carried us to Autun by midnight.

2 November: We came to Auxerre on the Yonne at dawn, and passed through Villeneuve and Pont-sur-Yonne, where, as other travellers had warned us, we experienced the insolence of the innkeeper, who was mayor of the town. The night seemed very long to me. It should be the last that I have to spend away from my dear parents.

We reached Melun and the happiest day of my life dawned at last. My dear parents will be rewarded for all they have suffered through my absence. We arrive in Paris at eight o'clock.

3 November: Ten o'clock in the evening. Can this really be my own room? Yes! Here are my table, my bed, my own belongings! Am I dreaming? Was it truly I who was imprisoned in Cadiz only two months ago? But the memory of my comrades, who are still there casts a gloom over my thoughts. I left Paris on 18 February, and now, on 3 November I am back again. Such terrible events have occurred in the interval. I think of those who fell at my side, whose eyes have closed forever without having seen their beloved country or their loved ones again. Now by Providence I return, almost alone!

4–9 November: Mystery surrounds all the events of our Spanish campaign. Villoutrey, who brought (details of) the surrender to France, is in solitary confinement. Prudence warns me that I should not stay here, and my anxiety to see and embrace a brother calls me imperatively to Pourvrai.

10 November: I shall leave tomorrow, with my parents.

12 November: Pourvrai at last! Scene of my happy childhood and my early dreams, when life seemed to open before me like a flower-strewn path; Pourvrai which is still the centre of my dearest affections.

13–15 November: Happy, peaceful days. Alas, the whirlwind will come too soon to tear me away from them. I can spend whole days lost in thoughts of the past, I feel seven years younger.

17 November: For many years I have heard the beauty and spirit of Madame —— praised. She is twenty-six years old, while her husband is sixty-eight. Tomorrow, I shall be able to judge for myself.

18–20 November: I am at Davière; these three days have passed like three seconds. When in less happy times, I wish to think of pleasant hours of innocent enjoyment, it is Davière that I shall remember. It is rare that peace, pleasure and innocence are united; all too often one of them excludes the others. I shall not forget Mademoiselle L——. How true it is that women are indescribable! Such a mixture of flirtatiousness and reserve, of forwardness and modesty (if, however, frigidity is virtue). Madame L——, her friend, is charming, but one has to be on one's guard in her company and weigh one's words; and this is always difficult for anyone who is less spirited than she or has more restraint. She maliciously draws attention to any word that can be ridiculed! But how her clever coquettishness can bestow charm on the slightest thing! In the entire world, only Frenchwomen know how to make their sex divine and if one is not careful, they can win a tender, all-conquering empire for themselves. There is a war between love and reason; it is to avoid the first and follow the councils of the second that, in spite of pressing entreaties, my brother and I leave this evening, to return to our good and peaceful Pourvrai.

1 December: Time rushes past, and I must tear myself away. How sad it is that unhappy hours pass so slowly while happy ones vanish like lightning. My movement order is coming to an end, and anyway, I have a strong desire to go where I can discover the fate of the man to whom I am indebted for my return to France and my family [*i.e. General Dupont – Ed.*].

2 December: I leave Pourvrai.

3 December: I reach Paris, and the same evening, meet Madame —— once more. It was she that I had seen at the window of the square tower, when I left my prison in Cadiz. I learn to my great anger that my good and faithful Schauss still remains in a Spanish prison, and that the rascal, Martin, has been brought back to me in his place. His hypocrisy, sustained over ten years, had deceived General Dupré, and he thought to trick me in the same way.

4 December: Today sees the end of my twenty-second year. Poor Wilhelmine. It is two years to the day since she and I enjoyed, together, the pleasures of a loving and virtuous friendship.

5 December: General Dupont is here, but in solitary confinement. I spend days beneath the windows of the Abbaye with a heavy heart. Generals Schramm, Le Gendre, Pannetier and La Plane are here for the same reason. God grant that, when the veil is torn asunder, the naked truth will be seen!
[*Editor's note: the Abbaye at Saint Germain des Prés was used as a political prison after 1789 and demolished in 1857.*]

6 December: I learn with joy that General Liger-Belair, to whom I owe so much, has returned to France. From what I had heard, I did not think that he would come back in good health.

7 December: I have lost seven horses in the course of a single year. I am to be paid for only one (that is to say, 400 francs), and 278 francs for my portmanteau. These two items together cost me more than 6,000 francs.

8 December: The Empress Josephine receives me in the kindest possible way and promises to give me a letter for the Minister of War.

9 December: Time passes. My movement order is still on my table, and it reminds me that I should already be in Maastricht.

12 December: I have left my beloved family once again, but this time, it is not to join the army. They are glad, but I am sorry for it.

13 December: Compiègne, Cambrai. I meet Collins again, and take him with me to Havrincourt. This evening, I happily embraced my dear sister and my brother-in-law, Henry, as well as Alphonse and my dear little niece, Stéphanie. [*Editor's note: Tascher's brother-in-law was Henry d'Havrincourt. The two children were Alphonse and Stéphanie, who later became Countess de Bondy.*]

15 December: Collins left me this morning, but I am to meet him again at Ghent on the 23rd, with his beloved Theresa.

22 December: I should have left today, but a snowfall – such as has not been seen for thirty years – has cut all communications and keeps me a prisoner here. I should bless this contretemps and my captivity, if poor Collins were not kept waiting for me.

28 December: I am still here; I am so happy and should be so grateful for the reason for it, but I know that this is not very friendly of me. If only I could bury myself in the snow; I am leaving tomorrow.

29 December: I had my boots on, ready to leave, when Collins came into my room; he was too kind to reproach me, though his very presence in front of me constituted a reproach in itself, without the need for any words. All I could say was: 'I'm sorry, I'm sorry.' He would not have treated me like that. What could I do to make up for my bad behaviour? We left at eleven o'clock and took a post-chaise at Cambrai to Lille, where we had to spend the night.

30 December: We reach the famous town of Ghent, which Charles Quint [*Charles V – Ed.*] admired so much that he said he could put Paris into his Ghent. All the townsfolk are convinced that their city is larger than Paris. Without agreeing with this exaggeration, I have to admit that it occupies a large space, partly because the town is very big and also because it encloses a great deal of land, on which there are no buildings.

31 December: It was with difficulty that, at dawn, I tore Collins away from Ghent – where, with his Theresa he could have forgotten the entire universe – and we set out for Brussels, which we reached at four o'clock; and Collins went off, post-haste, to catch up with his detachment.

1809

1 January: As I did not have to leave until seven in the evening, I spent the day exploring the town, which is handsome, rich and very busy: offering all the

resources and vices of big cities. It continually weeps for its lost magnificence and cannot forget that it was once a capital city with a royal court. The inhabitants do not like us very much. They are impatient, restless, and although lazy, are always prepared to seek a new ruler; the ruler they have at the moment is inevitably the one they like least. They neither possess the courtesy and friendliness of the French nor the sincerity and generosity of the Germans, claiming that these two neighbouring countries have nothing but faults. In business matters they are correct and industrious. The cleanliness of their houses is extreme, for they are washed, scrubbed and polished from morning to night, this being made necessary by the use of coal, the thick smoke from which blackens everything it touches. The houses have a strange feature, originating, no doubt, from a mixture of laziness and inquisitiveness. This is a little mirror attached to the outside of the windows, which can be moved from the inside, so that the ladies, seated at ease in their armchairs, are able to watch everything that happens in the street. The language spoken in Brussels is harsh and strange, consisting of a medley of French, German and Dutch. Nevertheless, they dare to call this dialect a language, and their newspapers, proclamations and books of record are written in it. They have their own grammar, and their own professors of the Flemish language, and one would be very ill received if one questioned its elegance and harmony.

2 January: I slept as I travelled through Louvain, Tirlemont and Saint-Trond and daylight found me in the dirty town of Liège, which lies at the bottom of a depression, from which coal is mined from the earth; this is the only fuel used in this country. The air one breathes is horribly smoky and filled with a fine coal dust, so that the whitest clothing becomes soiled within two hours. The roads are narrow and filthy, making Liège feel as if one is in the dirtiest quarter of Paris. The jargon they speak here is peculiar to the place and is not exactly like German or Flemish. The people are aggressive, quarrelsome and dangerous. Here, nothing is easier than to rid oneself of an enemy: for a few *escalins* [*small Dutch coin – Ed.*] one can have him thrown into the Meuse.

There are some very deep coal mines in Liège, into which it is dangerous to descend without taking some precautions, for sometimes the miners prevent you from ever returning to the light of day. There are several great foundries and arms manufactories here that enjoy a good reputation, although it is less than they deserve. Workers in Versailles buy a number of arms here, most of all the heavy guns, which they then sell on as their own produce at double the price they paid for them. I spent a few hours in Liège, and then travelled on to Maastricht, which I reached at nightfall.

3 January: I met five officers here, three of whom I already knew. There are six cavalry depôts, and two depôts of infantry, in this town. The accommodation for the cavalry is bad. Half the men are quartered in an unpleasant district, far

away from their horses, and the rest of the men are in the town. The horses are also dispersed among the stables of various inns.

4 January: This is a big, well-built and heavily fortified town. If there were to be a siege, between 12,000 and 15,000 men would be needed to man the fortifications. Fort Saint-Pierre is within a cannon shot of the town, which it dominates and protects, but that very fact makes its defence questionable, for once captured, it could render the town very vulnerable. Beneath the fort are underground passages, which were once quarries, and they are 5 or 6 leagues in length, with an infinite number of branches, forming a labyrinth where a traveller without a guide could become lost and wander until he died. It was once possible to travel underground all the way to Liège, but part of the mountain has collapsed, so I do not know if this can still be done. The walls of these enormous, subterranean tunnels are covered with names, some of them dated long ago, even from the thirteenth century. The Emperor Napoleon visited these tunnels.

5 January: I travelled to Liège to see Collins, and spent an uncomfortable night at Saint-Trond, where I met some Spanish officers, who had been taken prisoner in Denmark. What a strange encounter! Here, they are our prisoners, when, only five months ago, I was theirs!

6 January: Return to Maastricht.

10 January: A letter is received from the Minister, which orders my departure with the first detachment.

31 January: I am spending every spare moment in study. I go nowhere and see no one. When I leave Maastricht I shall miss my leisure.

1 March: I should have left with a detachment on the first of this month, but the order has not arrived.

15 March: I have learned from an unofficial but reliable source that I am to leave on the 22nd.

19 March: My instructions have arrived from the Minister. I am to leave on the 22nd with a superb detachment of 100 cavalry, to proceed to Strasbourg and march against Austria. To war! To war! The flame of glory burns distantly before my eyes. In its brilliant rays the intoxicating miasma of dreams of love disperse like a mist.

22 March: I leave Maastricht. All the officers accompanied me for half a league and lavished words of friendship on me. When they had gone, I found myself alone, and for the first time in my life, in charge of a fairly large command. I was, for a moment, anxious and preoccupied, for now there was no one to give

me orders and it was I who must give them. I contemplated the responsibility that rested on my shoulders and the extent of my duties.

We reached Liège at three o'clock. The care of my detachment of 100 *chasseurs* and 100 horses, both equally untrained, and for whom I was obliged to act as quartermaster, made it impossible for me to visit either the coal mines or the armament magazines of Berleur Brothers, the famous gunsmiths.

23 March: We leave for Terwagne, along the banks of the Meuse, which we crossed a league from Liège. Here, the Meuse flows between steep banks of craggy rocks.

24 March: Marche en Famine. This is a fitting name for this miserable town, which is made up of 500 or 600 dilapidated hovels.

The Ardennes start a league from Terwagne and the countryside becomes arid, mountainous and almost uninhabited. As soon as one has been able, breathlessly, to climb one hill, there is a steep slope to scramble down, and then one begins to climb again. I could imagine myself in the Morena Sierra, if there were not barren heathland all around in place of pomegranates, oranges and clusters of oleanders. But it must be said that the oak trees, the hornbeams, some scraps of pasture, the scattered huts and the brooks – above all the brooks – remind me that I am no longer in Spain, or suffering the terrible thirst I then endured.

26 March: Saint-Hubert. Our road took us through the same countryside as yesterday: mountains, heathland and forests. It was a surprise, when we reached the little town of Saint-Hubert, to see a superb church and a handsome abbey in the midst of such a poor and uninhabited area. The astonishment was even greater when one went into the church; there is a fine organ and the nave and stalls are decorated with exquisitely carved wood, particularly the carvings on the right, which depict the life of Saint Hubert (those on the left, of Saint Bruno, are less beautiful).

A single monk, the only one of this populous abbey remaining to weep for its downfall, showed me around the church, pointing out every detail. At last he took me into the sacristy to show me the little silver box that contains the Holy Stole, which was brought down from heaven by an angel and given to Saint Hubert by the Blessed Virgin. This Stole is greatly venerated in the country, and has given rise to many miracles; these are still performed daily, upon people who are suffering from rabies. In fact, it is only this Stole that brings prosperity to the village by means of the pilgrims it attracts, and by the rings and other items of goldsmiths' work that are sold here as a result. People from 200 leagues around have recourse to Saint-Hubert to 'cast out rabies' (the local expression). The ceremony is as follows: the monk, who alone is permitted to perform it, cuts a tiny morsel from the Stole, makes a minute cut in the forehead of the patient, raises the skin and inserts the fragment, then closes the incision. He only performs this operation upon those who have already experienced the first paroxysm of the illness. The monk, who showed the Stole to me and explained these details, seemed to be modest, but educated and free of superstition. In the course of the twenty months since he had returned to Saint-Hubert, he had already performed 680 of these operations. Without believing that he could, at will, dispense divine miracles, he knew how strong is the power and certainty of cure upon the mind of the sick; without explaining this to them, he maintained the people in their belief. The Stole had been in the possession of the Church of Saint-Hubert since AD 800 and although fragments had been continually taken from it, it grew no smaller. During the Revolution the Church was required to raise 30,000 francs to prevent its destruction. This monk saved it. He asked for, and obtained, permission to make a collection in the neighbouring towns. Ghent alone subscribed 10,000 francs, and the collection preserved, for an impoverished countryside, a church that brought it wealth.

28 March: Arlon. This is a larger village than Neufchâteau and stands on a hill. Just 6 leagues have produced a complete alteration in the language and the behaviour of the inhabitants. Here, we are in Germany, a region of the Duchy of Luxembourg and part of the German Empire. German is normally spoken here, while, since leaving Liège, a more or less corrupt version of French has been in use.

29 March: Luxembourg. Seven years ago this town was besieged and taken from the Austrians (the besieged, to excuse their surrender, claimed that they lacked water, wood and salt); but the inhabitants are still German at heart and accordingly, hope for a change of government. I was struck by the contrast between what the eye now sees and the warlike appearance of the ramparts. Only a few years ago they were bloodstained and bristling with cannon, threatening death and destruction. Today, nature is regaining her dominion; children and flocks and herds abound on the former glacis; huts and gardens cluster at the foot of the formidable fortifications; flowers, vegetables and fruit trees grow on the same land that was so recently furrowed by cannon balls and that still conceals the dreadful debris of war.

31 March: Thionville. This is a fortified town on the Moselle, where there are many barracks, warehouses and military buildings. The Moselle flows within the ramparts, and the bridge across it is unusual in that it has a roof.

1 April: Metz. Here I am, for the third time, in the large, handsome city of Metz. The School of Artillery is still here. This town, wealthy and well-populated, can offer, to some extent, both the opportunities and the dangers of Paris.

2 April: Solgne. This is a tiny village. The Emperor's carriages passed through yesterday, on their way to Strasbourg.

3 April: Vic is a village of about 3,000 inhabitants on the little River La Seille. The remains of a fine château that once belonged to Cardinal Montmorency can still be seen. Two years ago it was still intact and prisoners of war were lodged in it. When they left, the concierge, wishing to be rid of the straw on which they had slept, set fire to a pile of it at the foot of the walls and the château was burned down within two hours.

5–6 April: Maizières and Sarrebourg.

7 April: Saverne. Now we are in the Vosges; the nearness of Germany is apparent in its dark forests, and I see again the curtain of mountains, on which I had to gaze for six months when I was at Schlestadt.

I am lodging with a rich rabbi and today is the eve of the Sabbath. To take advantage of the experience, I dined with twelve Jews. Although I did not enjoy the unleavened bread, as recompense, I was oversupplied with grimaces, play-acting and the prayers that were chanted in various tones.

8 April: Strasbourg. I have now completed the first stage of my journey. This town is full of troops; the suites of the generals (Berthier, Masséna and Lefebvre) are here and the Emperor is expected any day. Troops have been passing through the town for a month. Strasbourg brings back so many memories for me, especially this Hotel, the Cigogne. I was here three years ago . . . what a great deal of experience I have gained since then, and so often, to my cost!

9 April: A review is held by the general of Beaumont's division. I am to join detachments of the 1st and 2nd Chasseurs to form a squadron; other detachments from regiments that are in Spain arrive daily, and are then incorporated at the depôts of various formations of the Army of the Rhine. I have found that the depôt of my old regiment of hussars is here; my heart was heavy at the meeting, for I feel myself to be a stranger to them now.

10 April: Oberhausbergen. I was ordered to come to this pretty village, today. It is a league from Strasbourg on the Saverne road. Before leaving Strasbourg I explored the famous cathedral that was built in 1015; its bell-tower is visible from far away. Worn out by my sightseeing, I left Strasbourg regretfully, without having seen the magnificent mausoleum of my namesake, Maurice, Marshal of Saxony [*French general (1696–1750) – Ed.*].

11 April: I have received orders to leave tomorrow and wonder if, when I cross the river that borders my homeland for the second time, it will be for the last time, as it was for so many of those who made the first crossing with me.

12 April: Bischofsheim. The first stage of my journey. Leaving the cantonment before dawn, I joined the detachments from the 1st and 2nd. This squadron, made up of 280 men, was paraded and I took command of it. We marched off on the road to Kehl. Here, the old pontoon bridge has been replaced by a fine wooden one. All the trophies and pyramids celebrating the exploits of the French Army that lined the road during the first Austrian campaign have now disappeared. We march along the same route; it is our responsibility to replace these forgotten trophies with other new ones. Prince Berthier left this morning for Augsbourg.

13 April: We were lodged at the village of Bietigsheim. All the women here plait their hair and decorate it with black ribbons. The plaits, two or three in number, reach far down their backs and the ribbons fall as far as the ground. The skullcaps worn by the men are edged with the fur of the marten or badger.

15 April: A halt at Pforzheim. I was happy to see this delightful town again and its pretty square. When I went back to the house where I previously lodged, I took my hostess, the wife of the Minister (who had tried to convert me), a little present. How my outlook on life has changed in three years! What things I have seen!

16 April: We passed through Waihingen and on to Schwiebaden, where we lodged in the little village of Munichen. I was amazed at the amount of wildlife to be seen in the fields; one could not take thirty paces without disturbing three or four hares, yet the peasants hardly dared to throw a stone at these animals, which devour their harvests under their very eyes. Hunting, I was told, is reserved exclusively for the King. Tonight, Napoleon passed through on the road to Ulm.

17 April: We passed through Cannstadt, leaving Stuttgart on our right. The traveller sees, spread before him, a pretty river, mountains, forests, fertile fields and prosperous villages. Signs of comfort and affluence are everywhere visible, although war has raged here for many years and two armies, in turn, have ravaged it.

I have today received new orders and I must take my squadron to Donauwerth.

18 April: Gmünd. Catholicism is powerful here, and to judge by appearances, the inhabitants are zealous in their faith. All their houses are painted to the roofs with depictions of the divine mysteries and the walls are decorated with mouldings of saints and other religious imagery. To the left of the road, on the mountainside, can be seen chapels, grottos and places of pilgrimage with little shrines placed at intervals to indicate the stations on the pilgrim's way.

19 April: Heidenheim. Having abandoned the road to Ansbach, as it appeared to be occupied by the enemy, and travelled 2 leagues across the mountains, I

regained the route at Weissenstein and reached Heidenheim to halt for the night. The Austrians have crossed the Inn, and after they had already begun hostile action, they declared war on Bavaria. All the Tyrol rose up in their favour and handed over to them, as prisoners, all the French and Bavarian troops who were there. Some of the enemy army is at Munich, and we are taking up our position on the Leck.

20 April: We have halted at the village of Alsteim, near Dillingen. The King of Bavaria, who was forced to leave Munich, is here with all his court. The peasants in this part of the world wear long red jackets with a row of silver drops, placed very close together; these buttons represent, to them, the greatest possible luxury and they take great pride in them.

21 April: We are at Redlingen, near Donauwerth, a small town, made important by its location and its bridge over the Danube. My hope of joining the regiment was quickly disappointed. Since we left Heidenheim we have been crossing wide, well-cultivated plains, where the villages are so near to one another that there is barely a quarter of a league between them.

22 April: Neuburg. We crossed the Leck a league from Donauwerth, where many workmen are employed on fortifying the bridgehead. There is a great deal of activity, too, on the fortifications of Neuburg. I lodged in the village of Lichenau, near Pruch.

A bloody battle took place on the 18th and 19th at Ratisbon. The town was taken by the Austrians and then retaken by a French assault. Shellfire set part of the town on fire and greatly damaged the rest of it. The Austrians are in full retreat. Prince Charles has sworn that he will never leave his position and that the first general to retreat will be hanged.

[*Editor's note: on 19–20 April the Battle of Abensberg took place, where Lannes with the Bavarians and the Württembergers forced the Austrian left wing back to the River Iser. The Battle of Eckmühl took place on 22 April, when Archduke Charles – brother of the Austrian Emperor, Francis I – was thrown back to Ratisbon; the town was taken on the 23rd, when Napoleon's foot was bruised by a shot.*]

23 April: Artheim. When we reached Ingolstadt I found the town full of wounded, stragglers and prisoners; full, in fact, of all the problems that follow in the wake of an army. On my way down the Danube I found a picket of my regiment at the bridgehead of Vohburg, and the sight of their uniforms was as pleasant to me as the sight of land to an anxious sailor. I had been separated from my regiment for two years, and to find it again reminded me of the provisional regiments and of my unhappy campaign in Spain. Could it be that fortune will, at last, smile on me?

I felt no regret at resigning command of the squadron I had brought with me. Finally, after travelling a league, I came upon the whole regiment bivouacked near Ortheim, where I handed over my 100 conscripts; they had been a heavy and wearying burden to bear, and throughout the four weeks of the march, had brutally strained my patience and my lungs.

24 April: We have not moved; our patrols are encountering the enemy at a distance of 3 or 4 leagues.

25 April: Ratisbon. We started out at two in the morning and marched across a rocky, mountainous countryside through thick forests. Passing through Altmul and Riendenburg, we arrived at Leman, a town the enemy had evacuated only yesterday, and where, a few days earlier, he had had 40,000 men. After a rest of two hours, we marched off again, reaching the walls of Ratisbon at midnight, having covered 16 leagues, and found ourselves to be in a most miserable bivouac in which to recover our strength!

26 April: Those who have no experience of war would find it impossible to form any idea of the dreadful state of the town of Ratisbon, with its half-burned houses, its blood-stained walls and of the wounded with which it is filled. We reached Regenstauf, and the regiment bivouacked before Burglengenfeld. I was sent as advance guard to Saltendorf, on the Schwandorf road.

27 April: We marched on Schwandorf, but the enemy was no longer there; he is at Neuburg, so we went in that direction, and a picket of 100 men chased the *Uhlans* [*from the Polish word* Ulan, *meaning 'lancer' – the term was used by the German and Austrian armies – Ed.*] into it. We returned at ten at night to Schwandorf, and left it again at midnight.

28 April: We regained the road between Burglengenfeld and Regenstauf, where we took a few hours' rest, of which we were in great need after so many forced marches. On the road again, always in pouring rain, we set out for Cham. After travelling 6 leagues in the mountains we rejoined Montbrun's division, near Falkenstein.

30 April: Today, we covered only 1 league, crossed the Cham and bivouacked near Fufligen. In this same house, in this very room where I, a humble captain, am writing these notes, the Archdukes John and Ferdinand were lodged only yesterday. Prince Charles was on a hill within cannon shot, and the Austrian Army was in an excellent position. It appears that the Emperor Napoleon ignored the left flank of the army and attacked the enemy on the right; the Austrian Army continues to retreat before him.

1 May: The general of the division, General Montbrun, today inspected us and he watched our manoeuvres near the River Cham. The division is made up of the 5th and 7th Hussars, and the 11th and 12th Chasseurs.

2 May: The 2nd company, with the addition of forty *chasseurs*, giving it a strength of 150 men, and under the command of Major Ameil, was today

dispatched as support. We set off towards Chameret, forded the Regen, which we were almost forced to swim, then we rested at Kötzting and again at Viechtach. We had followed the course of the Regen and crossed it twice, halting in the small village of Linden. The countryside here is fertile and well-populated, but still mountainous and covered in forests.

3 May: We continued to follow the course of the Regen, over mountains and through forests. After a brief halt in the pretty town of Regen, where we learned that the enemy was only 4 or 5 leagues away, we went on to Zwiesel, where preparations for an attack were made. Unhappily, we learned that the Austrians, numbering about 1,200 men, had entrenched themselves deep in the forests and among mountains inaccessible to cavalry. The squadron remained near Zwiesel. I left with eighteen men to probe the enemy forces, which the Major intended to harass from another direction. On leaving the town, one is suddenly in the mountains of Bohemia. As I advanced, I found myself among steeper mountainsides and ever deeper forests. At last, near Bömischeiffenstim [*probably Bömischeisenstein, a village on the frontier of Bohemia – Ed.*] the road was cut by a torrent and the bridge blocked. At the same time, gunfire warned me of the presence of the enemy. As I was ordered to advance no further, I contented myself with returning fire for half an hour, until I received instructions to withdraw. If the enemy had known his profession better, he could, without risking a single man, have killed or put most of my men out of action. We returned to bivouac near Zwiesel.

4 May: Grafenau. We passed through Schönberg to lodge in Grafenau, a little village in a valley so deep that the church steeple cannot be seen from 200 paces away, until it suddenly appears as one comes round a hill.

5 May: Eisenbirn. We rejoined the regiment when we left Grafenau, and then took the road to Passau. The Danube and the Inn meet beneath the walls of this fine, large town, around which numerous fortifications have been built on the hills. The fir trees that previously covered them have been entirely cleared from the hills, and several hundred peasants, including women and children, are still occupied in the work of fortification.

After crossing the Danube and the Inn at Passau, we continued on our way in the direction of Linz. Soon, the signposts, painted in white and in blue, vanished and were replaced by black and yellow: informing us that we were leaving allied country and entering that of the enemy. Deserted and ravaged villages provided even better evidence of the passage of the army. We halted a league from Saint-Jacob at Loch, near Eisenbirn.

6 May: Having passed through Payerbach and Watenkirch, we halted at Kerling, 3 leagues from Efferding. We are ordered to return to Passau. Return! Return to the rear, while our troops are pushing forward and are only a few

leagues from Vienna! I should gladly have born the hardships of advancing if I could only have fought, but to be denied the opportunity of taking part in this campaign – and such a brilliant campaign! To be reduced to listening to the exploits of our comrades instead of taking part in them! What can possibly compensate us for this unbearable act of obedience, and who can appreciate the cost to us?

7 May: So, we retrace our steps, passing through Payerbach and reaching Passau at nightfall, where we halt.

8 May: It appears that a bloody battle took place near Vienna, and that victory remained faithful to us. The Prince of Ponte Corvo has joined our army, to the rear of us.

[*Editor's note: on 3 May at Ebersberg (or Ebelsberg), Masséna forced the road to Vienna during the course of a hard battle. The capital itself fell on 13 May, following three days of skirmishing and cannon fire, greatly annoying composer Ludwig van Beethoven, not yet totally deaf. As for 'the Prince of Ponte Corvo', this was the title Napoleon bestowed upon Marshal Bernadotte following the victory at Austerlitz in 1805.*]

10 May: The Prince of Ponte Corvo has arrived. We went to see him, and had the satisfaction of confirming for ourselves, by the graciousness of his welcome, that the reputation he has for kindness is indeed true.

11 May: I have never seen, in any other town, so many charming women; not that they are remarkable for their beauty or regularity of feature, but rather that they have an air of propriety and grace, together with a delicacy and lightness of figure. Their clothing is always simple, elegant and well-fitting and their deportment graceful. Few ladies are seen who are not comely, for theirs is a type of beauty, that survives the passing of youth, and so the number of attractive women is naturally increased. This trait applies to all classes of society, and it must astonish any stranger to find, within the town walls, so many women deserving of the homage due to beauty.

And yet, I have seen in neighbouring villages, some women who, in their manner of dress, seem as alien to those in the town as would an Asiatic in the midst of a town in France. The clothing of the women in town clings to their elegant figures, but that of the village women is quite the reverse. These women look deformed and unnatural. Thick skirts, piled one upon another, distort and wrap them from hip to knee, making the youngest girl look like a woman about to give birth. Two breastplates, one in front and one behind, encase the area between hip and neck. The breast is made particularly odd by an outer garment, that is shaped to bulge from one shoulder to the other. Cut sharply across from right to left the woman presents the appearance of a wooden moulding, and if several women of similar size were placed side by side their resemblance to a picture frame would be perfect.

12 May: The regiment left Passau to seek forage. I was sent to Grafenau and returned to spend the night at Eberharfreit, a village on the road between Passau and Schönberg.

13 May: We are ordered back to Passau, and after a league, a counter-order sends the Staff to Dillingen and us to the miserable village of Brömin, 5 leagues from Passau.

16 May: We are now at Wuderlingen only 2½ leagues from Passau.

17 and 18 May: We are still idle, suffering all the hardships of war, while being deprived of all its excitement. The news of the exploits of our comrades makes our inactivity even harder to bear. What shall we say to those who, believing themselves to be speaking to the victors of Ratisbon, Ebersberg and Vienna, ask us for the details of those glorious days?

19 May: Heiligenberg. We mounted at dawn to set out once more on the road to Passau, which we already knew only too well. We travelled 13 leagues, through Payerbach, and lodged at the village of Heiligenberg on the road to Linz.

20 May: We travelled through Waitzenkirchen and halted at Efferding, a pretty little town with a beautiful fountain in its handsome square, which is surrounded with attractive houses and opposite the château of the Prince of Rosenberg. The priest who lives near the château invited us informally to dinner with him. His house proclaimed him to be a man of wealth and good taste, and his conversation revealed a man of letters and education, who had used his wealth to improve his knowledge. He is a naturalist, antiquarian and above all, a writer. He seems to be a great admirer of the French and showed us with pride, his collection of engravings of our triumphs. According to him, there are many rich and educated people who wish for our rule. If this man is not sincere, at least his views are shrewdly in tune with the circumstances in which he finds himself.

Some of the militia have returned to their homes, and the authorities everywhere have sworn fidelity to Napoleon. We have continued on our way to Linz.

22 May: We have left Linz on our left and passed through Traun to Ebersburg. The town and its surroundings demonstrate only too clearly the horrors of battle, and will continue to do so for a very long time. The rows of isolated chimneystacks, the broken-down walls, the roofs, half-collapsed and still smoking, the rubbish filled streets, walls that are splashed with blood and pock-

marked with bullet holes. This is the dreadful appearance of the town of
Ebersberg today. What am I saying? The town! The town no longer exists.
What is seen today is no more than the skeleton of a town! This is no more than
a heap of smoking ruins and corpses; in this terrible rubble one searches in vain
for an intact building or a living being.

23 May: We continue through the village of Aschbach on the banks of the
Grasnich, and regain the road to Vienna at the small town of Amstetten.

The first village on our way is that of Griskirch. It is in a lovely position, on
well-wooded hillsides, with fertile, cultivated fields watered by many streams.
Nature, aided by good husbandry, has been kind to this land. How beautiful
this village must have been a few days ago! Now, not a living soul is to be
seen, and the village is nothing but a hideous prospect of still-smouldering
devastation. A dreadful scene of death and destruction has replaced the vision
of rural abundance and peace. Where the remains of a well-cared-for interior
can be seen through a collapsed wall, the sense of loss is sharp. Further on, an
orchard filled with blossom may cheer the eye for a moment, but then the sweet
scent of springtime is overwhelmed by the foul smell of the animal corpses,
with which the ground is strewn, and one must turn away in horror. Sometimes a whole area has been burned, although here and there, a single tree
covered with buds and blossom may still stand. But, all around, nature is
profaned and the signs of returning spring are polluted by the evidence of
destructive war. There can be no happiness here, only bitter regret.

We proceed to Neumarkt, leaving the road to Erlauf and we lodge in the
magnificent castle of Danaudorf, owned by Count Zchermin [*perhaps Czernin –
Ed.*]. This castle stands on the banks of the Danube, which flows beneath its
walls. The countryside around it is delightful: forests and fields clothe the
riverbanks. On the summit of a steep crag can be seen the Austrian Emperor's
superb Castle of Baisenhaibach.

24 May: We leave Danaudorf and pass through Melek and Erlauf. As we come
nearer and nearer to the army, so the signs of wretchedness increase, and
burned villages become more frequent. Our march continues through the
steep, thickly forested mountains of this region. We halt at Rubrichshofen.

The lawlessness of the stragglers is horrible, and a quarter of the army is
occupied in this looting. Many villages are half-empty and others are entirely
deserted; all is ruined and shattered. It is dangerous to try to stop the robbery,
unless with a force greater than that of the culprits; four *chasseurs* of the 11th
have been murdered. Even more audacious, some bandsmen combined and
organized themselves, obtaining the uniforms and epaulettes of generals and
colonels and pieces of clothing worn by officials, and so in this way, made
themselves masters of a little town. From this place they made sorties, demanding taxes, arresting the French, stealing their money and watches and treating

them as thieves. It was only with difficulty that they were stopped, four of them were shot and the rest fled into the mountains.

25 May: The attractive little town of Saint-Pölten on the banks of the Traisen, has been spared destruction; its elegant houses and fine architecture bespeak its proximity to the capital, from which we are, in fact, only 16 leagues distant. On leaving Saint-Pölten we passed near Heiligen Kreutz, a magnificent church, and then we halted at Langmamersdorf. This village was completely deserted and we were forced, as in Poland, to search everywhere, and even dig in the ground, to find something to eat. As a result – sad but unavoidable – the village, which was empty of everything when we arrived, we were obliged to abandon full of wasted supplies. The normal beverage in this country is cider, but there is also a white wine with a flinty taste, which is very pleasant.

26 May: We marched on the road to Vienna for about 3 leagues, then, leaving the capital on our right, we passed through the big village of Saint-André and bivouacked in the hamlet of Wochtern. It is refreshing to find that the inhabitants here do not flee at the sight of the French. The mobile columns have restored order, and at least the bread that we eat has not been watered with the tears of the unhappy peasants.

27 May: Leaving Saint-André for Vienna, we enter the Kalberg [*i.e. Kahlenberg – Ed.*] mountains. There is an easier and much shorter route along the Danube through Klosterneuburg, but the Austrians can fire from floating batteries upon those who travel on that river. We pass through Dornbach, but as we arrive at the gate of Vienna, there is a counter-order, which sends us back to Saint-André.

28 May: Leaving (Saint-André), we follow the Danube and halt at Adelsfeld, a fine castle belonging to the Prince of Lichtenstein. I notice that this château, as well as many elegant houses and even some palaces, have shingle roofs.

29 May: We leave Adelsfeld at four in the morning to come down from the mountains, and take up a position at Altenburg; this is a village on the banks of the Danube, and now only the river separates us from Austrian forward positions.

At midnight the enemy moved, in three boats, into the village of Greifenstein, just 200 paces away from us. Fifteen *chasseurs* were there, seeking forage; five of them were taken prisoner and Sergeant Pyroley, who came with me from France, was mortally wounded. The gallant Corporal Mijon charged the enemy with his picket of four men and received a mortal wound; all of us jumped into the saddle and galloped to the attack, but the darkness and the difficulty of the terrain gave the enemy time to re-embark before we could catch up with him. I took over the command of the company.

31 May: The day was spent in patrolling. Our position was in a narrow gap, with the Danube on our left and steep, forest-covered hills to the right. We mounted horses at midnight.

1 June: It was said that the enemy had disembarked at Tulln [*on the right bank of the Danube, about 12 miles/20 km above Vienna – Ed.*]. We went there with General Pajol and the 11th Chasseurs, reaching it at dawn. There had been no disembarkation, but several advanced posts had amused themselves by firing from one bank of the river to the other. We went back to our bivouac at Saint-André.

3 June: With the 2nd Company, I went to take up a position at Wolfpassing, a quarter of a league along the road to Königstetten.

We learn of the death of Marshal Lannes: both of his thighs were smashed by a cannon ball at the Battle of Essling on the 22nd. This battle, that lasted for three days, cost us eighteen generals, killed, wounded or captured, three marshals were wounded, 15,000 men were killed, and it is said that 22,000 wounded were sent back to Vienna on the following day.

[*Editor's note: According to rough estimates, the Battle of Aspern–Essling, which prevented Napoleon from crossing the Danube in force, cost the French around 23,000 in killed, wounded and missing. Among the twenty-four generals listed among these losses, Lasalle, d'Espagne, St Hilaire and Pouzet were killed. The Austrians lost a similar number of casualties.*]

6 June: I hope today will bring me good fortune; it is the anniversary of the fight at Valdepenas. I have just learned that a 4th Squadron is to be formed, and that I have been proposed as captain of it.

8 June: At three in the afternoon, we received the order to present ourselves at Schönbrunn at six o'clock, to parade before the Emperor. The weather is appalling and the roads almost impassable. We crossed the mountains, passed through Kierling and Klosterneuburg. On leaving this town we saw the mountain on whose summit there stands an old convent, which gives the town its name. It is a very picturesque place, and in the distance, can be seen the whole of Vienna, with its magnificent buildings as well as the palaces, parks and gardens surrounding it. As the Danube winds, it divides into branches, forming an infinity of delightful islands.

The time fixed for the parade had passed when we reached Schönbrunn; fortunately, it has been postponed until tomorrow. We lodge at Weinhaus, half a league to the east of Vienna.

9 June: The brigade assembles before Schönbrunn. Just as the parade begins, General Pajol hands the Colonel the brevets for the officers who have been recommended for promotion. I am promoted to captain from 6 June. A happy anniversary of Valdepenas.

The Emperor reviews the parade, and we return to Weinhaus for the night. I am lodged in the palace of Count de Hadisk, who commanded part of the Hungarian uprising. The palace is furnished luxuriously and with taste and elegance, but, as usual, it has a shingle roof.

10 June: The 4th Squadron is formed today and I take over the command of the 6th Company.

11 June: We are manoeuvring near Schönbrunn, in the presence of, and under the command of, Marshal Bessières, Duke of Istria.

14 June: Both days are spent in manoeuvres, and theory is studied every day. The Emperor is using this moment of inaction to educate his army. Every regiment is actively and enthusiastically engaged in instruction and manoeuvres. An artillery company has been assigned to each infantry regiment and every battalion is to have a cannon.

17 June: I leave Weinhaus with my company and establish myself in the village of Harnals, near one of the gates of Vienna.

18 June. Today I visited the hospital. This hospital in Vienna must be the finest in Europe. Everything in it indicates evidence of the most enlightened charity. The main courtyard, filled with plants, has a fine fountain in the centre; all the rooms are spacious, clean and airy. In addition to the main courtyard, there are several others, surrounded by buildings in which the sick are accommodated according to their illnesses. This enormous building is regulated with wonderful propriety and economy. Our wounded owe a great deal to the care lavished upon them by the German surgeons. The sight of this place will do much to soften hearts embittered by the horrors of war! What a tribute it is to humanity, and how greatly it is to the honour of the Prince who is responsible for this sublime institution. I am afraid of seeming to exaggerate if I give the number of sick and wounded who are here, but it comes to several thousands.

To a considerable extent our emotions depend upon our surroundings. What our eyes see is mirrored deep in our hearts and gives rise to kindred feelings. When I saw the thousands of mutilated soldiers in the Vienna Hospital, I hated the evils of war, but as I walked round the Arsenal, I experienced more martial feelings.

During our first campaign, the Arsenal had been despoiled of its principal attractions, and more recently, when they evacuated Vienna, the Austrians had taken away everything they could carry. But there was still much to be admired by the art connoisseur and even by the idle visitor. For the principal beauty of the place could not be vandalized, as it is to be found in the columns and the ceilings; these are made entirely from arrangements of different weapons. Designs consisting solely of weaponry cover the doors and form all the decorations and mouldings. Often, the columns supporting, or rather adorning, this immense square gallery are made out of field guns, while others are composed of spirals of pistols. The number and variety of the weapons and the clever patterns in which they are arranged on walls and ceilings is remarkable. Two spread-eagles, representing the coat of arms of Austria, appear on the ceiling at each end of the gallery; they are composed of daggers, swords, bayonets and even the component parts of guns, each feather of the birds is a bayonet or dagger blade.

We had already found 10,000 guns in the arsenal. There were also a large number of model figures, which must have been intended to display armour, for each was labelled with the name of a different prince. However, someone has had the wisdom to remove them, for fear that we should be tempted to carry them off to Paris, as has been the fate of so many other art treasures that now enrich that capital, which is already crammed with the spoils of Europe.

25 June: The Emperor today held a review of nearly 40,000 men at Schönbrunn. The grenadiers and the light infantry of Oudinot's corps, all the Imperial Guard, our light cavalry division and an enormous amount of artillery were involved. The people of Vienna have become very hostile towards us and they are suffering the pangs of hunger. They help prisoners to escape, hide spies and pass information as to our movements to Prince Charles. The city of Vienna is full of spies, and it is impossible for us to prevent them slipping into our camp and then going back into that of the enemy.

26 June: Fighting continues in Hungary. Raab has been taken. The Army of Italy is making progress; elsewhere, the Austrians are advancing into Saxony, while the Saxon troops, who are fighting on our side, are wretchedly unhappy that they are not in a position to defend their own homeland.

29 June: We mounted at daybreak, left Hernals, and as we passed Schönbrunn, I saw enough of the park and the gardens to make me regret I was unable to see more of them. Even as I galloped along the road, I could see the superb fountains, pyramids, obelisks and monuments, as they vanished from my sight. I passed beneath an archway, built by Maria-Theresa, and came into the most beautiful avenue in Germany, perhaps in the whole of Europe. It is composed of chestnut trees, is perfectly straight, and nearly 4 leagues in length, and leads to the lovely village of Laxenburg, which must be the St Cloud of Vienna. The Emperor and his court live there for six months of each year. The homes of the sons of the Emperor, the Ritterschloss and the Launeschloss, the palaces of Prince Esterhazy and Prince Schwarzenberg and the home of the Emperor with its parks and pheasantry make up the chief beauties of this village, set among delightful pastures.

30 June: I intended to spend the day in exploring the different palaces in this lovely village, but my time was even more agreeably occupied. I met

Montgardet, the bravest and most good-natured man I have ever encountered. What terrible, bitter memories we recalled together! Only we two remain out of two regiments! We thought once more of our unhappy comrades of Bailén and Cadiz, and gave vent to new curses upon those who had so savagely defended their – admittedly righteous – cause. We hunted in the Emperor's pheasantry, where I killed a pheasant.

1 July: Weary from the hunt, I fell asleep, forming happy new plans for tomorrow. At midnight, the trumpet sounded and the regiment assembled at Biedermansdorf, a quarter of a league from Laxenburg, on the Vienna road. We marched along the Wiener Canal and through Maria Lanzerdorf, the church of which could be seen from far away. A large, black iron statue of the Virgin stood on the rooftop, seemingly intended to terrify the passer-by. We took up our battle-order only a cannon shot from the Danube and remained on horseback from six in the morning until five in the evening, under a steady downpour of rain. There was great activity near the bridge. All the army was gathering and concentrating, several regiments were sent onto the Island [*i.e. Lobau – Ed.*] as reinforcements. We received an order to return to Biedermansdorf for the night; but our pleasure is only deferred.

2 July: Cannon fire roared all through the night. Let it roar! When it is our turn we shall be there.

3 July: All the Hungarian Army has crossed over the Ebersdorf bridge. Our forces are concentrating and there will be some serious conflict. We are ordered to leave tomorrow, at eleven in the morning. So, while waiting, I make another visit to beautiful Laxenburg; it is so well worth exploring. Having examined the buildings of past centuries I was anxious to see a little of those of the present time.

I paid a visit to the Launeschloss, a whimsical castle built by the Empress. It is a sort of Chinese house of a strange appearance. The outside is decorated with dogs and cats lined up in a row like larks on a spit. There are turrets at each of the four corners of the building, which contains only one room. The light from windows of coloured glass, blue, yellow and violet produces a very odd effect. The kitchen is painted with devils and flames, like a picture of hell, while the walls of the little music room are scattered with small extracts of the music of different composers. Going up a little staircase, one expects to find the attic, but no, it is the cellar! The name of this curious house is well-deserved [*i.e. 'Moody Castle' – Ed.*].

4 July: We left Biedermansdorf at eleven o'clock and marched towards Ebersdorf by the same road as before, but this time it will be to some purpose. We move into battle position on the plain before Schwechat and are welcomed, as before, by a terrible storm. I think that the coming night will be harsh.

The entire army assembles: the Army of Italy, that of Dalmatia, the Saxons, the Bavarians – in other words, everyone who fights for Napoleon. From daybreak, the troops file over the famous bridge, which this time does not break down, but over which so many of us will never return. Each rider gathers from the fields all the wheat that he can, and loads it onto his horse. At nine in the evening, it is our turn to cross. The main bridge, which is built on piles, is a masterpiece of the art. It has railings and lights and is intended exclusively for the use of the cavalry and the artillery: the infantry crosses on the two pontoon bridges to the left and right of the main bridge. Now here we are on the famous Island of Lobau, to which the French Army withdrew following the fateful Battle of Essling. The Danube is behind us and the enemy army is in front. Tomorrow we must win or die! The day that is about to dawn will decide the fate of two great empires, and the lives of many thousands of individuals – 400,000 men who hate no one, who would, perhaps, like each other if they were to meet – are crushed together in the small space of 3 square leagues, and wait only for the signal to tear out each other's throats. What is soon to come dominates our thoughts, and our minds fill with sombre apprehensions.

Torrential rain falls as we sleep in the mud and in complete darkness.

The bombardment started at ten in the evening. A terrible uproar began as the mouths of 200 cannon vomited death. The tumult of exploding bombs on the fiery horizon produced a thunderous pandemonium and the whistle of bullets mingled with the sound of the wind. Lightning flashed in the distance, thunder growled, came nearer, and combined with the roar of artillery. Finally, the terrible anger of nature united with the rage of men to form the dreadful scene we saw unfolding before us.

5 July: The day dawned. Yesterday, and during the night, the whole army had moved onto the island; so now only a narrow stream, less than 20 feet wide, separated us from the left bank. At daybreak, three bridges were thrown across, and at seven in the morning, we set foot on the opposite bank. Three hours later, we were within cannon shot of the enemy. We were stationed on the right wing [*consisting of Davout's corps, to which Montbrun's cavalry division was attached – Ed.*]. The main thrust of the battle was in the centre and on the left wing, where the enemy entrenchments were placed. The small town of Enzersdorf had been in flames since the morning.

Ten at night. Ever since the morning, we have manoeuvred under the guns of the enemy artillery and the attack of their cavalry. There has been resolute fighting everywhere, and all the manoeuvres have been carried out with the same order and precision as if on parade. There have been few or no charges; every advance has been *en masse*; we have gained a great deal of ground, but the enemy has not, for one moment, been thrown into confusion. Nothing has been decisive. A huge artillery barrage has continued to thunder for twenty-four hours, and the outcome of the battle will depend upon this. The horizon is in flames, and nightfall, which came upon us by surprise, brought no cessation of the barrage. The two armies are lined up, within cannon shot of each other, near the village of Markgraf Neusiedel, which we still have not taken. There is an accursed square tower there that we shall remember for a long while. We spend the night, our bridles on our arms, amongst the wheat, waiting for the morning to shed its light upon the new struggles that lie before us.

6 July: Night drew to a close but the fighting went on. Here and there, the guns ploughed fiery furrows between the two armies. The murderous fire grew more accurate as day broke at last. For a moment, exhaustion and the lethargy of sleep dulled our senses; then, all at once, the whole of the Austrian line, from one end to the other, opened fire, their vigorous attack put pressure on us at every point. A multitude of bombs and shells darkened the air and brought a deadly hailstorm crashing down onto our heads. Cannon balls hissed and ricocheted in our ranks, furrowing the ground at our feet. A mass of infantry approached, bayonets sparkling ever nearer through the clouds of smoke. The cavalry moved off, and shouts of rage and impatience made themselves heard in the midst of the pandemonium of the artillery. This sudden, swift movement caused an instant's confusion in our ranks. A crowd of *cantinières*, servants and baggage wagons, which had come up during the night and mingled with our ranks, fled precipitously, and this noisy flight added to the perplexity and uncertainly of the soldiers. But soon, amazed that we had allowed ourselves to waver for a single moment, we quickly reformed and engaged the enemy in our turn.

Meanwhile, the Austrians, who, according to the promises of their generals, had been certain they would throw us back into the Danube and had, on the previous day, purposely yielded a little ground to us, now started to regret their withdrawal. They began to be alarmed that Prince John had failed to arrive, for he was to have cut our retreat to the bridges across the Danube. Fearing to let victory escape their grip, the French redoubled their efforts; all the artillery fire was concentrated on the unfortunate village of Neusiedel: fires burst out on all sides and the enemy force was obliged, at last, to abandon it. The redoubts were attacked at eleven o'clock and carried at bayonet point. Their left wing, commanded by Field Marshal Prince Rosenberg, was overwhelmed and turned. It was in vain that Prince Charles [*i.e. the Archduke – Ed.*], twice wounded and twice dismounted, when his horses were killed under him, deployed all the skill of a great general and the audacity of the bravest soldier imaginable. Covered with his own blood and that of the orderlies at his side, he dashed forward at the head of his cavalry; sometimes, sword in hand, he charged with his grenadiers on foot. Fortune failed to reward his courage. Napoleon had made himself master of the fate of the Austrian armies; they were pushed back from their positions, forced to yield on all sides, yet every regiment, even as it was overwhelmed, sought to save its honour and bring distinction to its defeat.

The left wing, which we were pressing hard, continually reformed a few hundred paces further back; little by little ceding ground along its front. On our right, it gained some ground, overrunning us in our turn and attacking our flank furiously, overwhelming three regiments, and for a moment, once more casting our victory into doubt. However, not being supported in strength by the infantry, the Austrian cavalry was repelled with great loss and abandoned the ground even more quickly than it had taken it. We advanced, thrust them back at all points, and only nightfall brought our victorious pursuit to an end.

Hunger and the heat had, for these two days, caused us great suffering, but thirst was the worst torment of all. *Chasseurs*, while skirmishing, were seen to dismount and tear grass up, to eat; others had collected their urine in bottles, to quench their thirst. We had only a very small quantity of bread, but our terrible thirst prevented us from eating it. One tried, in vain, to chew the bread and swallow, but the teeth refused to chew and the throat would not open to receive it. A mouthful of bread could be held in the mouth for minutes at a time, but the parched palate was aware only of a chalk-like lump.

Note: From eleven o'clock we were, for a long while, exposed to the fire from a battery that, from time to time, cut down both our men and horses. I was in command of the squadron since the morning. Worn out, dying of thirst, I stretched myself out on the burning earth, still holding the bridle of my exhausted horse as it lay at my side. Even the bullets falling around me could not keep me awake. Suddenly, there was an order to move off, by platoons, to the right. In a moment, I mounted and set off at a gallop to execute the movement. Just at that instant, a bullet hit my horse's head. It fell dead and I fell with it, trapped beneath it, unable to move. My orderly, Kapel, and Corporal Garnier, dismounted at once and freed me. A little dishevelled by the fall, I collected my saddlebag and my pistols and set off to find another horse, while the faithful Kapel removed all the accoutrements from the dead animal.

As I withdrew on foot, the enemy cavalry, which had disengaged itself along its front, charged us vigorously on the flank. The 1st and 2nd Chasseurs and the 7th Hussars were completely overwhelmed, and I soon saw the enemy cavalry rushing down upon me at a headlong gallop, with their sabres upraised. A dismounted horseman presents a dismal aspect in such a situation. I could see before me no alternative but capture or death, or at least, to be crushed beneath the galloping hooves. *Chasseur* Delbon, already encumbered with my possessions, again tried to give me his horse; I refused. Two other *chasseurs*, one of them wounded, also offered me their horses. I again refused, but asked them each to grip me by one arm. I gave myself up to their control, and off they went at a gallop. This exacting activity could not last long. One of their horses became unmanageable and the *chasseur* was obliged to let go of me. I fell heavily, but I was out of danger. I managed to reach the village of Markgraf Neusiedel. Half the houses were in flames and the rest were being looted; the wounded and the dying lay amongst the burning debris. A wretched, injured soldier seeing the flames advancing towards him, screamed to his comrades, but in vain. Without replying, they passed close by, intent on braving the flames for plunder. At one time, I saw six men wounded by a single burst of gunfire. I dragged one away, but as I could not help all these unfortunates, I quickly turned away from the sight and went into the first undamaged house I came to, in search of food. A moment later, a tall young man followed me in. His face was thin and burned by the sun, and he was covered with blood and dust and was leading his wounded horse. He called me by name. It was Albin de Brouville, who I had last seen at Orléans, the elegant man of fashion in that society. How two campaigns can transform a man, and how different was the setting now from that in which we last met! Just for a moment, by this happy meeting, I recalled my home and my family even in the midst of all the horror. And with what joy I saw Kapel arrive with my second horse, already saddled! 'We must return to our post, at once,' was my first idea. But death was nearer to me than I had thought, for before leaving, hoping to find a few oats for my horse, I went into the loft to look for some. There were some pigeons on the roof and an infantryman fired at them from below: the bullet went through the roof, scraping my face and covering me in dust and broken tiles.

I wandered for a while on the battlefield before, at last, rejoining my regiment, and looking anxiously among my old friends to see if all of them were present. Alas! Poor Grobert had just died. We followed the enemy until night fell; then we spent the night among the wheat near a little village, which had been given over to the depredations of the soldiery.

The battle was nearly over and only occasional shots could be heard. An officer named Freney had moved off with a few skirmishers, when one of his *chasseurs*, approaching him from the rear, killed him. The same bullet killed three horses. The regiment only lost two officers killed and twenty-seven *chasseurs* killed or wounded in the course of the battle.

7 July: The enemy is in full retreat, but is withdrawing in good order, and we are following them and taking several prisoners. A hussar of the 5th is shot. All the villages present a terrible sight, deserted and sacked: they are full of French and Austrian wounded. The immense plains are covered with burning crops. Having marched to Volkersdorf, we turned back and rejoined the bulk of the army outside Wagram.

8 July: We marched directly towards Moravia, following the main road to Brno. There is a wonderful harvest here, but the destruction we are causing is incalculable. Everything is devastated, wrecked and looted; even if, when we

arrive, a few peasants still remain, they do not stay long. Perhaps from neglig-
ence, perhaps from other motives, whole villages are soon reduced to cinders.
The country here is flat, open and rich in grain and forage.

9 July: We leave the road to Brno at Mittelsbach and move to our left towards
Bohemia, following the frontier between Moravia and Austria. We pass
through the little village of Laab, crossing the River La Taya, which separates
Austria from Moravia. We are crushed by heat and exhaustion. A little soup is
very precious when one has been hungry for so long! We are still pursuing the
enemy, who continues to retreat in good order, and we take a few prisoners.
The territory is wet and swampy.

10 July: We marched towards Znaim across vast marshes. Encountering the
enemy about half a league short of the town, we opened fire at midday.
Believing that only a few stragglers were involved, or at most, a rearguard
protecting the evacuation of the town, General Montbrun, having placed
Pajol's brigade in position, wanted to continue his advance. Gunfire broke
out among the vines and narrow pathways that surrounded the town, and
resistance increased with every step. However, supported by the brigades of
Jacquinot and Colbert, and the Bavarian infantry, we forced the enemy
advanced posts back and won some ground on the right. Even as we went
forward, so the gunfire grew heavier and more intensive on the left wing. There
is a chain of mountains overlooking the town, and artillery fire, aimed in that
direction, forced the enemy to deploy those of his forces he had, until then,
concealed. While this was taking place on the left, General Marmont arrived
with the Army of Dalmatia. General Montbrun, aware of the arrival of this
support, pushed hard to the right, and having taken several positions, reached
the town, where he encountered part of the enemy army. He seized a hill,
skirted the town and charged the enemy cavalry, pushing it before him, so that
we soon found ourselves on the edge of a ravine facing the entire Austrian
Army. This was deployed in three lines, occupying a position protected on all
sides, and impossible to outflank. As the enemy wing that rested on the town
had not moved, we found that, on our left wing, our front had been reversed.
The strength of the Austrian Army now extended before us, made us realize
the situation was more serious than we had thought. Our predicament became
more critical every moment. We had advanced too far. Behind us extensive
marshland and a narrow gorge would make our retreat extremely dangerous, as
well as slowing down the march of troops that might attempt to support us.
The enemy, although shocked by the energy of our attack, was rallying with
impressive speed, and seeing that we did not follow up our advantage, hoped to
regain any ground not strongly defended. This is what would have happened, if
those who opposed us had been French, but instead of putting as much energy
into their riposte as we had put into the attack, they brought up several

batteries against us. General Montbrun's courage saved us; we stood firm, and remained for a long while exposed to the artillery fire without making a single movement. We gained time; night was coming and our strength was increasing. At last, we retreated slowly and waited, lying in the mud, until returning daylight would enable us to compete on equal terms once more.

There was a terrible storm and we passed a dreadful night, nearly as bad as that of the 4th/5th preceding the Battle of Wagram. At three in the morning, as there were so few of us and our situation was so critical, the generals formed all the servants, *cantinières* and led-horses into a battle formation behind us, to simulate a second line. Worn out with hunger and weariness, it was not until ten in the evening that we were able to dismount. We could not sleep, for the deep mud forced us to remain standing up; we should have been so happy if we could have had a little fire, but we were all too tired to light one, and it would have been impossible in any case, for the rain fell in torrents. As our horses had had nothing to drink all day, a journey of a league had to be made to water them. We had only just returned from this duty, when dawn began to break and the call to mount again was sounded.

11 July: We once more took up the position on the right of the army, which we had occupied yesterday. The Emperor arrived at nine o'clock with the Imperial Guard; other corps appeared in turn, and by noon, the whole army had assembled.

The right flank of the Austrian Army now rests on the town of Znaim. On one side are the narrow pathways, the vines and the little valley, through which the Taya flows; the hills on the opposite side are covered with trees, through which a frontal attack would be very dangerous and which makes it impossible to outflank the enemy. All along the enemy's front there is a deep ravine, while his left rests on thick woodland, which is protected by a lake and swamps, so that it is equally impossible to outflank this position. Our army finds itself compressed onto a narrow plateau, and forced to attack in strength to its front, as it lacks the ability to deploy with marshland and ravines behind it. On the contrary, the Austrian Army, deployed in three lines, is spread over an immense hillside along the far side of the ravine and it remains there, motionless, awaiting our attack.

It is six in the evening. Since this morning, neither the right wing nor the centre has moved. There is heavy artillery fire on the town, and our infantry is firing near the gates. An Austrian trumpet is heard, calling for a negotiation. For about three hours, trumpets sound from time to time. At last night falls. Tomorrow morning we shall know if we are to embrace each other or murder each other.

12 July: At dawn there is a trumpet call to mount. Both armies remain in their positions while negotiations are taking place. At three o'clock, we are told that a

ceasefire has been agreed. Fires are hurriedly lighted and we are able to eat some soup, of which we have been deprived for eight days.

We move off on the road to Brno at six in the evening, reaching the village of Misslitz at midnight. It is impossible to imagine the terror that seized the townsfolk, or their sudden joy when they realized that we did not come as enemies. Several women fainted when they heard this unexpected news. In this part of Moravia, into which we have just come, the language spoken is Polish, mixed with a Bohemian dialect.

13 July: We pass through the villages of Franspitz and Pohrlitz to rejoin the good main road. On the way, we meet various Austrian regiments; yesterday we should have rushed upon one another with upraised swords, today we salute each other courteously. We enter Brno, an imperial city on a hill. A strong citadel named Spielberg dominates it, and this is filled with prisoners of the state. The people of Moravia are very patriotic and look upon us with an unfriendly eye. Fertile and well-cultivated fields surround very large villages with their low, thatch-covered houses.

It is impossible to calculate the damage we have inflicted on the countryside around Znaim; a magnificent harvest stood ready for the reaper, and across the wide plain, the corn was so dense that, as we trotted through it, our horses' legs were impeded and grain fell from the ripened ears of wheat. The unceasing torrential rain made the ruin we left in our wake even worse, and only an hour later, a sea of mud heaped with rubbish replaced the handsome harvest. What a sad sight for the unhappy farmer!

Chapter 5

Armistice, Marriage of the Emperor, the Empress Josephine: July 1809–June 1810

1809

14 July: We marched off on the main road to Olmütz and with my company, I occupied the little village of Inrievitz, 2 leagues from Brno. As we advanced into the countryside, the Austrians retreated before us. In accordance with the terms of the Armistice, they are to surrender the areas around Znaim and Brno to us.

15 July: We pass through the village of Rauznitz on the main road, leaving the battlefield of Austerlitz on our right, and have now halted in Wischau. It was in this little town that, during the Austerlitz campaign, the hussars of the 9th Regiment were besieged for thirty-six hours by a force ten times stronger than they. In the town's square there is a monument, surmounted by a pyramid, which was built more than a century ago to commemorate a terrible plague. It was the sculptor's intention to represent clouds and angels. However, from a hundred paces away, the column looks more like a gnarled tree trunk. All the towns and villages of Moravia are full of such cloudy columns, crowned with Holy Virgins or the Trinity.

16 July: Near Wischau there are mineral waters containing iron oxide, to which the local people attribute wonderful qualities. Their effect, due to the carbonic acid gas they contain, is very strange. When they are mixed with wine, it foams and sparkles like Champagne; after a few minutes, the wine becomes blackish in colour and has a spicy taste that the local people find very pleasant.

18 July: I go, with my company, to the village of Einvanowitz, and find it occupied by Colonel Barco's Hussars. They claim that the village is within the environs of Olmütz, and that I must withdraw. I maintain that it is under the administration of Brno and that he must surrender it to me. Colonel de Barco is unable to decide anything himself as he is under the orders of Count Starenberg. We both write letters and await the arrival of instructions from our superiors.

19 July: I remain master of the ground and the Austrians withdraw from the village.

20 July: I receive instructions to occupy Dresfit and Nebstich on my left and Schabevitz to the right, and to command the line of demarcation that, at this point, separates the two armies.

24 July: My daily duties are interesting but complicated and unending; I have not a moment of free time, nor am I able to move even a step away. I have to observe all the enemy's movements, to collect all possible information, to receive the reports sent to me from every point along the line, to interrogate deserters – of whom eight or nine arrive each day. From all this information I have daily to compose a report in duplicate, one copy of which I send to Marshal Davout, by way of Major Meuziau – the Commander-in-Chief of the line – and the other to my Colonel, for him to send to the General of the division, Montbrun.

25 July: I receive a letter from the Minister of War that informs me I have been appointed as aide-de-camp to His Highness the Prince Viceroy [*i.e. Eugène de Beauharnais (1781–1824), Napoleon's stepson and Viceroy of Italy – Ed.*] and ordering me to join him immediately. However, I also hear that Louis de Tascher de la Pagerie has actually been made an aide-de-camp to the same prince, so I think that an error has been made in my appointment, and therefore, I stay prudently where I am, until matters are clarified.
[*Editor's note: in the archives of the war, the file of Colonel Count Louis de Tascher de la Pagerie contains a copy of a notice dated 3 July 1809 from the Minister of War to His Highness Prince Eugène de Beauharnais, Viceroy of Italy, to announce the names of the following officers as nominations to his suite as aides-de-camp; Tascher, Labédoyère and Desève.*]

26 July: Very often, it is pleasanter for a man not to have to decide his own fate. To begin a new life, a new career at the heart of a court in the service of a prince who is my relation, and at the age of twenty-three, to be left to my own devices with the certainty of attracting envy, and most certainly without friends, as well as being faced with the prospect of having to bid farewell to my own country; this would have needed a great deal of thought.

There is much to be said for living peacefully with one's comrades, at liberty to do as one wishes in any spare time left over from one's duties; I am in suspense, but unworried; I await my destiny, whatever it might prove to be, without either hope or fear; but how anxious and undecided I should have been if my fate had been in my own hands. I wonder what inner voice is telling me I shall continue to be a contented captain of *chasseurs*, but I feel that it will bring me happiness.

9 August: A letter arrives from Louis de Tascher telling me of the mistake that led me to believe myself an aide-de-camp to Prince Eugène. I relinquish the idea without regret; I had never really entertained it, and I have spared myself a useless journey.

10 August: Troops are concentrating and the line is being fortified; the period of truce comes to an end and everything now seems to indicate that the war will soon begin again. I was dreaming happily of the prospect of passing a peaceful winter in Germany. Four years of weariness, danger and hardship in Prussia, Poland, Spain and Austria have taught me how to enjoy an hour of quiet and study to the full. Just a table, a chair, a few books and a tranquil room, followed by some pleasant company with whom to enjoy the moments when study is over, that was my dream. But now I must adjust all my thoughts utterly. To war! To war! Because there is no alternative.

15 August: In every place to which the Emperor's power extends – that is to say over most of Europe – his birthday is celebrated today. In order that the festival should be the same in each country, and so that every place accords a national holiday to Saint Napoleon, every soldier receives 30 *sous* and each officer 12 francs. The Generals call together representatives of each regiment. The colonels provide a meal for the corps. A huge banquet took place at Austerlitz, where Napoleon gathered one of his immortal palms. But the songs of victory are seldom heard, save in the midst of tears; even in the tumult of the celebrations, a fire broke out that devoured half the town. Sobs of misery were once again intermingled with shouts of joy. At Brno, the Marshal wanted the townspeople themselves to participate in the general rejoicing. How can it be possible, when the flower of their youth has just perished defending their homeland, while farmers have been driven from their peaceful homes, when all their wealth has been destroyed, and when an enemy army is firmly established in their country, to demand of these unhappy people that they demonstrate joy and then to believe that they are sincere? The balls given by French officers for the wretched inhabitants of Moravia painted, in my imagination, a picture of savages dancing around their captives, before serving them up to be eaten at a triumphal feast.

31 August: The hours, the days, rush past like moments. I think with dread of the fact that I have been here for forty days and that this happy time will come to an end. I dare not think of the future, so I close my eyes to it and am content to savour the delicious present.

Only a year ago today, I was far from my homeland, a prisoner, helpless and without hope, burned by the sun and surrounded by murderers. Oh, how this memory, and the way in which it contrasts with the present, makes the air that I breathe and the delightful country surrounding me seem even lovelier.

5 September: Today I leave.

6 September: Niscowitz. Now, I find myself alone in an uninhabited presbytery. I have four ruinous walls, with a rickety table, a chair and a few bales of hay upon a worm-eaten wooden bedstead as my entire furniture. The dilapidation of the window and the filth that encrusts the glass, would limit my view to a distance of 6 feet if the occasional broken pane did not allow me a view of the neighbouring cemetery.

7 September: I have just visited the handsome castle of Stanitz, where the Regimental Staff is established. The castle belongs to the Prince of Lichtenstein, the wealthiest landowner in the Empire, and it would seem, in Europe. One is assured that he owns eighty-nine spacious mansions, not including farms, woods and other properties (I know of nearly fifteen of these). His income is 6 million francs; and even after deducting the money he gives to his brothers as their inheritance, and paying his taxes and the salaries of innumerable employees there still remains 2 million for him to spend as he wishes.

10 September: As I have already remarked, I am living in an old, abandoned presbytery, where the most profound silence reigns all the week. However, on Sunday, my home provides the best place from which to observe the customs and the dress of the people of the village and its surroundings, for they assemble here for Mass, which is celebrated by an old priest from Austerlitz. The peasants, who throughout the week present an aspect of the most disgusting filth, look entirely different on Sunday.

Their dress consists of trousers in the Hungarian style, often elegantly braided and held up by a tight belt, with a long robe of sheepskin against the cold. A sort of thick white hood, edged with a piping of different colours, is worn on the head. When the sun shines, a strangely shaped scrap of fabric floats from their shoulders to serve, doubtless, as a hood. The hats they wear are completely original. I can do no better than to compare the head and hat together with an upturned flowerpot placed on a melon. The hair is cut all around so that an inch of it protrudes beneath the hat, producing an effect at once Gothic and strange.

The dress of the young girls is much more attractive. Their skirts barely reach their knees so that their brilliant scarlet stockings can be seen from afar, and their blouses are beautifully pleated and have long cuffs of lace. They take great care of their hair, which is plaited, with ribbons floating down to their shoulders.

11 September: I have visited the nearby battlefield of Austerlitz, as well as the Austerlitz Castle, which belongs to Prince Kaunitz. It seems that this was, at one time, furnished very elegantly, but fear of the French has caused everything that might tempt their rapacity to be removed. There is one wonderful

room in the castle, one to which all the others have been sacrificed. It contains eight beautiful chandeliers and seems worthy of an imperial palace. It has, indeed, been occupied, in succession, by Emperor Alexander and by Emperor Napoleon. The gardens are enormous and enclosed by high walls.

I travelled over the battlefield with the greatest interest and studied the positions that the two opposing armies occupied. Looking at these fruitful fields, thick with corn, seeing the peaceful peasants with their flocks and herds, it was tragic to realize that this earth must now conceal the corpses of so many men. In this little valley the cavalry of the Guard charged, and many magnificent, nameless, actions took place. But where is the glory of a hero who died for his country if, three years later, the illustrious are as silent as the earth that covers them? What strange thoughts these are for a soldier. Phantoms of glory! Earthly vanities! How many noble virtues are sacrificed in your name!

Here is the village of Sokolnitz, where the outlines of entire regiments could be traced by the rows of corpses. Now, where peaceful flocks stray and peasants sing at their work, the earth where so many died shows not the slightest trace. A stranger who had read the details of this bloody battle might ask, surprised: 'Is it true that three years ago the destiny of Europe was decided by such an outpouring of blood?' For there is no more to be seen here than if two sparrows had fought over a grain of wheat. As for the soldier who cheerfully confronts death in the name of glory, and in the hope that his courage will earn him immortality, let him be mindful of the silence of these furrows that cover the dumb and forgotten dead!

> One day, a labourer in these same fields / Where lies the wreckage of so many battalions / Will, with his ploughshare, strike these sad remains / And find, with dread, the rusty spears / Hearing them ring against the helmets of the brave / Then, with frightened eye, look upon their bones.

14 September: We are ordered to prepare ourselves for a review before the Emperor. This is usually the prelude to a great battle, and that the truce is about to end.

16 September: We leave the environs of Austerlitz, bidding a long farewell to the ghosts of our comrades, and go towards the Hungarian frontier, halting at Mutiguez, the last town on the Moravia side of the border. The whole countryside is covered with grain that has been cut and abandoned beneath the sun that ripened it. The peasants and their horses are always subordinated, not just to the needs, but also to the caprices, of their conquerors and they are forced to watch while the corn, which cost them a whole year's work and on which their life throughout the coming year depends, is left to rot.

17 September: The Emperor's parade is postponed until tomorrow. Already, although we have travelled only 6 leagues, the dress and the ways of the people

confirm that we are near Hungary. Both the speech and the clothing are national. If the peasant sometimes has an oafish and rustic air, yet his bearing is proud and his deportment warlike. His fierce moustache proclaims the fact that he considers himself to be more than a mere peasant.

18 September: At eleven in the morning, the six regiments that make up Montbrun's division are drawn up in battle order near Goding, with 5,000 cavalrymen, all rested and well-equipped, in a single line. Proud under Napoleon's eyes, their ranks are a magnificent sight, as they stand within view of the enemy, asking nothing more than orders to attack. The Austrians, watching from a short distance away, must feel uneasy.

The Emperor arrived at two o'clock and made several appointments, granted several requests and postponed others with the words: 'When the time is ripe'; then he made us perform a charge, got back into his barouche and vanished.

All the appointments the Emperor made, and his choice of individuals, announced the coming of war unambiguously. After the parade, no one doubted for a moment that very soon the overture of a great orchestra would be heard.

The Emperor said something we thought amusing to Colonel Dery. He remarked that the shakos worn by other regiments had chinstraps and those of the 5th did not, pointing out that the head would be unprotected if a sword blow knocked off the shako. 'Sire,' responded the Colonel, 'My hussars always see the enemy's blows coming, and so are never hit.' 'Ah,' replied the Emperor, smiling, 'and if only I had a million pounds a year!'

19 September: The neighbourhood of Goding provides the best hunting country in the Empire. It is to this place that the Emperor [*i.e. of Austria – Ed.*] and the imperial family come every year.

It must not be thought that pheasants, hares and wild boars are not of great concern in the political relationship of Austria and France. The Austerlitz campaign has already cost the lives of innumerable roebuck, hares and pheasants, and our long stay here has cost them even more dearly. The Emperor's parks provide no sanctuary from the French. The deer and other game are amazed to find themselves killed, spitted and munched by the humble French soldiers, even in His Majesty's parkland. The gamekeepers are dumbfounded and admire (even as they groan at) our audacity, and the peasants, who without daring to complain, have previously been obliged to watch the animals eat their grain, are delighted at the slaughter of their enemies.

21 September: Staff Headquarters is in the little town of Auspitz and the squadron is at Tracht. When I arrived, I was pleased to hear German being spoken. This village was completely plundered by the French at the time of the battle at Znaim.

25 September: I go with my company to Unterwieternitz, a village at the foot of the mountains, and then on again to the little village of Altenmark. It must be written somewhere that we are not to be allowed a moment's peace! There is to be a grand inspection by the General of the division.

26 September: The inspection carried out by General Montbrun was very detailed and strict; afterwards we were kept occupied by manoeuvres until nightfall.

27 September: Now I am back at Altenmark, the inspection is over, and I was hoping for a little peace; my table was prepared, my books and papers taken from my portmanteau, plans for my work were clear in my head. Then suddenly a damned order arrives, doubtless dictated by the demon of awkwardness. It tells me that I must leave tomorrow, travel 14 leagues, visit forty villages one after the other, in order to find and seize all the horses.

28 September: I set off on my task, accompanied by an army of 110 men: fifty from the cavalry, fifty infantry and ten from the artillery. I finally reach the little village of Obrowitz, a suburb of Brno, wet, muddy and hungry, having had nothing in my stomach while travelling 14 leagues in the mud and heartily cursing the weather, the horses, and the duty I am engaged upon.

29 September: Having 'declared war' – that is, when I had informed the bailiff of my less-than-noble proposal to take all his horses, either by agreement or by force, I went away to organize my plan of campaign. Having seventeen strongholds – or villages – to overcome, I made my dispositions like a great general. I ordered my combined forces to different places, and tomorrow at dawn, I shall myself ride to deliver the decisive blows.

30 September: It is hard to believe to what extent the entire race of horses has been exhausted by this war and its endless requisitions: of the 400 horses I have just seen, not one of them is worth a florin.

1–2 October: I inspect the bailiwicks of Lesch and Kritschen.

3 October: I relax from my unpleasant duties with a visit to a German theatre. Although I can only speak the language very badly, yet I find it easy to appreciate how far this theatre is from the perfection of our own. As far as I can judge, from about fifteen plays I have seen, they are generally only muddles that would not be tolerated in France. Pathos and gravity, comedy and tragedy are confused together without order or authenticity. Their only merit, in the eyes of the audience at least, seems to be the frequent change of scenery. As for the music, it is as superior to ours as one would expect in a country where everyone is a musician, and where a noisy or inattentive member of the audience offends everyone and commits a crime that makes him as many

enemies as there are people in the room. They let us drink their wine, they let us cut their trees, they let us steal their horses and make love to their women, 'so be it!' they say. But to disturb their music, to whisper in a neighbour's ear during a fine passage! Ah, that is too much!

If it is possible to judge public feeling from the mood of a large gathering, I must mention an opinion that I have formed. At a time when the country is impoverished by taxes of every sort, and the people are subjected to hardships of all kinds, when nearly all those capable of bearing arms have died in battle or been driven from their homes; when, in truth, it seems that the French authorities are determined to steal everything that can be stolen and to ruin all that remains; when, it seems to me, that every citizen must see each French-man as an object of execration, yet nothing seems to affect their immutable good nature. They are not blinded by patriotism; they know how to distinguish between the individual and the government and do not confuse the weapon that wounds them with the hand that directs it. Up to that point, this shows a friendly, generous good nature, and I admire it. But when I see a woman whose husband is perhaps a prisoner or even killed, chatting freely with a French officer, when I see young girls indulging in flirtatiousness, or at least, in too great a complaisance and encouraging the bold advances of the soldiers (all with the approval of their parents), when I see them attending the theatres and other public places at a time when they should be weeping tears of blood for the wretchedness of their homeland, even as I enjoy this convenient behaviour, I judge that the patriotism of which they boast comes more from the tongue than the heart. This is no longer good nature, it is apathy and culpable weakness, and my heart indignantly rejects the disgusting thought that Russian or Austrian officers could receive a similar welcome from our sisters and wives if France were to be overcome. But no, I am sure, that although the armies of France may have penetrated the heart of Germany, no enemy army can ever reach the walls of Paris.

4 October: I am approaching a place that brings back happy memories. I marched for half the night and slept for a few hours at Rausnitz. Some old man, recalling the happy days of his youth and reliving twenty-four hours with his beloved, would not have felt more enjoyment than I, when I again saw this castle, where my days had passed so peacefully and alas, so swiftly. Monsieur Luisignan received me, not as an enemy officer arriving at a billet, but rather as a friend who had come to bid a sad farewell. The day passed quickly and I tore myself away from this well-loved place, which I shall never see again. Night had already fallen when I left to pass the night at Wischau.

6 October: I had to leave Wischau this morning, and resume my arduous and unpleasant duties as the 'Grand Inquisitor', and having inspected the horses around Rasschitz, returned to sleep at Brno.

7 October: My duties are now finished, and I have disbanded my 'army' and set off to follow the regiment by way of Kostel and Altenmark.

9 October: I am now at Lundenburg, a big village on the frontier between Moravia and Austria. Only the River Taya flows between them. This is the finest hunting country in the Empire. Every species of game is preserved in the parks here. Each separate species of game has its own park, wherein deer or wild boar may be seen in their hundreds.

11 October: To my great annoyance, we are forbidden to go into the parks, but the countryside is full of hares and I take advantage of that fact. This morning I performed very well, killing seven hares, one with every shot.

14 October: Today, the Emperor announced the anniversary of the Battle of Jena, while crowning a glorious campaign by a no less honourable peace.

24 October: Among the population here lives a different sort of people, who have their own language and distinctive dress. These individuals are nearly all employed as servants, and are called *Cravatines* [*i.e. Croats, whose mercenary soldiers introduced the cravat into France – Ed.*] by the Germans. They speak a tongue that is a mixture of Hungarian and Bohemian and their clothing, filthy for six days of the week, becomes quite different on the seventh, when the women decorate themselves with ribbons and lace, dress their hair carefully and even clean the boots that they always wear.

25 October: There is still another sort of people here, scattered in small families, who are less than human, but rather half-man, half-brute. They are truly savages, living in the woods on roots and fruit and always sleeping in the open. Sometimes, forced by hunger or extreme necessity, they may approach a little village and try to steal the vilest scraps of food from the animals. Some children and two or three women of this race live near here and often come to beg. Their speech is quite incomprehensible to me; it seems unlike any human language. They have a few phrases that they articulate strangely. Their hair is long and as black as ebony, their skin is copper-coloured and their faces are quite hideous.

26 October: The General Staff has just moved to Billowitz.

2 November: We are ordered to leave tomorrow.

3 November: The entire French Army moved off today, to evacuate Moravia. We have only to take fifty paces to find ourselves in Austria. We cross the Taya and sleep in the village of Bernadstahl.

The priests, the mayors, and the bailiffs, whose right to be spared the task of providing us with billets we have failed to respect, heave a great sigh of relief as we leave, like a man who, in a bad dream, thinks he has a heavy rock on his chest and awakens at last from his nightmare. But this rock, however, was no dream to them! The people, the unhappy people cry: 'The French leave today, but the Austrians will arrive tomorrow; we have always to cook the soup so that others may eat. We are like the ass in the story whose burden remains the same – only his saddle changes.'

5 November: We march along the banks of the River March [*i.e. Morava – Ed.*] for 5 or 6 leagues, until we see the fertile Hungarian plains and we halt at Marcheck, where I am to lodge in the castle with a Saxon general and all the Red Dragoons of Clémentz. I look in vain for Lieutenant Hauns, but he is not here. However, I find the brother of Baron Unruhe, with whom I lodged in Poland. Clémentz's Regiment, whose 8th Hussars proved so brave at Jena, was in Lasalle's division at Wagram, where it defended the most dangerous positions with a courage that earned the admiration of both the French and the Austrians. These same Saxons and the same Frenchmen, marching shoulder to shoulder, at that time spilled their blood at Wagram in the same cause. Perhaps in six months' time, a new treaty will lead them to fight against us in the ranks of the Austrians, who were their enemies on 6 July. Thus, blood, noble courage and a soldier's very life are prostituted to political considerations or sold to the wealthiest, like the labour of a mercenary!

6 November: Leaving Marcheck, we turned towards the Danube, and with my company, I occupied the villages of Prama, Croatisch, Wagram and Strandorf.

8 November: I left Prama to go to Strandorf, where I am barely a league from the battlefield, on an immense plain covered with fine villages. But this fertile land has been ravaged and exhausted by the two armies, which have occupied it in turn.

14 November: I hear that a family friend – Madame de Vertamy – is, at present, in Vienna.

I have travelled from end to end of this battlefield [*the fields of Aspern–Essling and Wagram – Ed.*], made forever memorable by the four days of carnage (21–22 May and 5–6 July) that it suffered. After four months, I had not expected to find so many traces of it remaining. Marks of men's fury and signs of death are still deeply engraved on this unhappy land. I can identify our positions and those of the Austrians. Here are the redoubts where so many died, and the entrenchments where numberless French were killed, and here is the square tower that was to be the scene of conflict by 300,000 men for twenty-four hours! I walk across the detritus and reach the miserable village of Grossaspern and the notorious Esslingen – taken and retaken so many times. There are deep ditches, heaps of earth, decomposing bodies, and even worse, the dreadful clouds of ravens, reminding the horrified spectator of the scenes that so recently took place here. The town itself no longer exists, though the rows of chimneys, the charred beams and the remains of broken walls, form a hideous skeleton of a town. The lead-covered bell tower, half-melted in the fire, had collapsed onto the priest's house, while a half-burned tabernacle still remains in the bullet-riddled Sanctuary. I searched for a place where a man might have stood to be safe from a mortal blow, but could find one nowhere. I looked uneasily at the earth that covered so many corpses and feared to see their blood spurt up between my feet. I sleep at Vienna.

15 November: Vienna. I spent today with a delightful gentleman as interesting as he is kind; this is the Prince de Ligne. He is seventy-nine, but has preserved the activity and habits of a young man. While retaining the vivacity of a seventeen-year-old, he combines the gallantry of a young soldier with the sophistication of a forty-year-old courtier. He was the friend of Frederick the Great and of Catherine of Russia, with both of whom he corresponded; these letters, he tells me, are in print. The Prince – in his manners, taste and habits – expresses his love of France as well as his antipathy for the Germans. I found his judgement of the Austrian court and generals too favourable to be able to agree with his opinions; in any event, I do not know how much military knowledge he possesses. According to him, the councils of the Austrian Army have been guided by ill-considered enthusiasm, stupidity and chaos. Their army had attacked without making provision either for victory or for defeat, and it embarked on the campaign before any real plan had been prepared. I met Collins again and spent the evening with him.

16 November: Before leaving Vienna, I went to inspect some of the ramparts. What a sight for anyone with any feeling for his country. All the fortifications have been blown up and have fallen into the moat. This operation, which was much more of an insult than of practical use – for the suburbs would have prevented the use of heavy guns – has deeply wounded the feelings of the townspeople. They pardoned our victories, and the inevitable misery of the conquered, far more easily; but the humiliation and stain on the honour of their capital city for no military reason, has alienated many hearts and fermented civil unrest.

17 November: I am doing, on a small-scale, what conquerors do so very often. I am sending home my spoils from the conquered countries, but my trophies, at least, have not caused anyone to shed tears. I have asked Madame de Vertamy to take with her to Paris the notes I have made in different places, some maps, some drawings and some souvenirs of the countries. When I am at last at peace in my home, these things will remind me of my travels in distant lands. This notebook, too, will take its place in my father's house; reading it will cheer my dear father and remind him of the campaigns of his own youth. It will make my kind mother tremble as she learns of the dangers past and alert a brother, still a

child, and make him cry: 'I too will go to the war when I grow up.' Such thoughts as these make writing the journal a pleasure; but I see there are still many blank pages to be filled, who knows where I shall be when I write in them?

18 November: We receive the order to leave tomorrow.

19 November: The regiment gathers near Esslingen, and we march right across the battlefield [*of Aspern–Essling – Ed.*]. Something that I could not have believed if I had not seen it with my own eyes, as well as the dead horses, the cannon balls and debris of all kinds that cover the plains, there are also many bodies still in view. It is possible even to identify, from the rags of uniform, the regiment to which these cadavers belonged. Some are stretched out along the road and for five months, have vainly begged the passer-by to perform the last sad office of burial. The ravens, following their natural instincts, help them to the oblivion they crave by hastening the destruction of these tragic remains. What a sight this is! To write of it demands the pen of one able properly to express the tragedy and the dignity! But all creatures show their feelings in their own way. Soldiers, watching the hordes of croaking ravens, shout out cheerfully; 'Look at the rascals, they are eating our friends' eyes!'

Who knows what diseases will flourish in the heat of summer? One cannot blame the country people for having failed to bury these dead, for the miserable inhabitants have enough troubles of their own. Sickness has cut down those who escaped the flames and starvation has carried off nearly all the others. An eyewitness has reported that fourteen burning villages could be seen from Vienna on 22 May; and on 5 and 6 June, all those places that had escaped in May, were destroyed. These plains, populous and fertile a year ago, present a spectacle of utter devastation, and only silence – as of a vast cemetery – reigns there. The earth is everywhere scored by shot, so that I crossed a considerable distance without seeing one spot where a man could have stood unscathed. What a slaughter there must have been of the infantry battalions!

We entered Vienna, and lodged in the suburb of Mariahilfe. I saw the Prince de Ligne and his family again.

20 November: We mounted at eight in the morning and the brigade formed into battle order under the walls of Vienna, where we remained for twelve hours without moving, exposed to the freezing cold. This was one of the most unpleasant days of the whole campaign. It is said that there have been difficulties concerning the taxes that have been exacted. We slept at Kitzing.

21 November: We took the main road to Saint-Pölten and the regiment stationed itself near Sigartz Kirchen. The Staff is at Zweitendorf and I am at Trasdorf, 9 leagues from Vienna. This is a horrible place.

4 December: This is my twenty-fourth birthday. Time has flown past and the uncertainty of the future has reduced to very brief time that which once seemed to stretch interminably before me.

12 December: This is a horrible hovel. My room is cold, the food is filthy and there is no company. Time is passing for me, just now, like a very old man bowed down with infirmities; but my studies profit from my loss of pleasure.

15 December: We are to leave tomorrow.

16 December: The 2nd Squadron is ordered to form the rearguard of the army. Today, we leave this nasty village, something that we may be reduced to regretting in the future, and reach Wasserburg. It is impossible to convey the extent of the suffering endured by villages like this one. Nevertheless, we are kindly received and there are more supplies here than one would have expected. It is hard to say which is the more astonishing, the availability of food in these places, which have been plundered daily for eight months, or the typical German good nature still displayed by the inhabitants, quite unaltered by the outrages and losses they have suffered. They are wise enough to bear the curse of war without rising up against those who inflict it.

17 December: We stop at the little village of Heinrichstein. Those who wish to gain some idea of the ravages of the vandals, need only look at the big houses near the main road. Apart from the usual marks of avarice, signs of stupidity and sheer wickedness are visible everywhere: it is clear that these bandits in the guise of soldiers have perpetrated evil acts just for the pleasure of doing them; pictures have been slashed with swords and bayonets, stoves smashed with rifle-butts, chandeliers smashed to a thousand pieces, cabinets of porcelain completely shattered, and so on. How such excesses dishonour our armies and force a groan from those who hear the words: 'This is the work of the French.'

18 December: We go through the small town of Melk and halt at Erlauf, villages that were burned to the ground during our earlier passage. It is cheering to see that some of the houses are being rebuilt in the surrounding ruins.

19 December: To appreciate the meaning of the term 'muddy' in the fullest sense of the word, it would be necessary to see us after we have travelled 8 or 9 leagues. Roads that have been impossible to repair during the war have been churned up in the bad weather by the passage of the artillery and baggage wagons of the whole army. What a pleasure it is to form the rearguard of the army in these circumstances!

20 December: We have at last crossed the River Enns, which should mark the end of this second stage. At least a rest might make up for the weariness of the journey; but no, after marching for about fifteen hours in the snow and the

mud, we arrive at the home of an unfortunate peasant and have to squeeze into a smoky hovel and try to dry our uniforms. All too often, on the following day, we have to put them on again, still soaked in the rain of yesterday. Tomorrow, at least, we may rest on our straw until midday, if we want to, and this is a small consolation.

29 December: I am now in the village of Oberndorf, a league from Enns, and visit the famous convent of Saint Florian, though this is not a good time to do so. The war has caused great suffering here, the convent has been pillaged several times and a large part of the building is being used as a hospital. The immense revenues of its ecclesiastical owners render them powerful landlords; they might be compared to rats in a hermitage made out of Dutch cheese. The church here is very beautiful and very wealthy, possessing two organs, one of which is reputed to be the finest in Austria and has, at present, an organist worthy of the instrument. In the galleries, the pictures are more remarkable for their number than their quality, although it is true that our known taste for stealing works of art has caused the finest pieces to be hidden away. However, the most interesting room in this fine monastery is the library, where there are more than 30,000 books as well as some precious manuscripts. My attention was fixed on a large volume, in which the writing of many interesting individuals had been preserved. I examined it for a long while before I became convinced that it was an engraving, but I still could not comprehend how the irregularities of a hundred different pens could have been reproduced so exactly with a chisel.

31 December: Tomorrow there is to be a rigorous inspection by General Montbrun. This means we shall spend ten or twelve hours with our feet in the snow and the icy cold. What a wretched Christmas present!

1 January 1810: The General's inspection has been cancelled and we are warned to be ready to leave the day after tomorrow.

3 January: The regiment crosses the Traun at Ebersburg. This is a name that will long be remembered by the French as both glorious and terrible. The town now resembles a convalescent at last attempting to take a few uncertain steps, and who, while having escaped death, still bears its imprint: half-burned beams serve to support newly-built roofs; blackened walls, pock-marked with bullet holes, are ornamented with new doors and windows. The cheerful look of these houses in the midst of the ruins, makes the debris surrounding them appear even more tragic. After marching for twelve hours, we camp by the light of torches in the farms around Schmidnig.

4 January: We again travel along the Traun and through Lambach, where I am shown the spot where we first encountered the Russians in the Austerlitz

campaign. We march through Schwanenstadt, a name that has attracted different meanings; town of the swans, of sponges, of pigtails or of pigs. The desolate time of year makes the latter name more suitable. We halted at last in the village of Alsbach.

5 January: At last, I find myself in one of the good billets such as are seldom grabbed by junior officers; it is sad that Messieurs, the senior officers, have sensitive noses in such matters and will soon find me and throw me out. Then, as is the custom, I shall find myself worse off than the others, having preserved nothing of my former comfort except the memory – and the trouble of moving.

My host is a senior cleric, very rich, well-educated, fond of good living and of hunting. Among all his compliments and attentiveness, I search in vain for true German warmth. I think that he is deeply egotistical, but this is well-hidden behind an appearance of smiling friendship.

15 January: Thirty *louis*, fruit of my economies, that I had intended to devote to the well-being of my company, has just been stolen from my senior sergeant.

19 January: I was not mistaken about the secret aim of my clergyman's courtesy. As long as I was the only person here, I was, according to him, the best educated, the friendliest and the best brought up of all the French officers: all this flattery was with a view to ensuring that he had to billet as few men as possible. Since the arrival of the General at the Kepach château, I seem to have lost many of my good qualities – or rather, the flattery has been sent to a different address. A secret request has been made to remove this delightful captain, who had been so very welcome a few days earlier. The service and the food at the château have so much to gain from the goodwill of this cleric that it was impossible to refuse him a request, from the effects of which, after all, only junior officers and a hundred men would suffer. By one of those miracles, which must be believed rather than understood, it was found that an area which, before making the acquaintance of the priest, could support two squadrons, is today unable to accommodate a single company. Whatever the reason, I am ordered to leave tomorrow with my company to go 8 leagues, near to Haag.

20 January: Now, here I am once more, established in a hamlet of four houses, alone in the middle of the forest, in the house of a poor, and very dirty peasant, who is far from welcoming. My lodging is no different from that of the lowliest *chasseur* in the company; in all the previous six years I have never had one that was worse. This delightful place is called Vinessling, and is a league and a half from Haag.

23 January: At last, I must tell you about my precious money. I am now waiting for a storm to burst over my head. I know that this affair may prove to be a trap

spread at my feet, but a well-ballasted ship can await a storm with confidence and I am determined to confront whatever may happen.

24 January: For the first time in many long years, soldiers hear talk of leave and of retirement; but, and this is difficult to believe, the longing for it has almost ceased to exist in most of them. The passage of time, absence, and a different way of life has loosened the bonds that tied them to their families and to the places where they were born. And as a man must attach himself to something, custom has led them to form new families among their comrades to replace the old ties. Very few men have expressed a wish to put off their uniform. Army orders seem to indicate that there will be a long peace. A reorganization in the cavalry is also spoken of.

25 January: The storm has burst. The priest, while writing the most complimentary letters to me and busying himself with having restitution made to me for the theft I suffered has, at the same time, secretly stirred up complaints against me, and finally denounced me himself. I received an order to return the money and to remain under close arrest. As for the second part of the order, the weather makes it impossible to do anything else; but as to the first, I refuse to comply. When all is known, it will be seen which of the two has the right to tell the tale.

N.B. The theft took place in the absence of Duquet, without the lock of the chest having been broken; two similar thefts from the French had been perpetrated at the same inn – under my questioning the innkeeper was terrified and promised restitution. The bailiff repeated these promises but he put me off from day-to-day, reiterating his vows and promises. When we were leaving, he told me that he would pay nothing. I had the innkeeper arrested; he offered me the money, and I left a sergeant to receive it and went away. The General arrived, and caused the money to be given up to the thief. I seized the community's horses and wrote a threatening letter to the bailiff. With the most flattering words, the priest offered to mediate while, at the same time, making a formal accusation against me.

26 January: I receive the money by way of the priest, and on the 25th am placed in close arrest in accordance with his recommendation. I refuse to return the money. I write to the General of the division and produce letters that prove the bailiff's double-dealing, and demand that the matter be brought before Marshal Davout. I do not mention the fact that I have in my possession orders from the Colonel authorizing my actions, so that he could appear to disown me.

27 January: The brigade has undergone a rigorous inspection near Thalem. My close arrest has deprived me of the incomparable pleasure of standing for seven or eight hours with my feet in the snow. While my comrades shivered, sword in hand, I lay peacefully stretched in an armchair with my feet towards the stove.

31 January: My close arrest has been lifted and I remain in possession of the money.

8 February: Now here I am at Payerbach, a little town on the way to Passau. My host is a good old priest, who has neither the servile eagerness of the last one nor the harsh, sullen aspect of some of the others.

25 February: Days pass here with a gentle monotony, divided between walking and studying. Some good books in two languages occupy the many leisure hours my duties leave to me. Horse riding in the neighbourhood relaxes the mind while it tires the body, and the sharp air from the snow-covered mountains ensures that the fireside is fully appreciated when one returns. I know that, when I return to my lodging, I shall find a friendly welcome, a modest meal willingly offered, and good-natured and interesting conversation. There are many officers who would laugh to see a young French captain, alone in the midst of half a dozen German priests; one who prefers their conversation to the noisy shouts of his comrades. But each word of this talk, in a foreign language, brings me both difficulty and triumph. Every phrase I utter is a problem overcome; every correct phrase is a pleasure that rewards my tedious studies. Above all, my pride is satisfied and I can happily say: 'I achieved this by myself!'

1 March: The Colonel came to say 'goodbye' to us, yesterday. He is leaving for France. Perhaps I shall follow him soon, I do not know, but except for my family, I have no wish to go. All the feelings that draw me towards France are concentrated in the narrow circle of ties of blood; even the thought of leaving Germany makes me unhappy. Certainly, I shall feel moved when I reach the left bank of the Rhine, but I shall look over my shoulder at the other shore with regret and tenderness.

7 March: We have been ordered to go with all speed to Braunau, there to provide an escort for the future Empress of the French. We shall leave tomorrow, at dawn.

8 March: Today has been the same as a day on campaign. Leaving Payerbach at dawn, we covered 14 leagues in the mud and pouring rain and find ourselves, hungry and weary – as necessity knows no law – sharing military lodgings in the hamlet of Saint-George with the Portuguese. What a subject for thought! The Portuguese, transplanted from the banks of the Tagus, are following the French eagles into the depths of Germany, while the armies of England, France and their own people are disputing the remains of their divided homeland.

9 March: At dawn, we were on our way to Braunau, but the order was countermanded and we set out for Obernberg, a pretty little town on the banks

of the Inn. A plain, covered with woods, villages, farms and hamlets, stretches as far as the eye can see, and there is a magnificent waterfall just outside the town walls. When spring arrives there will be nothing left to wish for.

10 March: I had scarcely installed myself in my billet and unpacked the last item in my portmanteau, when I had to mount my horse again and set off once more in the mud. I was to occupy a miserable hamlet called Oberfreiling and take up residence in a mill. The four walls of my room are made out of planks, very badly joined together. A bench, built into these walls, runs right round the apartment. Although I can take no more than three paces in any direction, I possess five windows, and it is still too dark to see clearly even at midday. Bad food, dirty maidservant, horrible lodging!

12 March: How one moment can change our ideas, our plans and our future! Just when I expected it the least, I learn that permission for three months' leave has arrived for me at Headquarters. However, I shall not be granted this leave yet; I am also told that I am to be retained until the end of our present duty.

14 March: Although it is for only a day, one must seize any opportunity when it is offered. I leave my room – or rather my coffin – in Oberfreiling, and go to the small hamlet of Oberndorf. On my way I notice that the houses in this area – at least those in the villages – all have a wooden, painted balcony covered with an awning.

16 March: At last the day has dawned when the future Empress of the French must take a solemn farewell of her native land, and place herself in the hands of her new subjects. Her accession will surely promise a time of happiness, but this has not yet arrived, for the rain continues to fall upon us in torrents, and all the warmth of our enthusiasm does not suffice to dry us out.

We leave our shacks in the darkness of a stormy night. We reach the gates of Braunau after travelling for 6 leagues by land and water. The brigade assembles in the most magnificent uniforms; the infantry are in white breeches, at least that is the intention, but the surrounding mud makes it impossible to distinguish the colour. Twenty-two thousand men are under arms. The white pipeclay spread on their equipment proves, at least, that pains that have been taken to appear clean. The floating plumes of the cavalry, intended to bestow a martial and gallant air upon them, are now all spiky and limp in the rain and makes them look like unhappy, defeated gamecocks. Half a league from Braunau an elegantly decorated wooden pavilion has been prepared; it is divided into three apartments. At either end of it float the banners of France and Austria, each of its doors is painted in the national colours. The Noble Guard of Hungary is stationed along the avenue that leads towards Vienna, French troops occupy the exit in the other direction. It is in the central room that the exchange, that is to unite and mingle the interests of the two peoples, will be made.

At two o'clock the Archduchess Marie-Louise arrives, escorted by the two Archdukes, her brothers, and by Duke Arrighi and Prince Berthier. She is received, in her room, by the Queen of Naples [*i.e. Caroline, Napoleon's youngest sister, who had married Marshal Murat, now King of Naples – Ed.*], who should have assumed the title of 'Stewardess of the House' but had refused to do so, being beneath her dignity as a queen. After having spent about an hour in the pavilion, the whole escort set off towards Braunau, where all the church bells rang among shouted acclamations and the repeated salvoes of the artillery. These same bronze cannon that, only eight months earlier, had brought death to the Austrian ranks and shook the throne of Emperor Francis I, today celebrated, with a less menacing uproar, the accession of his daughter to the throne of France.

Night fell, and when the rain stopped for a while, illuminations were lit. A rainbow, appearing in the sky, seemed to form a triumphal arch above the new Empress as she entered her new country. But the soldiers nodded crossly and said: 'There'll be more rain tomorrow.' The peasants, greedy to observe marvels, viewed the sight as a miracle, presaging a long period of peace. However, the night wore on, leaving the hungry soldiers in the mud. Officers of the three cavalry regiments gathered to celebrate the event with a sumptuous and noisy meal; wine warmed heads, and one forgot that one was wet and would be forced to sleep on the floor.

17 March: We mounted at dawn, and escorted the coach of Marie-Louise for 2 leagues. Her face shone with calm and serenity. Through the door on the other side of the coach, one saw the Queen of Naples, whose glance, swift and coquettish, followed the young man galloping at her side: her looks were too eloquent to be misunderstood. One might dare to gaze into her eyes, sparkling with youth and voluptuousness. The Queen noticed this and smiled. Then the coaches disappeared, everyone dispersed. As for me, I left my company and returned to Oberndorf, where I changed horses and left immediately for Payerbach. I rode through Ried and Spitemberg. I rode all day, without stopping for rest or food. Nightfall, at last, halted my journey at Riedau and on the morrow, the 18th, I was again in the home of my kindly priest at Payerbach.

The joy of the people there was as sincere as it was universal; everyone behaved like a person who had been delivered from great danger, especially the peasants on whom the burden of war had fallen most heavily. The wretched Bavarian peasant, who has been repeatedly plundered by both armies, now dares to hope he might be allowed to reap the harvest he has sown. He dares not allow himself to contemplate the possible union of the French and the Austrian armies into a single scourge. The memory of the misery inflicted on him by their quarrels is too recent!

19 March: I am on my way to the Headquarters.

20 March: My journey brings me to the Château de Tholet, where the Staff Headquarters is stationed. The thaw has made the roads very dangerous; for melting snow has made the earth so soft, one might be in the middle of shifting sand and many of the pathways have turned into torrents. I spent the night at Greiskirchen, where the Headquarters suite is lodged.

21 March: This morning I took leave of my comrades, received their assignments for France, and dawn found me on the main road to Paris.

22 March: Passau. I left Payerbach and the regiment yesterday. All travellers experience abrupt and swift changes of scene: yesterday I was peacefully at the home of a kindly priest, and today find myself in the confusion of a city. One can hardly move in Passau, for the town is so full of officers, coaches and wagons etc., etc. I find a friend in Maastricht, a sincere and virtuous friend, but I find also, a dangerous siren, the sight of whom brings back the memory of past mistakes. So it is that in life a poisonous fruit is found near to a flower. One of the officers of the regiment is to be my companion on my journey. Our affairs are settled and a barouche purchased. Tomorrow we shall set out on a journey that will only end when we are reunited with our families.

23 March: We should have been on our way at dawn, but it was not so easy to free oneself from the embrace of pleasure. I do not speak of myself, for I played the part of Mentor, tearing Telemachus from Calypso's Isle. I notice – to my great advantage – how demeaning an attachment to someone unworthy can be. Nevertheless, by eleven o'clock we are on our way. Marie followed us to the first stopping place (Wilshofen), where, by a painful, last effort, I contrived to separate my too amorous companion from her. Now we are at Pleinting, where we are to spend the night, for there are no fresh horses to be had. We have only travelled 17 leagues, but it is something to be on our way.

24 March: Six leagues were covered before we had our breakfast in the village of Dingolfing, and then we continued on our way, crossing the Iser at Landshut.

25 March: After travelling all through the night, at dawn we changed horses at Freising and reached Dachau just as high mass was ending. A lot of peasants had gathered in the square. I should have liked to conjure up, as if by magic, a dozen of our French villagers, so that I could enjoy their mutual astonishment, for no part of Germany has so impressed me with the singularity of the costume worn there. The women are encased, front and rear from the waist upwards in large shields made of light planks or painted pasteboard, while the layers of skirts that they wear give them the appearance of an upside-down funnel.

But even as I examined their grotesque clothes, our barouche set off again. The weather was fine and the countryside flat so that by nightfall we reached Augsbourg, where we enjoyed a few hours' rest.

26 March: Our journey today ended at Ulm, a place memorable and glorious to the French, where, four years ago, it became the brilliant prelude to the victories that marked their progress. I looked on this place that I remembered as ruined and desolate, with great surprise and pleasure, for it was covered with vines, well-cultivated gardens and pretty houses. For thus kindly nature and men's labour combine to repair the destruction that rage so endlessly inflicts.

We left Ulm at nine in the evening. The road being as flat as a promenade, we hoped for a comfortable and swift journey: but towards midnight, just as weariness was closing our eyes, we received a rude shock. We were overturned; I was underneath with d'Evry on top; we crawled out of our cage on our stomachs. The peasant responsible for crashing us into a milestone, fearing our justified anger, yelled at the top of his voice that he was dead (demonstrating his perfect health by the noise he made); meanwhile, my unfortunate servant, who had been on the box seat, had been thrown 10 feet away and now rose, groaning, with a broken wrist. However, we had to set the smashed barouche back on its wheels, repair it as far as we could, and grumbling and swearing, travel another 5 leagues to Geislingen, arriving at dawn.

27 March: We arrived in the domain of the King of Württemberg. Fortunately, it was late, otherwise we might have traversed the kingdom of this potentate without having eaten or drunk. The condition of my servant made it necessary for us to pass the rest of the night at Vahingen. This is the third time I have been in this lovely countryside; it could justly be called the garden of Europe. The towns and the villages are wealthy and populous; the faces of the people proclaim health and happiness.

28 March: As a French officer, it is delightful to travel post through Germany. When the post house is reached, there is nothing to pay; do you wish to leave at once? Everyone hurries to help you (so as to get rid of you as quickly as possible). If you ask for nothing except horses (free of charge, of course) you are admired for your moderation. If you wish to sleep or dine, you are taken to the best inn, and when you leave, are rewarded by the lowest of bows. Such is the hospitality and good nature of the Germans, and these virtues are only matched by the insatiable voracity of the insect parasites to be found there. But, should a French traveller reach a town where authority is in the hands of one of his compatriots, he will experience a thousand difficulties, a thousand restrictions; there is no help for him. Selfishness has grasped everything. A French commandant shows himself to be more rapacious towards the citizens than they are towards a stranger, or even towards an enemy.

We changed horses at Pforzheim; memories of this place made me feel four years younger. Then, I was eighteen years old, a lieutenant of hussars at the start of a career and in a country where everything was new to me. How quickly time has passed; I wonder if time will rush past so rapidly in the future?

We stopped for new horses at Ettingen and they took us as far as Rastadt. We continued on our journey, ending the day at Bischofsheim.

29 March: Strasbourg. Today, at eleven in the morning, I stood once again in my homeland. As I crossed the famous bridge that has become the path of victory for the French, my heart was filled with so many emotions, it would be impossible to describe any one of them. I thought of the multitude of French, who like me, had crossed this bridge and whose bones now lie far from their homes. More fortunate than they, I return to all that is most dear to me, and yet I look back to Germany, of which I have such pleasant memories. I feel like a child, who returning to the arms of a beloved mother, must tear himself away from a childhood friend who he may never see again.

Having speedily completed our business in Strasbourg, we packed ourselves into our carriage again, every limb aching, and obtained post horses, but there was this difference: from now on, we should have to put our hands in our pockets. Only the thought that I should not have to stop again before reaching Paris, made me oblivious to my weariness.

30 March: We had lunch at Saverne, dined at Lunéville, drunk our dessert wine at Nancy and come what may, are spending another night on board our carriage.

1 April: I arrive, at last, in plenty of time to give my parents a delightful April Fool's surprise. There was so much to talk about after an absence so long, and involving so many dangers. There were so many accounts begun and interrupted, restarted and interrupted again by loving embraces! All the weariness of nine days in a cramped barouche was forgotten in a moment. Such a meeting could wipe out any amount of pains and suffering.

2 April: Today I saw with my own eyes, a great event, the influence of which will be felt in all the courts of Europe. I was in the gallery of the Louvre to witness this forever-memorable union. It is for the historian to describe the details, for the poet to honour it and for the painter to depict the spectacle – the most imposing and magnificent in all of history. I shall not speak of the sumptuousness of the clothes or the splendour of the ceremony. As an obscure spectator, lost in the immensity of the crowd, I shall describe only those details I found most striking. All eyes were fixed upon the Emperor. Despite the solemnity of his progress, consciousness of his glory and his state shone in his face. That of the Archduchess Marie-Louise expressed majesty and decorum; one saw that her heart could not contain all the emotions that beset it; quite

apart from the thoughts the occasion must have awoken in her, she could not have forgotten that the throne she ascended was still stained with the blood of her unhappy aunt [*i.e. Marie-Antoinette (1755–1793), Queen of France – Ed.*], and that the insolent hand, on which she was about bestow her own, had just shaken her father's empire to its foundations! Five queens carried the new Empress's train, but the Queen of Holland seemed to bear most of the burden, and it appeared to weigh heavily upon her! It was the same cloak that, at a happier time for the family, had been worn to the altar by her mother, the Empress Josephine. A similar sorrow, but one endured with nobility of spirit, could be discerned on the face of her brother, Eugène, the Viceroy of Italy. But anger could also darken a brow that wore a crown! An insulting glow of delight in her good fortune, shone in the eyes of the Queen of Naples, and was reflected to some degree in the faces of her relations. The bearing of Madame Mère [*i.e. Letizia Bonaparte, Napoleon's mother – Ed.*] was the most dignified and imposing of any of them; in it could be read the pride that filled her maternal heart as she contemplated the heights to which her son's destiny had elevated him. As for the spectators, there was none of the tumultuous joy that had formerly burst from these noisy, cheerful people; the long, sorrowful years had, at last, subdued their gaiety, but surprise, admiration and hope could be seen on every face. A man, suddenly snatched from danger and strife, still remembers his past struggles too vividly to appreciate immediately the prize of peace he is about to enjoy.

[*Editor's note: the 'five queens' that carried the Empress's train were, in reality: Hortense, Queen of Holland and wife of Louis Bonaparte; Julie, Queen of Spain and wife of Joseph Bonaparte; Catherine, Queen of Westphalia and wife of Jérôme Bonaparte; Napoleon's first sister Elisa, Grand Duchess of Tuscany; and Napoleon's second sister Pauline, Princess Borghese. Napoleon's third sister Caroline, Queen of Naples and wife of Marshal Murat, walked in front of the Empress; as did Augusta Amalia, Princess of Bavaria and wife of the Viceroy of Italy.*]

9 April: Having enjoyed the happiness of seeing my dearest relatives again, it is only right to visit the rest of the family, and with my mother, I shall leave tomorrow for Orléans.

10 April: I wonder if, after long absence, I shall always be fortunate enough to see again all of those I left behind.

11–14 April: I have spent the days very happily with the friends with whom I grew up, and in whose company I first left home to begin the turmoil of military life. Now, like pigeons scattered by a gust of wind, we now, at last, find ourselves all returning to the dovecote. I say 'all' but I am wrong. Sainvilliers is still far away in a foreign country – that evil country, the theatre of crimes and horrors [*i.e. Spain – Ed.*].

16 April: I return to Paris.

10 May: Now that our family is sufficiently separated from the court we are no longer obliged to play a part in matters of importance to the country. Tomorrow, I am to go with my father to visit one who, for a while, occupied the French throne and who still reigns in our hearts.

[*Editor's note: a reference to Tascher's distant cousin, the Empress Josephine (1763–1814). Born Marie Rose Josephine Tascher de la Pagerie, she married Vicompte Alexandre de Beauharnais in 1779 at the age of sixteen; was widowed in 1794; and married Napoleon in 1796.*]

11 May: We began our drive to Evreux at dawn; so beautiful was the country through which we passed that it was less like a drive on a public road than a promenade in a lovely garden. On our left, the Seine wound its way through fertile fields and smiling valleys, with handsome mansions and exquisite gardens to claim our admiration at every moment. As we passed by, the old Château de Rosny caught my eye, the modest retreat of a great and powerful minister, a faithful subject and generous friend [*Sully, a minister under Henry IV – Ed.*]. At last, when we had gone through Evreux, we reached the end of the handsome avenue that leads to the Château of Navarre [*Napoleon sent Josephine to this castle, several miles from Evreux, to keep her out of the capital when his new Empress, Marie Louise, arrived – Ed.*]. The sight of this castle, once the cherished home of Henry IV and now occupied by a deposed Empress, moved me deeply. If the ghost of the great Henry, who, they say, still haunts this spot, could speak to his illustrious hostess, he would hold out his hand to her and say: 'How happy I am to see you. You have cared for my people; you are worthy to reign over them, for you still reign over their hearts.' Today, with my mind full of thoughts of Henry IV, I look around to see if I can discover traces of him, but alas, they no longer exist.

12 May: The whole of the evening yesterday was spent in gilded salons filled with equerries, chamberlains and ladies-in-waiting. As for me, in an effort to preserve my composure while conforming to the strict rules of etiquette, I would perhaps approach a lady, as I searched my vacant mind in vain for some suitably gallant remark, or perhaps I might approach a group engaged in quiet conversation and when someone spoke, I would smilingly agree, without having understood a word that was said. From time to time I cast an envious eye on the children who were running about in the lovely gardens, I should have been so happy to join them. This morning, early, one of her Majesty's coaches came for us to take us to lunch. Before presenting myself 'on parade' and knowing that the Empress had still not arrived in the salon, I slipped away to look around the estate. I should have liked to examine the place in more detail, but I saw, at a window, my father waving to me and making urgent signs

for me to return to the salon, where the Empress was about to make her entrance. I made haste to add to the number of her courtiers.

Immediately after luncheon, a drive through the woods was organized. The woods that belonged to Navarre and were part of Napoleon's gift extended for about 19,000 *arpents* [*an* arpent *is about an acre and a half – Ed.*] and paths had been opened through them to offer vistas of the castle and surrounding countryside.

On our return from the drive an elegant and sumptuous meal was served, which went on until nightfall, when we were permitted, at last, to escape from ritual decorum and return to our beds at the inn.

We had planned to leave early, but the slightest wish of a 'great one' is an order. The Empress had indicated that she wished us to remain longer, and so our departure was postponed. In the morning, one of the coaches from the court came early to fetch us. All the courtiers were gathered on one of the terraces, all in morning dress. Josephine soon appeared, accompanied by the Princesses of Baden and Arenberg. The greatest skill and the most elegant simplicity in her toilette had been combined to repair, 'The irreparable insult of the years.'

Her gracious and ethereal smile made her attractive, even before she spoke, and her gaze, at once sweet and charming, expressed an inner beauty that confirmed she was as good as she was lovely. Yes, beautiful and seductive in spite of her forty-five years. From what I saw this morning, it could be said, without hyperbole, that she was the elder sister of the Graces.

When all the courtiers were gathered together, it was proposed that a walk through the gardens should be enjoyed before luncheon. We began in the Garden of Hebe, where we admired the streams that flowed swiftly over pebbles by the side of the pathways, the thickets of roses and of lilacs in flower, delighting in the fresh, scented air. My only criticism would be that here I found the lawns too closely cut, the pathways too smooth. In a word, art had been allowed to intrude too much where nature's charm alone should have reigned.

The Isle of Love, to which we went next, must be the happiest of retreats for the gentle refugee of Navarre. It is a sort of amphibious garden, half-land, half-water. Wherever one looked there were cascades, pools, waterfalls, fountains; at every step one thought a spring might burst forth. Perhaps it might be objected that there were too many naiads [*i.e. a water-nymph – Ed.*], but everything was so beautiful that, no matter how far one wandered, one dared not find any fault.

After lunch, when everyone retired to dress for dinner, we slipped away to our inn. Thanks to the speed of the post horses and the good road, we reached Paris on the same day.

19 May: I am at the home of my sister, Madame d'Havrincourt.

25 May: Today, I went with my father to visit the Empress Josephine at Malmaison. Of all the delightful houses that surround Paris, this one is most admired for its situation. Even before a royal hand had beautified it, nature had given it a well-deserved reputation. Enormous expense, guided by perfect taste, has added every possible advantage to this happy spot. This mansion, appearing from the outside to be a simple dwelling, is a veritable miniature palace within.

2 June: Cannon fire proclaims the arrival in Paris of the Emperor. This is a moment longed for by the people, who are always avid for spectacle, and by foreigners, who have come from afar and at great expense. Now their curiosity, excited by accounts of these sights, will be satisfied.

3 June: The celebrations of monarchs are hardly ever enjoyable. Pleasure is a nervous child, frightened by noise, and who, when summoned at great expense, seldom keeps the appointment.

While awaiting these pompous pageants, which may, perhaps, occupy a few pages in the history books, I took my part in a more modest festival that will not be remembered – except in the annals of happiness. There are many places in Paris devoted to public entertainments; the city itself is full of them. It is in them that, most often on Sundays, ordinary people have their gatherings. Here, too, men of all ranks divest themselves of their ranks and titles, and gladly mix with the crowd in simple everyday clothes. Among the assemblies of this type, the one that best contrives to unite liberty, pleasure and decency, the one in which the different classes of society can meet without confusion, and that offers the best variety of amusements is, without doubt, the Tivoli Gardens. It would need the brush of Delille properly to depict the happy sights and spectacles to be seen here. In time to delightful music, couples dance, chatter and laugh. Near the woods, mothers of families with their little children sit around and admire the skill of Olivier the famous illusionist; the peasant from the outskirts of the town watches, his eyes wide and his mouth hanging open, uttering only cries of amazement, while the shop assistant, in his new clothes, sneers and points at him and with a knowledgeable air, explains how simple are the matters of which he does not understand a single word.

Some distance away, a group gathers round a gurner [*a grimacer or face-puller – Ed.*] to admire the amazing flexibility of his face. Here, two or three flirtatious girls have separated an unsophisticated young man from the crowd and fight over him with their brazen chatter. Over there, a happy couple sees a longed-for opportunity, and steals away swiftly from the watchfulness of a worried mother or the anxiety of an unfortunate husband, and rushes into the darkest pathway where, seeing no one near them, they feel themselves to be alone in the world.

When night falls, the gardens become a magic palace. The sunlight is brilliantly replaced by thousands of lamps around the circle where groups of people now gather, curious to see some wonderful spectacle. It may be the intrepid Guernerin rising in his hot-air balloon, or perhaps Madame Sacchi, or Ravel or Forioso, suspended in midair, enchanting and terrifying the spectator with their skill and courage. Now a flash of light is followed by thunder, and fireworks burst out on all sides, criss-crossing in the air. Suddenly, at the summit of a pyramid of fire, a beautifully dressed woman appears, a white plume floats from her head and in her hand, is a magic wand. She sways gracefully in the air; there is something ethereal in her movements, as she advances confidently through the intensifying fire. The spectators gasp their admiration, but soon, true emblem of human fallibility, the light dims, the fire pales, everything vanishes, leaving only a thick haze and smoking debris. The crowd quickly disperses, silence reigns; the solitary onlooker, torn abruptly from his reverie by the harsh voice of a patrolling soldier, feels like one who has been woken in the night from a delightful dream.

5 June: I read today a verse by Delille that inspired in me a wish to visit the Monceaux Park, which has now become a public place within the bounds of Paris. Here, efforts have been made to imitate nature, rather than to subdue it artificially. With its pretty stream, its woods and meadows, Monceaux has become a charming place to walk; the eye can rest upon fresh verdure and the ear hears nothing of the clamour of the city. It is as if one walked in the countryside, rather than within the walls of noisy Paris.

10 June: A celebration, given by the capital city of the greatest of empires to the most powerful of rulers, is certain to provide miracles of luxury and magnificence. I can only convey an idea of it by saying that each was worthy of the other. In spite of the incredible numbers of those invited, augmented by the merely curious, the police so skilfully performed their duties that no accidents occurred to mar the memorable day. The food, the decorations, the illuminations and the fireworks surpassed anything that Paris had previously witnessed. Among the different firework displays, there was one that excited particular admiration. The old heraldic device of Paris was seen to descend towards the Seine; it was a double-decked ship, complete with all its cannon. A multitude of lights outlined the sails and the rigging; a broadside of rockets was fired from the gun ports. Art, in fact, was made to improve upon the original.

11 June: This morning, my father, my mother and the rest of the family left for the country to enjoy a rest from the distractions of the capital. Only my older brother and I remain here, and I find that Paris, so attractive to most people, seems empty and sad when bereft of the people that one loves best.

12 June: This morning I went to Charenton. There were two reasons for this: the first was to compensate for the absence of my family by seeing my good

friend Collins de Ham, *sous-lieutenant* in the 8th Hussars; and the second reason was so that I could visit the school of equestrianism, usually called the Alfort School. This school was set up and is maintained at government expense; it contains, apart from skilful horsemen, excellent professors of anatomy, agriculture and botany etc. Each regiment is obliged to send an officer and an NCO there, but this ministerial decree is not always observed. Each regional prefect also appoints to the school an individual usually selected from a poor family. These young men are fed and educated at the cost of the state. When their course of instruction is ended, and they have taken a final examination, they are qualified as veterinary surgeons and they practice in the provinces. The course for military personnel lasts for two years.

Chapter 6

The Russian Campaign:
July 1812–January 1813
(Transcribed by Ferdinand de Tascher)

My brother Maurice's revised notes end on 12 June 1810. He had the habit of carrying a small notebook with him, in which he wrote brief, succinct notes every day: these he would rephrase and transfer to an exercise book when he had the time. As soon as one exercise book was full, he would add it to the earlier ones at our home in Paris. It is for this reason that we have been able to preserve those that I have transcribed above.

In the course of the Russian campaign, the last exercise book was lost; he had begun it and would have been very conscious of its loss. Nevertheless, in the portmanteau that contained the few possessions that remained to him in Berlin, I found two little notebooks containing the daily notes he made until 8 January 1813 – the day on which he fell ill at Marienwerder. There are, alas, many gaps in these notes.

Nothing, I feel, better demonstrates the courage and coolness of my brother, in the midst of such great danger, than his imperturbable determination to write, with his frozen hand, of the horrors of the retreat and of his own dreadful situation, of the appalling sights that were constantly before his eyes. It is because these facts seem so terrible to me that I have faithfully transcribed them here at the end of his revised notes.

These latter notes end on 12 June 1810. A short time afterwards, Maurice was at Saint-Mihiel, the location of his regiment's depôt. I went to see him there in June 1811. In December of the same year he was granted a leave, which he spent with his family in Paris; but before the end of this leave, he was forced by the outbreak of war with Russia, to return to Saint-Mihiel; his regiment left the depôt on the day that Maurice arrived there. From that day until 11 July 1812, his notes contained practically nothing but the itinerary of his journey through Germany, Saxony, Prussia and Poland. Although he notes the crossing of the Niemen on 24 June, he does not begin to give any details until 11 July. So it is from this place that I shall transcribe his daily notes.

Ferdinand de Tascher

The Campaign Diary Resumes ...

11 July (1812): In great haste, we passed over a bridge so frail that the artillery was unable to cross it. We travelled a further 5 leagues and bivouacked near the village of Sloboda, where there is a Catholic church with an organ and a dome. All the peasants had remained in their villages until we arrived, but ill-treatment then made them flee.

12 July: We remained here today; the country around is thickly wooded with many lakes and impassable swamps. All the ground is spongy.

13 July: We set off at dawn and marched to Druja, crossing the small River Drouika. A brigade was marching on either side of us; the enemy was encountered a league from the town. The Poles made a successful charge and pushed the enemy back into the town, which lies astride the River Düna. They burned the bridge. Our brigade has been positioned as a second line, behind a thick wood.

14 July: We stay in position all day. At nine in the evening, we learn that the enemy has rebuilt the bridge and sent four infantry regiments across it. We send all our wagons and led horses to the rear, and spend the night with our bridles over our arms.

15 July: Sotorosnitz. The enemy, formed up into three lines, attacked the brigade at dawn and pushed it back onto the wood. The General was away and there were no orders, so confusion resulted. The brigade was overwhelmed. The General arrived and was taken prisoner. The Poles and the 11th have lost 200 men. The regiment, which had hoped to conceal itself in the wood, was forced to retreat. We retired by echelons, recrossed the river, and turning to the right, travelled for 6 leagues before bivouacking at Sotorosnitz.

16 July: We marched 4 leagues along the road to Disna, joined the cuirassiers and the *carabinières* again, and bivouacked in the village of Maleserina.

17 July: Today we bivouacked on a broad plain between Druja and Drissa.

18 July: We retreated and bivouacked in a little village half a league further back. There is hunger and extreme wretchedness. The horses are suffering terribly.

19 July: The regiment mounted at midnight and made a general movement to the right. At dawn, I was sent out to reconnoitre near Léopol, where I found the enemy. We moved our bivouac in the evening, passing through Merista, and halting near General Montbrun's château.

20 July: Marched towards Léopol, which has been evacuated by the enemy, who has now recrossed the river. We moved along the Düna as far as Drissa,

where there is a good bridgehead, entrenchments and a huge camp. A map of it was made for the Emperor. Some small boats were burned; the enemy was encountered and fired on. We returned to the bivouac of the 11th near Poriau, after marching 16 leagues.

21 July: We left in a hurry at midday, marching towards Disna, and met two army corps on the way; we continued our march until midnight, and spent the rest of an unpleasant night standing in the midst of a fine crop of rye, a league away from the town.

22 July: We reached Disna, an uninteresting town built entirely of timber, it was abandoned and pillaged. We crossed the Düna by means of a deep and dangerous ford. We went through Lousouka and followed the right bank of the river for 10 leagues. The whole army was marching in the same direction on the opposite bank. No sign of the enemy. At last we find some food and some oats in the villages.

23 July: We left at two in the afternoon and halted in the village of Robna on the road from Disna to Polotsk. A large number of wagons containing sugar and coffee were captured just a league from the junction with the road from St Petersburg. The town was burned.

24 July: We went through Polotsk and sacked and burned it. It contained a fine church and a handsome Jesuit monastery. Astonishing signs of luxury could be seen, with elegant houses next door to wooden hovels. This is a town that was rising in the heart of a village. We continue on the right bank of the river in the direction of Vitebsk. The archbishop's fine château was pillaged. We bivouacked before the village of Strounya.

25 July: We travelled 6 or 8 leagues on an excellent road shaded by a double line of silver birch trees. There are seventeen regiments of light horse cavalry advancing on Vitebsk. The enemy attacked the 9th Hussars.

26 July: We continue to march along this good road. The enemy, who is following us, was charged by the 4th Chasseurs, at the head of our column, and prisoners were taken. We bivouac at the end of a long day near Poltevo, 5 leagues from Vitebsk.

27 July: We are followed by the enemy, who retreats in haste. All day long, a powerful cannonade was heard from the opposite bank of the river. We reach the town (Vitebsk) at four in the afternoon and are separated from it only by the river. The army corps deploys. The brigade, on the left, bivouacks near the river. We are ordered to leave at midnight.

28 July: We leave at dawn, and descend the river for 2 or 3 leagues in order to find a ford. We cross the ford and after passing over the battlefield where the

fight took place yesterday, reach Vitebsk. The Emperor and all the army are here. We march through this fine, handsome city, now completely filled with troops.

We set out on the road to Souraj, but the order is countermanded when we have travelled 4 leagues, and we cross the fields to the right, to find the side road leading to Smolensk. Men and horses are exhausted. We bivouac at last, in a wood, at eleven at night.

29 July: We continue to follow the side road to Smolensk, passing through Liosan, a little town built entirely of wood, and bivouac a league outside it.

30 July: We stay in position. I am with the advance guard.

31 July: We moved off at two in the morning to mount an attack and found the enemy near the small town of Roudnia, from which he withdrew slowly. We followed, and there was gunfire. A château was dreadfully plundered.

1 August: The division crossed the Berezina [*more likely the Beredzonina – Ed.*] at Roudnia, marched 4 leagues and positioned itself near Inkovo, on a hill. The terrain is very rough and marshy.

2 August: The entire army is at a standstill. I am now using my tent.

3–4 August: We remain in position.

5 August: The Cossacks appear to be about to attack us.

6 August: We parade for inspection. The enemy is prowling around us. We withdraw in the afternoon and the division positions itself at Lernitz (Lechnia). The 1st Brigade is to the rear of the castle, we form the second line near the church, and the foreign troops make up the third line.

7 August: The enemy is harassing the forward line. Tomorrow we shall have to withdraw to Roudnia. Promotion recommendations are received for the regiment.

8 August: The enemy attacked at dawn and Rouveau was killed. General Montbrun charged with a squadron of the 5th Hussars, pushed the enemy back, and returned. Our brigade went forward at eight o'clock, met the enemy, and found itself to be heavily outnumbered. We withdrew by echelons in disorder, the route being much obstructed in the confusion. My horse was killed. Devoted heroism shown by Corporal Leclerc. There are Kalmuks and Bashkirs [*peoples originating from that part of Russia between the Volga and the Don – Ed.*] with their arrows. We retreat to Roudnia.

9 August: Roudnia. Stench, depression and misery in the bivouac. The disaster we experienced yesterday was occasioned solely by disagreements between the

generals. The division, which previously had 2,000 horses, lost about 600 of them. The enemy had attacked with several battalions, 10,000 Cossacks and twenty-four cannon. My attempts to discover Leclerc's fate were unsuccessful. [*Editor's note: Details of this affair were contained in a letter Maurice de Tascher sent to one of his comrades who had remained behind at the Saint-Mihiel depôt: 'Now, I must tell you some sad news. News that my pen would refuse to write if I were not sure that you would soon hear of it from others. On 8 August we were attacked by greatly superior forces. I cannot, at this moment, give you all the details of this tragic day. Monsieur Rouveau who was in the advance guard, was one of the first victims. Felled by a bullet, he was then killed by the Cossack lancers. You, yourself, know what it is like to be obstructed at the entrance to a defile, with lances at one's back. One retreats at a gallop. I had remained a little to the rear of my squadron, and rejoined them in the company of a crowd of Kalmuks and Cossacks, even as a cannon ball cut Colonel Guilozat in two and killed my horse. Being captured or killed was inevitable. Miroir wanted to give me his horse, but I refused. Leclerc, the company sergeant, jumped from his saddle, freed me from under my horse, offered me his mount and was, at that instant, surrounded by the enemy; he to whom I owe my life and liberty, heroically paid for it with his own. All the officers of the regiment and the whole division – even the generals – express their admiration for the action, and Leclerc is promised a Cross, but is he still alive? Ever since that day I have been tireless in trying to ascertain his fate, but with no success. I have sent 25 louis to him by an intermediary and have explored every possible means of inquiry. I know that your kind heart will appreciate how my uncertainty grieves me.'*]

10–11 August: My enquiries continue and are fruitless.

12 August: Roudnia. I make renewed efforts, which are equally useless, to seek news of Leclerc by means of a parley. There is trouble concerning General Montbrun; General Sébastiani leaves.

13 August: Roudnia. General Pajol arrives. The whole army marches to the right for two days (I am of the advance guard). It is a matter for consideration that the army is made up of four different nationalities. The Cossacks have their outposts at the Lesnitz château.

14 August: Our division, acting as the army's rearguard, moves to the town of Liouvavitschy, where we encounter the Army of Italy and Louis Tascher. We pass by the town and bivouac a league ahead of it on the Smolensk road.

15 August: We continue on our way and reach Pokelnia, where we bivouac near a large swamp. We are to guard a bridge over the Dnieper, while the rest of the army doubtless celebrates the Emperor's birthday in a more exciting fashion.

16 August: We remain in position and hear a heavy bombardment. The army is at Smolensk.

18 August: We leave on the road leading to Smolensk. We cross the Beredzonina, and follow the Dnieper to bivouac near the village of Kousino.

19 August: We withdraw, recross the little river, and return to our old bivouac at Pokelnia. Cossacks are on the flanks and to the rear of the French Army; they take many prisoners and have cut the road from Liouvavitschy.

20 August: We leave Pokelnia and cover the same ground to bivouac once more near Kousino.

21 August: We travel along the Dnieper as far as Katan village, on our way to Smolensk, where we halt for a long while. The peasants are harvesting their crops but the troops seize them to feed their horses. Katan is burned. Our direction is altered and we march to the left, on our way to Inkovo. There are frequent fires as the soldiers search for honey.

22 August: We are passing through a beautiful countryside; it is hilly with many villages and fine crops. We reach Inkovo, where we join up with the Italian Division under Pino.

23 August: We return by way of Roudnia, turn back in the opposite direction to bivouac at Liozna. The sick and wounded are in a deplorable condition. The air at Liozna is foul.

24 August: We march on Souraj and bivouac near Zamchino, where the château is burned.

25 August: We arrive and bivouac at the fairly big town of Janovitzki, which is built entirely of wood. Only a few Jews remain here, and our soldiers plunder them. A large number of stragglers and marauders are captured by the Cossacks.

26 August: Our mission, the purpose of which we never knew, is now over. We change our direction and march towards the *Grande Armée* by way of Porietsche. We bivouac in a fine wood on the main road just after Pogni-Ponaroré; the villages here are very handsome but their inhabitants have abandoned them. A large quantity of clothing and other property is found buried in the ground.

27 August: We reach Porietsche – to the north-east of Smolensk – it is another large town built of wood, and it is quite deserted. There is a fine Greek church containing paintings on wood panels. The country around is heavily forested and the armed inhabitants have sought refuge in the woods, taking their families and their most precious possessions with them. Several patrols that strayed from the main body have not returned. Clémentz, etc., etc., have disappeared. I am in the advance guard.

28 August: We continue on our way, halting at Kharino, where there is a fine château to the left of the road. There is no shortage of supplies in the bivouacs. The army has not passed this way.

30 August: We pass through Doukouthtchina and begin to see traces of the army – that is to say, devastation, corpses and stench. What a contrast with the territory that the army has not penetrated. After a long march, we bivouac 8 leagues beyond the town. Not far away, a short distance back from the road, armed peasants watch us, keeping pace with us as we move forward. Anyone who wanders off or stops, disappears. The regiment has lost ten men.

31 August: We reach Dorogobouj and rejoin the main road between Smolensk and Moscow. Dorogobouj is like the skeleton of a big town spread out over seven hills. Rome, in the early days, must have been like this. There are castles and convents on the heights and buildings that are still burning. We meet Guyot's brigade. Seven leagues from the town, to the left of the road, stands the fine château of Prince Potemkin.

1 September: Marching along the main road to Moscow, the cannon balls and corpses strewn along the way indicate the passage of the army. We bivouac near a burning castle a league from Semlevo.

2 September: Our march is the same as yesterday and we halt near Viasma. The sight of this flayed and devastated land, covered with rubbish and bodies, fills the mind with pity and horror.

3 September: We do not see a single inhabitant as we march through the magnificent town of Viasma. From a distance it looks like a forest of bell towers, but the Russians have burned everything and destroyed 125 palaces, in order to delay our artillery among the ruins. Little remains to indicate the occupations of the previous inhabitants. The Holy Cross alone, rises triumphantly in the midst of the rubble, as on the Day of Judgement. We bivouac near Teplucha, having travelled about 8 leagues.

4 September: We pass through Teplucha, which no longer exists, and reach Gjatzk, where the Emperor, together with the whole army has assembled. The Russians are before them and preparations are made for a battle. We see the distressing evidence of an epidemic among the cattle in a deserted village. The *cantinière* has lost my portmanteau. At eleven o'clock, the Emperor hears that the Russian Army has moved out of its position.

5 September: We move through Gjatzk; I look over my shoulder when we have travelled about a league and see that this delightful town has been utterly destroyed. We march for 8 horrible leagues, always surrounded by flames. The wounded, who are being left behind, are in a dreadful condition. We bivouac a

league to the right of the road, behind Gridnira [*i.e. Grituewa – Ed.*]. The entire French Army is marching in close order in front of us.

6 September: We march 4 leagues through Gridnira and finally rejoin the army. We spend the night on the battlefield that will, tomorrow, be drenched in blood. We are in the centre of the army near the Château of ——.

7 September: We mounted at half past three in the morning and the first cannon shot was heard at five o'clock. At seven o'clock the whole army moved off under cannon fire. The first redoubt was taken; the army advanced on the right. At ten o'clock, we moved to the second position, near a ravine. We moved forward at three o'clock and prepared for a charge. We remained for nine hours under cannon and musket fire and slept on the battlefield. A terrible night; I took water to the many wounded. A buried Russian seems to be emerging from his grave.

8 September: There are terrible sights on the battlefield, in the wood and on the redoubt. Ten hours in the saddle. Cossacks are found within cannon shot. Charges and skirmishing occur. There are negotiations at four o'clock. We are deployed in front of the town of Mojaïsk, and are under fire until nightfall. Hope to be awarded an Officer's Cross [*i.e. the Légion d'Honneur – Ed.*]. The regiment had 280 mounted men present at start of the battle; 97 of these were killed, wounded or dismounted, ten of these were officers.

9 September: The Russians evacuated Mojaïsk during the night; leaving it filled with their wounded. We are pursuing their rearguard, which is made up of Cossacks and artillery. At ten o'clock they halted, deployed and began firing at us. We forced them back with cannon fire, at which they immediately retreated. This happened three times. In the evening the Prussians charged. Pajol was wounded. We travelled 6 leagues.

10 September: The same wearisome routine as yesterday. Nevertheless, they took up their position at four in the afternoon and retained it. We got lost and trotted until nine at night. We bivouacked in a wood, without water, bread or forage. We ate a horse. Our situation was miserable in the extreme. The regiment is reduced to six platoons. The Russians are burning everything, even the villages where their own wounded are lying. My telescope has been stolen. We covered 4 leagues.

11 September: The Russians have pulled back during the night. We mounted our horses at dawn. The Cossacks fired on us and retreated. There were negotiations and a hope of peace. The outlook improves. We cover a league and bivouac near a swamp.

12 September: We attacked at seven in the morning. The enemy put up a feeble resistance. We marched on rapidly for a long way and bivouacked

beyond the town of Kybinskö, 7 leagues from Moscow. There are rumours and speculations of infinite variety. My brother Eugène arrived in the evening. The Russians are continuing to burn everything. There is utter wretchedness.

13 September: The Russian rearguard made a stand and brought us to a halt several times. Our horses are dying of exhaustion. The company is reduced to twenty-three men. We are 4 leagues from Moscow when we bivouac to the left of the road, near a château.

14 September: We mounted at seven in the morning. The Russians stood firm for about two hours and then retreated rapidly. We reach their abandoned redoubts. The Emperor joins the advance guard. There is a parley. We enter Moscow. There are superb buildings and palaces of different colours. We are fired upon from the Arsenal and from windows. There is uncertainty as to whether this is due to mistake or treason. In the evening, the Russian officers are jumbled together with us. We bivouac a league from Moscow, near the château. There are explosions and there is fire in the town. Many of the French have warned us that there is some fateful scheme in prospect.

15 September: We move forward half a league. The Cossacks parley and agree to evacuate the village. The village is burned. All my belongings, notes etc., are lost. There is an abundance of supplies in the bivouac, which may be dangerous because of over-indulgence. Moscow is being pillaged and burned.

16 September: We mount at nine o'clock. The Cossacks are marching slowly in front of us. We parley. They give back a horse. Their weapons and dress are of Turkish design. The King of Naples [*i.e. Murat – Ed.*] arrives. Gunfire begins. We drive the Cossacks before us for 4 leagues. There are cannons in ambush and the King is endangered.

17 September: The arson and looting increases in Moscow. It is said that the Russians started the fires. All the inhabitants have vanished. The Emperor Napoleon is furious. Mines are exploding. We bivouac on a hill above a large village; I am with the advance guard. The Cossacks end their fire-raising and are reduced to a defensive retreat. The villages are lovely, well laid out and the woodwork is like lace.

We pass a terrible night on guard and move forward at four in the afternoon. There is a discussion and we return to the bivouac. I am hopeful of promotion.

18 September: News comes that the enemy is retreating. At nine o'clock the army marches off on the road to Riazan, and reaches the banks of the Moskova, where we find the enemy, who parleys and retreats. We bivouac near the village of Miatschkowo.

19 September: We remain here, and I visit the village church, where there are many little boxes and pictures, as well as tiny white books, the use of which I do not understand.

22 September: We leave Miatschkowo. The King of Naples arrives from Moscow at nine o'clock and informs the enemy of his intention to advance to Bronnitzk. We cross the Moskova by means of a ford and travel about 6 leagues. A very small rearguard of Cossacks retreats without firing a shot. They are no longer starting fires. A small number of peasants are remaining in their homes. The land looks prosperous, open and fertile. We bivouac near Bronnitsk, which is a little town near the Moskova, on the road from Kilomna. It seems that the Russian Army went another way.

[*Editor's note: Kilomna was on the Moskova, downstream, and to the south-east of Moscow. Murat travelled to the south, following the Russian Army and with or without the Emperor's acknowledgement, entered into negotiations with the Cossacks.*]

24 September: March to the flank, seeking the enemy who has tricked us. We are forbidden on pain of death from negotiating. We head towards Podolsk and travel about 9 leagues without seeing the enemy. The countryside is magnificent and filled with mansions and villages. The enemy has stopped burning everything and we find some peasants, but most of them are armed and sympathetic to the Russians.

25 September: At nine in the morning, after marching for 2 leagues, we come up with the enemy and fire on him. Prince Poniatowski [*Commander-in-Chief of the Polish troops of the Grand Duchy of Warsaw, Jozef Anton Poniatowski – nephew of Stanisław II, the last King of Poland – led Napoleon's V Corps in Russia, becoming a marshal of the Empire in 1813 – Ed.*] is marching on our right. We advance very slowly. At three o'clock, the enemy makes a stand and we halt. We bivouac in the village of Znabiszyna, surrounded on all sides by Cossacks. We cross the ravine at midnight. The night is horrible. We have left Podolsk on the right, to our rear.

26 September: There are endless alerts. The Cossacks are intrepid, and our small outposts with their crews are captured. We spend the whole day in one place. Snow starts to fall and we begin to suffer from the cold.

27 September: We are attacked at seven in the morning, and push the enemy slowly before us for nearly 2 leagues. The Cossacks are more numerous and far more determined than usual. We come upon the enemy army near the village of Awieczkina and all of us bivouac near the village of Satyna.

28 September: Remain in position. The army has drawn tightly together. There is hunger, for there is no bread or forage.

29 September: We advance a league, to the left of the road and surprise the enemy at the village of Kischewo. He retreats, and we pursue him as far as the village of Widewo [*possibly Vinkovo – Ed.*] on the banks of a little river. The enemy sends his infantry forward. As we have nothing with which to oppose him, we return across the ravine and bivouac at Kischewo at ten in the evening. We endure a horrible night in the rain and cold. All day long we have heard heavy artillery fire on the right flank, which is composed of Prince Poniatowski's corps.

30 September: Our foragers and servants are subjected to a *hourrah* [*Cossack war cry and the signal for a surprise attack – Ed.*]. We form the advance guard from two in the afternoon; I spend the entire night on horseback, with General Exelmans.

1 October: No movement today. The Cossacks are continually skirmishing around us, and seizing many members of foraging parties, servants and baggage. The company is reduced to fourteen men, and the regiment to four platoons.

2 October: I mount my horse at eight o'clock, and we are placed as an ambush in a wood near the river. All the army corps are moving to the right towards Kaluga. The Cossacks attempt to seize the baggage train and we remain at Kischewo until four in the afternoon to protect it. We reach our bivouac near the village of Usadiska at nine in the evening. Bitterly cold.

3 October: We left at eleven o'clock, and found the enemy near the village of Bogawlinia, after a three-hour march. We crossed a ravine and entered a wood. We began firing and pushed forward through the wood; the regiment charged twice. The enemy opened fire. We were engaged to our front and flanked on the right and the left; the infantry we asked for did not arrive. In the midst of the fighting and confusion ineffective efforts were made to rally in the wood, but there was a complete rout, involving the loss of a hundred men. We bivouac behind Bogawlinia.

4 October: All the morning we could hear a heavy barrage to our right; we moved off at nine o'clock and encountered the enemy at one in the afternoon, near the village of Spakt (The King of Naples is here). We chased a few Cossacks in front of us for a quarter of a league; some cannon shots came from behind a wood and all at once, artillery fire can be seen all along the enemy line. At three o'clock, the Cossacks rushed forward, supported by the Russian dragoons. Two or three charges were made, but they cannot shake us, and they retreat. We remained in position for about an hour, serving as a target for their gunners. At four o'clock the Cossacks, supported by a large number of cavalry, returned and our field guns withdrew, lacking ammunition. Lines of cuirassiers

came forward. There was a general scuffle, with the advantage first on one side, then on the other, until after nightfall. We returned to the bivouac at Ciecierowka, on the left of Spakt. All the regiments are reduced to four, three or two platoons. My company has only five *chasseurs*. The Russians are again burning everything.

5 October: We stay here all day. The countryside is fertile and not swampy, cut through by frequent ravines and covered with forests of oak, aspen and silver birch. General Lauriston has been named as negotiator.

[*Editor's note: General Jacques-Alexandre-Bernard Law, marquis de Lauriston (1768–1828), was appointed to negotiate with Tsar Alexander, but was detained by the Russians and not allowed to pass through their lines. The letter he bore – a peace overture from Napoleon – was carried to St Petersburg by Prince Volkonsky.*]

6 October: We are still in position. Negotiations continue. It is a courtesy war between the French and Russian Generals Bennigsen, Kutusov and Minevalovitsh [*i.e. Miloradovich – Ed.*]. The army is in a miserable state, living on vegetables, horsemeat and on ears of rye.

7 October: Still in the same position. The weather continues fine. The foragers have brought in some supplies, but the armed peasants and refugees in the wood are defending themselves against our soldiers.

8 October: There are ever-increasing difficulties in finding supplies, which must now be sought as far as 3 leagues away. The Cossacks attack every day and capture our foragers.

9 October: Still in position. I am with the advance guard. General Lefebvre has replaced General Saint-Geniez ...

* * *

There is a gap in Maurice's notes here, which does not end until 20 November. It is during this period that the retreat and the misfortunes of the French Army began. Meanwhile, allowing himself to be distracted by useless gestures of friendship, Napoleon was shut up in the Kremlin working on regulations for the theatre [the Comédie Française in Paris – Ed.], *even as the Russians' terrifying plan for the destruction of the French Army was taking shape. At the same time, in detailed bulletins, Napoleon was informing us of the distance from Moscow to St Petersburg and boasting that he held all the roads leading into the interior of Russia; the madman failed to see that the one leading back to his Empire was closed to him, and that a Russian Army was hastening from the Turkish frontier to cut the crossing of the Berezina. At last, the retreat was ordered on 18 October and the dreadful disaster for the army began.*

It was during this interval, in the neighbourhood of Smolensk, that Maurice found our unhappy brother, Eugène, in a state of utter destitution. Eugène had been wounded on 4 October near Kaluga. Neither of them has left us any account of this sorrowful meeting.

I resume Maurice's notes from 20 November; he is at all times travelling on foot, leading his brother, to whom he has given his sole remaining horse, as both of the unfortunate Eugène's feet had been frostbitten since Smolensk.

Ferdinand de Tascher

The Campaign Diary Resumes ...

20 November (1812): We travelled 6 leagues and halted half a league before Kokanov with the regiment. Efforts are being made to restore some order to the army.

21 November: There is a sudden attack on a division of cuirassiers, which is captured. We march in our ranks, the Cossacks, on our flanks, follow and watch us. We reach the fortified town of Tolochin at nightfall. Since we left Smolensk we have marched on a fine road, bordered by a double row of silver birches. There is a thaw.

22 November: We travel 8 leagues on foot and sleep at Pauver. The mud and the weather are dreadful.

23 November: It is freezing hard. All mounted officers are called upon to form a guard for the Emperor [*the so-called 'Sacred Squadron' – Ed.*].

25 November: We have been marching through an endless forest since we left Tolochin. Today, after 3 leagues, we are halted in a hamlet near the road. Eugène is in a desperate situation, for I am compelled to leave him in the care of only a single *chasseur*. We leave at nightfall and bivouac in a pine wood, near the château where the Emperor is staying. We lie in the snow, without any fire, in the bitter cold.

26 November: We leave at four in the morning and pass through Borisov, where we can see the fires of the whole of the Russian line along the Berezina. We bivouac at Klein Borisov. The river crossing is begun.

27 November: The honour guard assembles and remains in battle order from the morning until two in the afternoon at the bridgehead. Afterwards, everyone goes his own way. I bivouac and endure a cruel night near the bridge. I have lost my brother and my comrades.

28 November: I go to the bridge at dawn. The disorder and congestion is terrible. Several times I manage to avoid being suffocated, and struggle across after waiting for four hours. Half an hour afterwards, the enemy starts to fire and the crossing turns into a massacre. There is fighting at Borisov. An

immense number of men and horses are drowned. I go to find something to eat in a village near the river, but leave when I see the Cossacks. I travel 3 leagues along a narrow road that passes through woods and swamps and reach Zembin. Here I find my brother again.

29 November: We follow a narrow road that crosses the one running from Minsk to Vilna through woods and swamps. There is great hunger and wretchedness. We sleep at Kamen, a large village where the Prince of Wagram [*i.e. Marshal Berthier, Napoleon's Chief of Staff – Ed.*] is lodging. I have a fever.

30 November: After 4 leagues we lodge near the little town of Semlovitz.

1 December: We travel 7 leagues through a wild, deserted countryside that is thickly wooded. The Emperor is lodging in a castle. I remain in a village where the Headquarters is located.

3 December: We march through a wood for five or six hours and then across a long causeway over an impassable marsh. We halt at Molodeutsch [*i.e. Molodeczno – Ed.*], another town that is built entirely of wood and then rejoin the main road from Minsk to Vilna. There is an astonishing difference between the soldiers of the army and those who are newly arriving from France.

4 December: It is bitterly cold. We march in silence. What memories fill my mind; it is my birthday [*he was twenty-six – Ed.*] and my mother must be thinking of me with tears and agony even as I think of her. We travel 6 leagues and lodge in a village a quarter of a league in front of Headquarters. I have fever and diarrhoea. Eugène's suffering continues.

5 December: We reach the little town of Smorgoni, where we halt. There are supplies here, but we have to endure the misery of seeing them vanish into the hands of plunderers without being able to obtain any of them. I find a detachment of the regiment; it is astonishing to see well-dressed men in good uniforms.
[*Editor's note: it was on this day that Napoleon, having consulted his marshals, set off for Paris, leaving Murat in command of the army's survivors.*]

6 December: The cold is terrible. Many men are falling dead by the roadside, often being robbed and stripped before they die and left, still living, naked in the snow. We bivouacked with the Army of Italy, 2½ leagues to the rear of Headquarters.

7 December: Extreme cold. We march 6 leagues, to bivouac in a village 3 leagues beyond Offian, the winter Headquarters.

8 December: We are compelled by exhaustion, to halt for an hour along our way. We cover only 4 leagues and halt in a hamlet along the road, only 4 leagues from Vilna. There is joy in every eye, at the prospect of reaching Vilna!

9 December: We reach Vilna, but there is disorder, anger and congestion among those struggling to enter the gates. I lose my servant, Franz. I find a billet with a Pole. I note the attitude of the Jews. A bed and a good night. [*Editor's note: the considerable Jewish population of the city was supposed by the French to be responsible for hunting down and killing many officers who had sought billets in their houses.*]

10 December: The Cossacks entered the suburbs at dawn and we leave at eleven o'clock. There is tumult and disorder, the warehouses are plundered and wagons burned, our defeat is total. The Jews plunder the French and the French plunder the Jews. There are cannon fire and swift attacks along the road. The French Army is terrified at the sight of the Cossacks. We march until eleven in the evening and spend a terrible night, unable to rest.

11 December: We march 11 leagues and reach Zizmory [*i.e. Jimouroui – Ed.*].

12 December: We make a forced march on foot for 12 leagues. There is a gloomy, listless satisfaction in seeing that the Memel [*i.e the Niemen – Ed.*] is frozen. We reach Kovno at nightfall.

13 December: The warehouses have been plundered. The Cossacks are following us closely. We cross the Memel by means of the bridge and on the ice. The whole army is on the march without anyone knowing where it is going. We sleep on the road to Königsberg, 4 leagues before Stansheim.

14 December: March 10 leagues and sleep at Virsytz.

15 December: March through Wylkowyszki, and travel 2 leagues further in the village of Olvita.

16 December: My horse is stolen. The situation is desperate! I buy a sledge; the journey is slow, painful and beset by continual accidents. We pass through Virbalen, where the Guard has halted, and we sleep at Egerkirken.

17 December: I find Kapel here [*Tascher's orderly at Wagram – Ed.*]. A good sledge. My brother's condition is getting worse!

18 December: Gumbinnen. A visit from Monsieur Larrey, the Emperor's surgeon.

19 December: Insterburg. I am finding the journey very difficult.

20 December: We are still on the road to Königsberg and halt in a little hamlet, by the name of Kochkutheim.

21 December: The small depôt at Wehlau is being plundered. I retrieve my rifle and some of my other possessions. We are in an almost desperate situation and my brother's health is growing worse all the time.

23 December: We reach Königsberg, and I take my brother to the hospital. Exhausted by the search for billets. No. 12 Königsberg Street. A doctor, a warm room and a bed. Happiness that I am incapable of enjoying!

24 December: I am in terrible difficulty due to lack of money. I travel all over the town. I am evicted from my room and must leave for Elbing!

25 December: I am thrown out of my billet, but there is unexpected help from General Exelmans, who lends me 300 francs. I hurry to take this money to my brother and receive a dreadful shock. His condition is hopeless. I leave Königsberg at nightfall and sleep at an inn, 3 leagues along the road to Elbing.

26 December: I travel along the Frisches-Haff, and through the unpleasant little town of Brandenburg, sleeping 3 leagues further on, in an inn.

27 December: I still travel by sleigh on the Frisches-Haff. The Prussians demonstrate their hatred openly. The authorities and the ordinary people vie with each other to see which can make us most conscious of our dependence upon them. I have seen the Russian prisoners here receive the help and food that is denied to us.

29 December: We reach Elbing, which looks delightful. There are windmills, gardens and places of entertainment; how charming it must be in fine weather. I reach my lodging late and with difficulty.

30 December: I obtain permission to rest here for two days. I change my billet and go to No. 97 Fleischergasse.

1813

1 January: I am enduring weary and sleepless nights. I am roused daily by the croaking of a multitude of ravens. I am suffering physically and mentally. I receive permission to stay for four more days.

2 January: Disquieting news makes me anxious to hurry my departure. My health continues to be precarious.

3 January: The King of Naples and some of the Guard arrive.

4 January: Our departure delayed until tomorrow. I have memories of my host and his three daughters at 97 Fleischergasse, they would not take my money.

5 January: We travel 9 leagues, and reach the big fortified town of Marienburg with infinite difficulty. The countryside over which we have been journeying today is very low-lying and waterlogged. We crossed the Nogat at eight in the evening, to halt in the village of Damfeld.

6 January: We took a side road and recrossed the Nogat, travelling through woodland for 6 leagues and then sleeping at an inn. The country is very fertile and the cattle extremely large.

7 January: We reach Marienwerder after 4 leagues. Travelling in a sleigh is very difficult. We remain here on 8 January ...

* * *

This note, written on 8 January, was the last one penned by Maurice's failing hand. On the previous day, he had written to his parents to give them his news and to reassure them about his health. But the improvement of which he wrote did not last long. On the next day, the 9th, he set out again on the road to Custrin, where his army corps was to be reorganized. Although he complained of extreme weakness, he continued to travel on horseback as long as he was able.

At last, overcome by fever and exhaustion, he was compelled to allow himself to be carried on one of the carts that was following the army. In this way, he reached Custrin on the 20th and on the same day, was admitted to a hospital in the town. On the next day, his sergeant, Kapel, came to bid him farewell. Maurice exclaimed that he was being abandoned and that he wished to leave with him for Berlin. With death in his soul, he did then leave, reaching Berlin on the 23rd. When General Sébastiani learned of his circumstances, he sent him some money and offered to receive him in his own lodging. Maurice thanked him. Kapel also suggested that Maurice should stay with him if he wanted to remain in Berlin. However, influenced by fatal advice and perhaps, in the hope that he would there find the help, of which he felt himself to be in great need, the ill-fated young man made up his mind to go into hospital. He was admitted to hospital on 23rd, taken there by the faithful Kapel, to whom, as a result no doubt of a sad premonition, he handed his sword, begging him to take it back to the regiment, and to throw away his weapons, rather than abandon them. After this, the nervous fever from which he was suffering became even worse and he soon became delirious, after which his mind was filled only with thoughts of the loss of his brother, and of his family.

I left Osnabrück on the 22nd and reached Berlin on the 25th, where on the 26th I found Maurice in terrible distress, but even so, I did not fully understand the danger he was in. However, he did recognize me and said, in a broken voice: 'At last a moment of happiness in this vale of tears!'

How sad are the parallels in our fate! On 23 December, Maurice had taken his brother Eugène to the hospital at Königsberg; on the morning of the 25th he had gone there to take him the money that Providence had helped him collect. They would not let him enter, for they said his brother was dead. One month later, guided by the same Providence to Maurice's deathbed, I was to face the same refusal when I returned the following morning, but my urgency overcame the prohibition and I found the corpse of my brother on his bed. He had just died!

Ferdinand de Tascher

Appendix I

Notes on Napoleon's Russian Campaign of 1812 by Rosemary Brindle

Maurice de Tascher's notes of the terrible Russian campaign begin on 11 July 1812 and end on 8 January 1813. They were never elaborated, as were his earlier entries and as Ferdinand de Tascher makes clear in his final account of his brother's death, they consist only of aides mémoire. Although it is clearly impossible to make good the absence of Maurice's own narrative, the outline that he has given us may perhaps be supplemented by some details of the campaign to give a clearer picture of the events.

His victory at Friedland in June 1807 and the treaty signed at Tilsit with the Russian Emperor Alexander, had placed Napoleon in an apparently unassailable position as the ruler of Europe. He had responded by redesigning what had been the Holy Roman Empire and forming puppet states that were friendly to France. The Kingdom of Westphalia was handed to his brother Jérôme, brother Joseph was to have Spain and Murat was proclaimed King of Naples in place of Joseph. Only Britain remained hostile and unconquered, for at Tilsit, the Emperor Alexander had committed Russia to joining the Continental System, designed to bring Britain to its knees by bringing all trade between Europe and Britain to an end. This resulted in serious trade losses, not only for Britain but also for Russia. It was to enforce the Continental System upon the Peninsula that Napoleon had invaded Spain, a hitherto friendly country, and appointed his brother, Joseph, as king. What became known as the 'Spanish ulcer' resulted, with its endless drain upon French arms and resources. It has been estimated that the lives of 300,000 French soldiers were lost in this ill-considered campaign.

The treaty signed at Tilsit became more and more unacceptable to Russia and to Alexander himself. The economic disaster caused by the treaty was exacerbated by smaller, but no less aggravating insults inflicted by the confident Emperor Napoleon. Among them was the formation of the French satellite state – The Grand Duchy of Warsaw – on the Russian frontier. Open conflict became inevitable.

At the beginning of 1812, Napoleon gathered, from France and the subject nations of Europe, an enormous Grand Army. This eventually became an assembly of over half a million men (fewer than half of whom were French), together with 150,000 horses to pull the wagons, provide mounts for the cavalry and drag the artillery. It was in the heat of June 1812 that the vast army crossed the Niemen on its way to complete disaster. The intention had been for the French Army, by means of overwhelming numbers, to crush Russian resistance in a brief, but conclusive campaign lasting no more than three weeks. But the sheer size of the Grand Army induced the Russians to retreat before it, while the French horde was drawn after, through the stifling heat of the summer, always hoping for the decisive confrontation.

By the time Maurice de Tascher's notes begin, the French Army had suffered its first reverse. The terrible state of the Russian roads had thwarted Napoleon's determination to bring the 1st Russian Army under Barclay de Tolly to battle at Vilna, but the French had suffered a misfortune that would prove as devastating as a battle: for 10,000 precious horses had already died. Weakened by forced marches and fodder that consisted of green wheat and rye, the horses died in thousands when a terrible storm burst over the army as it reached Vilna, bringing icy rain in place of summer heat. Captain Coignet writes: 'Next morning a heart-rending sight met our gaze; in the cavalry camp nearby, the ground was covered with horses frozen to death; more than 10,000 died during that dreadful night.'[2] Inevitably, the supply system, already shown to be inadequate for the vast numbers involved, broke down. Hungry men resorted to undisciplined looting. Some elements of the army, composed as it was of disparate nationalities, and of many conscripts lacking experience and training, soon began to lose coherence.

From Vilna on, as de Tascher's diary makes clear, the Russian strategy of 'fight and fall back' wearied and exasperated the pursuing French, who suffered continual attrition through disease and the casualties of frequent encounters with Cossack cavalry and elements of the Russian Army. As discipline weakened in the French Army, unchecked looting and burning laid waste the countryside through which it marched; the Russians, too, burned towns and villages as they withdrew, to deny resources to the invading army. A swathe of devastation was left in the wake of the two armies. Thirst, as well as hunger, tormented the French, for the retreating Russians often poisoned the wells. His generals warned Napoleon of the state of his exhausted army, but he was determined to press forward.

Napoleon, with the eyes of Europe upon his spectacular undertaking, continued to follow the will-o'-the-wisp of the decisive battle that would bring victory, justify his actions and satisfy his pride. The Russian general, Barclay de Tolly again disappointed him of a battle before Vitebsk and fled onwards towards Smolensk. Napoleon hurried after him instead of resting his exhausted troops and replacing the wastage of men and horses. But, as General de Ségur of Napoleon's Staff remarks in his memoirs, 'happy had it been for him (Napoleon) if he had not mistaken the movements of his impatience for the inspirations of genius.'[3] The dazzling dream of Moscow was before him, promising immortal glory, peace, abundance and reimbursement of the expenses of war. This prospect drew him on, always expecting some sign of vacillation on the part of the Russian Emperor, but none was given.

The phantom of victory again escaped Napoleon when, instead of massing to protect Smolensk, the Russian Army withdrew, leaving the French to suffer losses as they battered the walls of the burning town, only to find it deserted next morning, when they had hoped a decisive battle would take place. Nevertheless, the assault on Smolensk and the fighting around it cost thousands of killed and wounded. Both sides claimed victory. Again, although still caught in the mesh of a logistical nightmare, Napoleon failed to halt and regroup; the Russians continued their retreat and the weary French Army toiled after them on the road to Moscow.

On 7 September 1812, the Grand Army, now much reduced by sickness, starvation and casualties, at last confronted more than 120,000 Russians at the bloody Battle of Borodino. Prince Kutusov, who had taken over the command of the Russians from Barclay de Tolly, had orders to fight to protect Moscow. It proved to be a terrible conflict: the French losses in killed and wounded amounted to about 28,000 and while no accurate estimate of Russian casualties has been made, it is thought to have been about 40,000. At last, with both sides again claiming a victory, the Russians withdrew in good order. Baron Louis-François Lejeune in his memoirs: 'The terrible struggle, so hotly contested, had won no results at all commensurate with the great losses sustained on both sides.'[4]

Kutusov had failed to protect Moscow, and Napoleon, with his depleted army, trailing its wretched sick and wounded, struggled on. The French Emperor, in poor health and horrified by the sight of the battlefield with its legions of corpses, still saw a triumphant conquest of the Russian capital as certain to compel Alexander to capitulate. Justification and recompense for French suffering must surely require only one more effort.

It was on 14 September, seven days after the Battle of Borodino, that Murat, at the head of a regiment of Polish hussars, rode proudly into the empty streets of Moscow, even as the Russian rearguard was leaving the city. No deputation met Napoleon at the town gates. Moscow seemed deserted. Napoleon took up residence in the Kremlin, but soon afterwards, fires were reported. Palaces and houses burst into flames, driven by a strong north wind and new fires leapt up in every direction. Realization that the Russians themselves were burning their own capital city came slowly, and it was not until 20 September that the flames were brought under control; but by then, the infuriated French were taking advantage of the disorder to sack and pillage everything in the burning town. Valuable sable robes were being sold among the troops, and passed into the hands of senior officers, who were enjoying the riches still remaining in the city. The Emperor himself packed his own trophies – among them the great cross from the tomb of the Tsars – into wagons and sent them off to Paris with an escort under the command of General Claparède.

Now, disappointed of his glittering triumph, Napoleon fatally hesitated, unwilling to face the prospect of retreat. Utter confusion reigned; his orders against looting came far too late. Food supplies were wasted, the troops loaded themselves with valuables, destroying what they could not carry. No word of capitulation came from Alexander, and General Jacques-Alexandre Lauriston, sent by Napoleon as a negotiator to the Russian Emperor, did not even earn a reply. On reading Napoleon's letter, Alexander reputedly exclaimed: 'Peace? My campaign is just beginning.'[5] Meanwhile, the Russian Army under Kutusov gathered reinforcements.

By the time Napoleon overcame his reluctance to abandon hope, it was already far too late: valuable weeks had been wasted and the Russian winter loomed nearer. His pride and his belief in his 'star' had betrayed both him and his army. It was not until 19 October that Napoleon at last quit Moscow; at the head of a much-depleted army of about 140,000 men and followed by a ragged multitude, laden with plunder and burdened with sick and wounded. He set off towards the rich province of Kaluga, with the intention of bypassing Kutusov's army. The Battle of Maloyaroslavets on 24 October, cost the French 6,000 killed and wounded and diverted their march to the north, again with the intention of avoiding Kutusov. Now, they were doomed to retreat over the ravaged land that had already been laid waste during their march to Moscow. The dispirited French soldiers found themselves marching over the corpses that still lay unburied on the battlefield of Borodino, though it was fifty-two days since that battle had been fought. The men began to abandon their loot as they went, but no preparation had been made for the terrible Russian winter ahead. Even the horses had not been suitably shod. Near the battlefield, in the monastery of Kolotskoie, were found thousands of starving wounded, now barely alive. Regardless of the lack of provision for them, Napoleon ordered that they should be taken along on the retreat. So gun-carriages, baggage wagons, and the private carriages of generals and civilians were requisitioned. Most of the unfortunate sick died quickly, of cold, of hunger and of the pain of their wounds. It was in no one's interest for them to survive. Russian prisoners, who had been marched ahead of the army, guarded by Spaniards, Portuguese and Poles, were found by the wayside with their brains dashed out. General de Ségur claims that 'we were cruel from necessity' and added that French prisoners in Russia were also ill-treated.[6]

Kutusov, as ever convinced that the Russian winter would prove sufficient to crush the retreating French Army, kept pace with it on its left flank, preventing it from turning towards the well-provisioned southern provinces, while still avoiding a major confrontation. The French, however, were not left in peace.

Cossack horsemen never ceased to harass them, and the threat of attack from Kutusov, Miloradovich and Platov continued. On 31 October, Napoleon, at the head of the retreating echelons, reached Viasma. Stretched out behind him on the Smolensk road was the rest of the army, with General Davout's I Corps bringing up the rear. Those in the rear were doubly miserable, for the muddy road on which they struggled was churned up, littered with broken down wagons and gun-carriages, dying and dead horses as well as the sick and wounded, who had fallen out of the ranks. Twice as many of the remaining horses, now growing progressively weaker, were needed to draw each heavy gun. Napoleon would not permit the artillery to be abandoned, to be claimed as trophies by the pursuing Russians. The line of march of the French Army now extended over more than 18½ miles/30 km. The experiences of those in front and those in the rear varied greatly.

Maurice de Tascher's brief notes do not resume until 20 November, by which time the weather had become more bitter than ever, and there was serious demoralization in the ranks. Numbers, already depleted by wounds and starvation, had been further reduced by the endless skirmishes in which the Russians tried to cut the French line. Only the inertia of Kutusov had saved the French from the attack of Miloradovich before Viasma, but even so, there were huge gaps in their ranks: some 4,000 had been killed or wounded. The army now trudged on, hoping to find supplies at Smolensk. Snow had been falling since 6 November. General de Ségur says: 'the heavens declared against us' and he speaks of the light garments in which the troops were still clad, and of their torn shoes and boots, as they struggled through the blizzard.[7] Many stumbled, fell and did not rise again. Others turned aside in search of food and shelter, but their earlier advance over the same ground had laid everything waste and they encountered the hatred of the armed population and of the Cossacks. From this point on, all was catastrophe. Every account of the retreat is an account of growing horror. A picture emerges of a pitiful mob, staggering forward through gales, snow and ice, clad in tattered summer uniforms, now augmented by the silken dresses and furs they had looted, and overcome by cold and hunger. Some 5,000 horses perished on the icy roads, for they, too, were weak and starving. Without winter shoes, they slipped and fell on the ice, where they lay to be eaten by the famished troops.

There had been hope that supplies would be found at Smolensk, although that town had been ruined and burned in the attack of the previous August. An attempt was made to admit only disciplined formations into the city, and the gates were closed against the starving majority. By the time this unhappy mass was admitted, after hours of waiting in the cold, hundreds of their number were dead and dying, unable even to join in the looting of the meagre supplies that remained. Convoys of food and cattle that had been collected in Germany were intercepted by Cossacks, and such as arrived were far below what was needed. The army that had left Moscow 100,000 strong had been reduced to little more than 41,000, but it was still encumbered with more than 50,000 unarmed stragglers and a long trail of baggage and artillery.

Napoleon and the imperial column left Smolensk on 14 November, followed at 24-hour intervals by the other formations. They marched towards Krasnoi, and then to Orsha in increasingly appalling conditions. It was as well for them in their weakened and demoralized state that their enemies could not believe how reduced they were, and that an almost superstitious fear of Napoleon seemed to prevent Miloradovich and Kutusov from pressing home the advantage that they certainly possessed. Frostbitten, hindered by deep snow, men and horses fell in terrible numbers as their comrades struggled on, marching over the snowy mounds that quickly covered the corpses. Skirmishes claimed more lives as they pushed forward in a desperate attempt to reach the Dnieper bridges ahead of the enemy. There was food at last in Orsha, and some fresh horses were found, but the River Berezina still lay ahead, the final obstacle between the army and possible safety. Orders had at last been given to destroy superfluous baggage, and unfortunately this had included the burning of the heavy bridging equipment. But General Eblé, in command of the engineers, had disobeyed his Emperor's direct instructions and had preserved some forges and other items that were to prove invaluable at the Berezina.

On 20 November, near Orsha, Marshal Ney, in command of the rearguard, was cut off from the main body of the army by General Miloradovich, but with magnificent determination, he and the 2,000 men with him, fought their way through, and Napoleon then reinforced his remaining men – about 800 – bringing the strength of the rearguard up to 4,000. But it was with only about 25,000 effective troops that Napoleon approached the Berezina, knowing that the Russians had already cut the Borisov bridge and already held the opposite bank. Orders were given to construct bridges at a ford several leagues upstream of the old one. The work was carried out thanks to the foresight and courage of General Eblé, with the bridging materials he had preserved from the general destruction of baggage, and on 27 November the crossing began. Maurice de Tascher's notes give only a glimpse of the horrors of that crossing. The scene was of utter disorder, as the thousands of stragglers rushed to the bridge, jostling and clamouring to cross. Again the indecision and hesitation of the converging Russian armies saved the remains of the Grand Army from obliteration at that terrible river crossing. Every eyewitness account tells of the utmost nobility and courage, as well as of the depths of human depravity and selfishness. All accounts are of almost unbelievable suffering and wretchedness. In all, the battle for the bridgeheads may have cost as many as 20,000 troops and perhaps 40,000 of the unarmed stragglers also died. The latter, many of them stranded on the Russian side of the river, were either killed by the Cossacks or died of exhaustion and hunger. But the pitiful remains of the

French Army had escaped complete annihilation, and now reduced to little more than a rabble, pressed on towards Vilna, pursued by the Russian armies who were, of course, also suffering the effects of the bitter cold and were much reduced in numbers. The Cossacks continued to attack and to take their toll of the fewer than 13,000 troops who remained with the French colours.

Meanwhile, news had reached Napoleon of a conspiracy that had come to light in Paris, involving a certain General Claude François de Malet. This individual, arrested in 1807 as an anti-Bonapartist agitator, escaped confinement on 22 October 1812 and attempted a Republican coup d'état, claiming the Emperor had died in Russia. Within a week, Malet had been caught and executed; but the disturbing news of his crazy exploit convinced Napoleon to quit the army for Paris, accompanied only by his Mameluk servants and General Armand de Caulaincourt. It was on 5 December, at the town of Smorgoni, that Napoleon left the remains of his army under the command of Marshal Murat, and sped off back to the capital. It was from this time that the cold, already severe, became truly terrible.

Although some order had been restored among the troops who had crossed the Berezina, the knowledge that Napoleon was no longer at their head combined with the murderous cold to complete the disintegration of the demoralized army. Murat, finding himself in command of a virtually ungovernable rabble, proved quite inadequate for the task. Although a brilliant, flamboyant, brave cavalry general, he lacked the qualities that might have been of use in such appalling circumstances. General de Ségur wrote: 'Hunger, devouring hunger had reduced these unfortunate men to the instinct of self-preservation ... which is ready to sacrifice everything to itself ... Like savages, the strongest despoiled the weakest ... With the exception of a few commanders all were absorbed by their suffering, and terror left no room for compassion.'[8]

There were rumours of cannibalism on the road between Smorgoni and Vilna, as the cold became more extreme. Thousands of lives were lost to frostbite, while starving soldiers cut chunks from the flanks of living horses, benumbed by cold. According to historian Edward Foord, 20,000 men were lost between 5 December and 9 December, when the remains of the army at last reached Vilna.[9] But there was little comfort to be found in this town, on which so much hope had been focused. As at Smolensk, an undisciplined mob stormed the gates. There was food in the town, but no organization by which it might be distributed fairly, and starving men were left to die, still waiting for the nourishment that might have saved their lives and which, on the following day, fell into the hands of the attacking Russians. Lacking orders and a clear command structure, chaos broke out again, terror was compounded by the need, once more, to retreat; commanders and such troops as still followed them, set out on the road to Kovno. The frozen slopes of the Ponary Hill lay in their path: a hill that proved to be an insurmountable obstacle to artillery and baggage wagons alike. It was here that the ultimate catastrophe took place; it was one that might have been avoided had there been even reasonable foresight and discipline. Now, even the private treasure wagons belonging to Napoleon were rifled in the mêlée, and the hillside was covered with broken, overturned carriages, dismounted cannon, dying men and horses. Colonel Noël, an artillery officer, expressed in his memoirs the shock he felt at encountering, on 9 December, the tragic remains of the French Army that had so proudly marched from Dresden in May. Noël had brought up reinforcements, including two artillery batteries, and he halted at the top of the Ponary Hill, reluctant to venture his horses and guns on the icy slopes. He and one other officer went forward to examine the situation: 'It is impossible to imagine a more tragic picture, and I was unable to comprehend what I saw, or to express the anger and despair that I felt. It was a rabble, a mass of haggard men, slovenly and in rags, which stumbled forward, lurching into each other seeming to see nothing, hear nothing and understand nothing. All ranks were muddled together, officers and troops, cavalry and infantry, French, Italians, Germans, without their weapons, clad in tattered finery, cloaks, sacks, the skins of newly-killed animals, and with footwear made from old clothes and hats.'[10]

Even the gallant Marshal Ney, the only commander whose orders were still obeyed, found that the troops of his rearguard had melted away, and he entered Kovno accompanied only by an aide-de-camp, where he attempted to rally the garrison. The Russian advance troops attacked again. Ney, with only four others, faced the Russians. Shamed by his bravery, a few others joined him and it was not until nightfall that, still fighting, he left the town and crossed the Niemen, the last of the Grand Army to quit Russia.

The melancholy narrative of Maurice de Tascher covers only a few more days of the retreat. He struggles on to Königsberg, and it is left to his elder brother, Ferdinand, to bring his story to an end at a hospital in Berlin.

It has been estimated that, of the more than half million men led by Napoleon into Russia, only about 10,000 returned. Thousands died as prisoners of war, thousands more were crippled by wounds and frostbite, and there were thousands who simply died of cold, famine and despair along the way.

General Kutusov has often been vilified for his inertia, his failure to complete the destruction of the French invading force on the many occasions when he seemed to have them at his mercy. His excuse was always the same: that the Russian winter would destroy his enemy, as indeed it did. Probably, without being aware of it, he was following Napoleon's own maxim: 'Never interrupt your enemy when he is making a mistake.'

Napoleon's mistake was indeed fatal; his reputation, one of his greatest strengths, never recovered. He himself acknowledged his terrible error: 'it was making war on Russia that ruined me.'

Appendix II

Notes on the de Tascher Family by Rosemary Brindle

The de Tascher family came originally from the region of the Perche known as Thimerais, of which Dreux forms the centre. Taschers can be found from the twelfth century, and the name is mentioned several times in the fourteenth century, but a direct connection cannot be made, in the absence of documentation, earlier than to a Guillaume de Tascher, who in 1462 married Jeanne de Chaumont. Their eldest son, Imbert, was the founder of the senior branch, that of La Pagerie, who adopted the name in the sixteenth century, this being the title of the lordship of La Pagerie, in the parish of Saint-Mandé, now the village of Viévy-le-Rayse (Loire-et-Cher). The younger son, Pierre, had only one son, Esprit de Tascher. This son had two children: Gilles, who gave rise to the family of Tascher de Guyenne (this branch moved to Bordeaux and had little contact with the rest of the family – its last representative was killed in 1917) and Pierre, father of Tascher du Perche or de Pourvrai, from whom Maurice de Tascher is descended.

The relationship of the author of this work to the Empress Josephine is, therefore, quite distant, for it is necessary to travel back to the fifteenth century, through ten generations to find a common ancestor: nevertheless, family ties between the Tascher de la Pageries and their French cousins were strong. Josephine, as well as having a very kind nature, had a very strong feeling for family ties, and if the Beauharnais and the Tascher de la Pageries seem to be more in evidence, she did not forget her du Perche cousins. As we shall see in the memoirs of Maurice, the army was not unaware of this. Moreover, the Arms of La Pagerie and du Perche were the same.

Maurice's father, Pierre-Jean Alexandre, Count de Tascher, born in 1745, was very young when he entered the service of the King and was a captain in the Penthièvre Dragoons when he left it in 1785. He did not emigrate during the Revolution and commanded the National Guard at Orléans, contriving to escape the Terror. There were seven children of his marriage to Flore Bigot de Chérelles, who was of an old Breton family established at Orléans. There were five boys and two girls: Ferdinand, Maurice, Eugène, Frédéric and Benjamin. Only the latter has left a direct descendant. Born in 1797, he served in the bodyguard and then in the cuirassiers of the Royal Guard. Following his marriage to Josephine de Montalivet, he went to live at Berry in the château of Thauvenay and died at Paris in 1858. Thanks to the patronage of Josephine,

Pierre de Tascher became a senator and officer of the Légion d'Honneur in 1804. From 1806 he lived in Paris at 23 Rue Saint-Guillaume, becoming a count of the Empire in 1808 and a peer of France in 1814. He died at Pourvrai in 1822.

The second son, Maurice-Charles-Marie de Tascher was born at Orléans on 4 December 1786 in the family home, 6, Rue des Cures (or d'Escures). He was educated at home under the direction of the Abbé Fousset, who must have been a humanist to judge by his pupil. He next entered the Fontainebleau School; then, after the necessary training at the depôt, was appointed a second lieutenant in the 8th Hussars. On the day after the Battle of Jena he was promoted to lieutenant in the 12th Chasseurs, and it was with this regiment that he fought the Polish campaign. Having asked to be sent to Spain, he was transferred to the 2nd (Provisional) Regiment of Chasseurs, where he served as adjutant-major. He was taken prisoner at Bailén and repatriated thanks to the good offices of General Dupont. He rejoined his regiment and was promoted to captain a few days before the Battle of Wagram. He received the award of the Légion d'Honneur in the same year, 1809. After a long spell at his regimental depôt at Saint-Mihiel, he left for the Russian campaign and aged twenty-six, died of exhaustion during the retreat, having vainly tried to save the life of his brother, Eugène.

Practically nothing is known of Maurice de Tascher, apart from his own diary notes, but these provide a remarkably clear portrait. This tall youth with gentle eyes and a far from forceful personality, engages one's sympathy. From Cadiz to Moscow, by way of Paris, Tilsit and Vienna, he is a companion in travel and in battle: always good-humoured, never complaining bitterly, either of people or circumstances, and always ready to endure hardship. Possessed of a calm and cultured mind, he is hungry to see and to comprehend, interested in everything in the lands across which he travels. If some artlessness resulting from the enthusiasms of his age – enemy of irony – may now make us smile, due more to the 'sensitive' style of his period, yet his notes are filled with youthful sincerity. For if Maurice de Tascher can sometimes appear argumentative he is never pedantic, and his style, if it may appear flowery to us, is never mere foolishness.

This young man is remarkably modest. There is no boasting: on the contrary, at the affair of Valdepenas, where he demonstrated great composure, he does not even mention the shot in his right side, noted in his service record.

If Maurice de Tascher's account brings no new revelations about the important personages and events of the period, it is valuable for the sense of mood and place that it contributes. The meeting at Tilsit is covered in two lines – enough for a young twenty-year-old lieutenant. But yet he makes us take part in the joys and pains of his campaigns, brings the people he meets and the countrysides he traverses to life. It should be remembered that from 21 July until 10 April 1810 he had spent less than six months with his family, and that, for the rest of the time – more than three years – he had sped across Europe on horseback, or by post-chaise from bivouac to bivouac, with Jena, Friedland, Bailén, Cadiz and Wagram as his points of reference. It is stupefying to consider, and when the Russian campaign is added to this, one understands better the weariness of the imperial armies by the time 1813 is reached.

One point is worth making: Maurice de Tascher, who speaks with youthful enthusiasm of fatherland and glory, never once refers with admiration or affection to the Emperor. Is this a throwback to an unconscious regret, learned from his family, for the loss of the King, or that Napoleon's grandeur made any comment seem futile? And yet, while he was in Spain, he expressed several harsh judgements upon the Emperor's policies. On the other hand, in the course of the Russian retreat, there was not one complaint or bitter word about Napoleon.

Maurice de Tascher fought because he was young and generous, because war was the normal state of affairs from 1792, but if he lost patience when he thought the army was fighting without him, he grieved with touching sincerity for the dead and wounded, as well as for the miseries of the civilians whose tragic fate he deplored on practically every page. Nothing could be more moving, in their brevity, than his notes on the Russian campaign, which were written in the midst of the most appalling sufferings both mental and physical.

Sadly, we are not in possession of the original text of the diary of Maurice de Tascher, but the copy of them that was made by his elder brother, Ferdinand de Tascher (born in 1779, he succeeded to his father's peerage and died in 1858) gives an impression of the utmost accuracy. This copy is a large volume of 537 pages, not including the foreword and title, bound in black calf and gilt edged. Each page consists of twenty-one lines of elegant, regular writing, clearly legible. The appearance of the manuscript, alone, vouches for the fact that Ferdinand brought a reverent care to the copying of his brother's notes, and we can rest assured that he changed nothing in them, either through carelessness or design, for he was honest enough always to indicate his personal reflections in notes that were inscribed in different script.

A final word attached to the endpaper bears the words that give us the history of the manuscript:

> This work was handed, as an affectionate remembrance to Madame Clémentine de Chabaud de la Tour, née de Tascher and niece of Maurice de Tascher, daughter of Count de Tascher, peer of France, who had copied the notes of his beloved brother having been present at his death-bed in the hospital at Berlin following the Russian campaign.

Clémentine de Chabaud de la Tour was the daughter of Benjamin de Tascher, youngest of Maurice's brothers. She bequeathed the copy of his uncle's notes to her son, Baron Chabaud de la Tour who was kind enough to entrust the publication to us (Plon).

Notes

1. Marbot, Jean-Baptiste, *Memoires du General Baron de Marbot*, Ch. 3, Vol. II, Paris, 1892.
2. Coignet, Jean-Roch, *Notebooks of Captain Coignet, Soldier of the Empire*, London, 1928.
3. De Ségur, Philippe-Paul, Comte de, *History of the Expedition to Russia undertaken by the Emperor Napoleon in the year 1812*, London, 1825.
4. Lejeune, Louis-Francois, *Memoirs of Baron Lejeune, aide-de-camp to Marshals Berthier, Davout and Oudinot*, London, 1897.
5. Palmer, Alan, *Alexander I, Tsar of War and Peace*, London, 1974.
6. De Ségur, Philippe-Paul, Comte de, *History of the Expedition to Russia undertaken by the Emperor Napoleon in the year 1812*, London, 1825.
7. De Ségur, *op. cit.*
8. De Ségur, *op. cit.*
9. Foord, E., *Napoleon's Russian Campaign of 1812*, London, 1914.
10. Noël, Jean-Nicholas-Auguste, *With Napoleon's Guns*, London, 2005.

Index